JOURNAL FOR THE STUDY OF THE OLD TESTAMENT
SUPPLEMENT SERIES
23

Editors

David J A Clines
Philip R Davies
David M Gunn

Department of Biblical Studies
The University of Sheffield
Sheffield S10 2TN
England

THE GLORY OF ISRAEL

The Theology and Provenience
of the Isaiah Targum

BRUCE D. CHILTON

Journal for the Study of the Old Testament
Supplement Series, 23

Sheffield
1983

Published by
JSOT Press
Department of Biblical Studies
The University of Sheffield
Sheffield S10 2TN
England

Printed in Great Britain
by Dotesios (Printers) Limited
Bradford-on-Avon, Wiltshire.

British Library Cataloguing in Publication Data

Chilton, Bruce D.
    The Glory of Israel.—(Journal for the Study of the Old
    Testament Supplement series, ISSN 0309-0787; 23)
    1. Bible. O.T. Isaiah—Criticism, interpretation, etc
    I. Title   II. Series
    224'1'06   BS1515.2

    ISBN 0-905774-46-9
    ISBN 0-905774-47-7 PbK

CONTENTS

The author dedicates this book to his parents.

PREFACE

The present monograph derives from my attempt over several years to understand the Isaian meturgeman (if that term may be used generically of the various interpreters who contributed to the Targum). The attempt was born of my conviction, argued elsewhere, that this Targum has particular affinities with the kingdom sayings of Jesus. Since reaching that conclusion, I have tried better to understand what the meturgeman stood for, and what situation he addressed, because in answering these questions we come to an appreciation of how and when the Targum as we know it took shape. At the same time, I have been comparing New Testament citations of Isaiah with the Targum in order to develop a clear perception of the extent to which exegeses similar to those in the Targum can be found in the New Testament.

The project was originally conceived of as a single volume, but it eventually became clear that anything like an adequate understanding of the theology and provenience of the Targum would have to be developed in a separate monograph, with the treatment of New Testament parallels left to another day. The research also demanded that I venture outside the New Testament field, in which I was trained. Targum study itself is today a thriving subject, and—as explained in the introduction—a certain refinement in methods currently in fashion seemed necessary if the Isaiah Targum was to be understood. Moreover, the study of Rabbinica and Intertestamental literature proved essential to the appreciation of this Targum in its context.

During the course of the project, I profited enormously from the advice of Martin Hengel, who encouraged me to publish my treatment of the Targum as a study in its own right. At a later stage, detailed comments on the manuscript were made by Peter Schäfer, which have been most helpful. The manuscript was finalized while I was teaching and researching at the Forschungstelle Antike und Christentum, University of Münster. I am very grateful to have enjoyed the six months of fruitful meetings and uninterrupted study which were involved, and wish to thank Karl Heinrich Rengstorf and the Minister für Wissenschaft und Forschung for them. In addition, the editors and staff of JSOT Press have worked long hours on the presentation of the volume. The index of primary sources was painstakingly assembled by David Olford, and the author index was compiled by Andrew Ahmed. My thanks are also due to the Sheffield University Press Committee, which provided a loan toward the initial cost of publication. Even with so much support, I am well aware that aspects of my thesis must be regarded as of a provisional nature. Nonetheless, I offer the present contribution as an honest account of the meturgeman's vital faith in the God who promises, and acts on his promise.

B.D.C.
The University
Sheffield

Abbreviations

AGAJU	Arbeiten zur Geschichte des Antiken Judentums und des Urchristentums
BETL	Bibliotheca Ephemeridum Theologicarum Lovaniensium
CBQ	Catholic Biblical Quarterly
JBL	Journal of Biblical Literature
JJS	Journal of Jewish Studies
JSNT	Journal for the Study of the New Testament
JSOT	Journal for the Study of the Old Testament
JQR	Jewish Quarterly Review
JSJ	Journal for the Study of Judaism
NTS	New Testament Studies
Rec. S. R.	Recherches de science religieuse
SBL	Society of Biblical Literature
SBLAS	Society of Biblical Literature Aramaic Series
SJT	Scottish Journal of Theology
SPB	Studia Post-Biblica
SVT	Supplements to Vetus Testamentum
VT	Vetus Testamentum
ZAW	Zeitschrift für die alttestamentliche Wissenschaft
ZNW	Zeitschrift für die neutestamentliche Wissenschaft

In addition, 'MS' is used for 'monograph series', and 'DS' for 'dissertation series'. Except in quotations from other scholars' work, abbreviated reference to Talmudic tractates (and Qumran documents, unless repeatedly cited) has been avoided. Tractates are cited as from the Babylonian Talmud, unless 'jer' or 'j' (for 'Jerusalem'), or 'm' (for 'Mishnah') precedes. Biblical works (and those in penumbra of the Bible) are referred to by the full spelling of the proper noun in their titles when first mentioned, or when they have not been mentioned for some time, and then by a conventional abbreviation. Similarly, 'Targum' is often abbreviated, appearing as 'Tg', and 'MT' does duty for 'Masoretic text'.

I

INTRODUCTION

The identification of the Neophyti Targum in 1956 as a version related to Pseudo-Jonathan, the Fragment Targum and the Cairo Geniza fragments gave fresh impetus to Targum study.[1] Díez Macho's 'discovery' was hailed as the confirmation of Paul Kahle's assertion that a Palestinian targum tradition antedated the Babylonian recension, and since that time, even though late 'Palestinian' exegeses have been recognized, a host of contributors have turned their attention to the recovery of pre-Christian elements in 'the Palestinian Targum.'[2] The very use of the last phrase as if in reference to an extant document has met the objection of Joseph Fitzmyer, who quite correctly points out that what we have to hand are various targum*im* and that the existence of an archetypal Palestinian source is an inference, not a fact.[3] In regard to both language and substance, the date and provenience of these Pentateuch Targums is not a matter of scholarly consensus,[4] and the present study, while obviously indebted to the movement initiated by Díez Macho and his followers, does not assume that they are correct.

There is a certain irony in the recent fascination with the possibility that the Pentateuch Targums contain pre-Christian readings: while the Talmud acknowledges the second-century provenience of its official Aramaic Pentateuch (Onqelos), it asserts that Jonathan ben Uzziel, a student of Hillel, composed the Prophetic Targums under the guidance of Haggai, Zechariah and Malachi. Moreover, the frequent citation of and allusion to Isaiah in dominical sayings would seem to make the Isaiah Targum attributed to Jonathan an obvious and somewhat overdue topic for inquiry from the point of view of New Testament study.

The relevant Talmudic passage is found in Megillah 3a:

> R. Jeremiah—or some say R. Ḥiyya b. Abba—also said: The Targum of the Pentateuch was composed by Onqelos the proselyte under the guidance of R. Eleazar and R. Joshua. The Targum of the Prophets was composed by Jonathan ben

Uzziel under the guidance of Haggai, Zechariah and Malachi, and the land of Israel quaked over an area of four hundred parasangs by four hundred parasangs, and a bath qol came forth and exclaimed, Who is this that has revealed my secrets to mankind? Jonathan b. Uzziel arose and said, It is I who have revealed your secrets to mankind. It is fully known to you that I have not done this for my own honour or for the honour of my father's house, but for your honour I have done it, that dissension might not increase in Israel.[5]

At least since the time of Abraham Geiger, it has been argued that, as Onqelos is the equivalent of Aquila, so Jonathan derives from Theodotion, another prominent figure in the development of the Greek Old Testament.[6] The suggestion is ingenious, but it suffers from obvious difficulties. First, as Jeremiah (or Ḥiyya) had no qualms about identifying the composer of Targum Onqelos with a second-century proselyte, it would seem odd that he should deliberately obscure the equation between Jonathan and Theodotion by insisting that the former was none other than the first-century disciple of Hillel. Secondly, the antique authority for the production of a Prophets Targum (Haggai, Zechariah, Malachi) is stressed in opposition to the relatively recent warrant for a Pentateuch Targum (Eleazar, Joshua). Thirdly, the bath qol here functions in an important way in respect of the propriety of the Targum; in the light of the de-emphasis of the bath qol's role at Yavneh and thereafter,[7] this may strike us as a primitive feature of the story. Fourthly, the purpose of Jonathan (viz. to decrease divisions in Israel) corresponds well to the haggadic understanding of the situation after Shammai and Hillel. We read (jer. Ḥagigah 77d): 'When their disciples increased in numbers and did not attend their masters as diligently as they ought, the divisions of opinion multiplied in Israel. They formed two parties, the one declaring unclean what the other declared clean; and things will not return to their former state (of unanimity) till the Son of David comes.'[8] Megillah 3a alludes to a time before the division became irreparable, i.e., to a period near to that of Hillel. When the Talmud says our meturgeman was Jonathan ben Uzziel, it would appear, rightly or wrongly, to mean precisely what it says.

Joseph bar Ḥiyya (fourth century C.E.), a head of the Pumbedita academy in Babylon, is also associated by name with the Prophets Targum. Zacharias Frankel suggested that this rabbi composed the

Targum, that his name was abbreviated with a yod, and that this provided the occasion for the identification of the compiler with Jonathan.[9] The same observations made in connection with Geiger's suggestion apply, *mutatis mutandis*, to Frankel's as well. Nonetheless, the Talmud does refer to this illustrious rabbi as one who discussed targumic renderings of Prophetic passages, and sometimes the reference implies translational activity on his part.[10] On the other hand, Joseph appeals to Targumic renderings as already extant and authoritative on two occasions.[11] This would seem to suggest that Joseph had a role in consolidating and affirming Targumic tradition in respect of the Prophets, but it is hardly an exegesis of the Talmudic texts involved to say that he exercised a creative function as the Targum's author.

Obviously, Talmudic attributions cannot be taken at face value as modern historical assertions: the work of Jacob Neusner has taught us that rabbinic literature, even more than the New Testament, speaks to us in a variety of idioms, and therefore that we make the facile equation between a given text and our own conception of history at our peril.[12] For this reason, it would be imprudent to assume, even as a working hypothesis, that Jonathan or Joseph is what we would call the 'author' of the Prophets Targum. But it would be equally unwise to ignore two implications which the Talmudic passages, in aggregate, would appear to make: (1) that the Prophets Targum took shape over a very long period and (2) that rabbis were intimately associated with its formation. Each of these points must be considered in the light of the present consensus on the growth of the Targumim.

The introductions of George Foot Moore, Roger Le Déaut, John Bowker, Martin McNamara and Donald E. Gowan all rightly stress the importance of synagogue worship as the matrix of targumic activity.[13] The need to render the Bible into Aramaic was pressing,[14] and it attended the need, particularly in Prophetic passages, to explain biblical imagery.[15] In the Talmud, we are given vivid testimony to the influence of popular opinion on the use of Targums (Megillah 21b):

> Our Rabbis taught: As regards the Torah, one reads and one translates, and in no case must one read and two translate. As regards the Prophets, one reads and two may translate, but in no case may two read and two translate. As regards the Hallel and the Megillah, even ten may read. What is the reason? Since the people like it, they pay attention and hear.

It comes as no surprise, then, when we are told rabbis consulted with

speakers of Aramaic to recover the proper phrasing in translations.[16]
The conclusion is warranted that a coherent Targum tradition could
only evolve out of generations of synagogue practice.

Yet it is also obvious that the evolution of synagogue practice alone
does not explain the existence of written, authoritative Targums. The
usage of centuries might lead to a certain amount of consolidation and
common custom, but the step from rendering those passages which
happen to have been read in public worship to translating an entire
corpus is a considerable one. The passage from the Megillah tractate
shows that some variety in practice was countenanced by the rabbis
for good, pastoral reasons; it also shows the rabbinic concern for and
involvement with targumic tradition, as do all of the Talmudic
passages cited in this introduction. Such concern and involvement
would have been very natural, of course, but it is also necessary to
postulate in order to explain the development of ad hoc paraphrases
into actual versions of Old Testament books which evidence contact
with rabbinic discussion.[17] Hence, while the Targums might be
characterized as 'popular paraphrases' in respect of their liturgical
function, substantively they are the outcome of a dialectical relationship
between the beth knesset and the beth midrash.

Once the Targums are understood in this fashion, their importance
for the student of early Judaism becomes evident. Mishnah, Midrash
and Talmud present us, in the main, with intramural rabbinic
discussion. Targums provide us with some insight into how those
discussions found expression in a more public, less expert context, i.e.,
in the worship of the faithful. We may say this without being so rash as
to imagine that the standard rabbinic translations were everywhere or
consistently accepted, or that there was an exclusive norm among the
rabbis themselves. The large number of extant Targums, as well as the
Talmudic passages discussed, militate against the acceptance of such a
picture. The Targums better represent a process than an ideal, but a
process distinct from, even though cognate with, that which produced
Mishnah, Midrash and Talmud. Since this is the case, the problematic
relationship between Targumic halakhah and haggadah and those
expressed in other rabbinic literature is quite natural. For this reason,
it is simply inappropriate to argue that the divergence of a Targumic
reading from mishnah (if I may use the term broadly) demonstrates
that the reading is pre-mishnaic.[18] Such divergence might be explained
by the distinctive purposes of targum and mishnah, or by the reflection
in a Targum of non-rabbinic, popular, but not necessarily primitive

opinion, or by divisions within rabbinic discussion about which we may or may not be informed. All of this is to say that Targums can no more be measured by mishnah alone than synodical proceedings could be said to furnish an adequate criterion for dating parochial sermons. Rabbinic literature provides one possible index for the sort of material found in the Targums, but it is not a solely sufficient or even primary standard for the evaluation and dating of Targumic readings.

The reader of the Targums is therefore left, as is the reader of the New Testament,[19] to infer the date of the document from allusions to datable historical events or circumstances. This programme was carried out by Pinkhos Churgin in his classic monograph on Targum Jonathan; we will cite some of the evidence he adduces and proceed to consider his conclusions. The reference in Targum Isaiah 28.1 to the deplorable state of the priesthood seemed to him to presuppose that the Temple still stood (pp. 23, 24),[20] and in our exegesis of characteristic terms in the Targum Isaiah we will see that there are many indications that material presented in chapter twenty-eight derives from this period. Churgin saw in 65.4[21] an allusion to the erection of Tiberias (p. 25) and in 54.1[22] an interpretation designed to address the conditions prevailing in the Roman occupation (pp. 27, 28). Targum Isaiah 21.9[23] was plausibly related to the presecutions in Sassanian Babylon (pp. 28, 29). But Churgin did not feel he could perceive allusions to later periods (p. 29):

> On the other hand, the fall of Babylonia is with the author still a desire ... There is no other allusion in the Targum to the Arabs. So that this allusion to Babylonia affords us a terminus ad quem.

While one can only concur with Churgin's demonstration that this Targum presents a startling range of historical allusions,[24] one must approach the conclusion just cited with circumspection. Just as a reader in the Sassanian period could understand Is. 21.9 to apply to his own situation, even though the political régime in question was not the one the prophet had to endure, so a reader in a later period, especially if he lived in Babylon, could apply this passage to his experience without introducing changes into the text. The further complication must be borne in mind that 'Babylon' can be used symbolically (cf. I Peter 5.13), and in this sense it has no terminus ad quem.[25] Tg Is 21.9 is taken only as an example to suggest that two principles of Targumic formation restricted the inclusion of historical allusions: (1) as

renderings of Old Testament texts, such Targumic allusions would
have had to have been seen as consistent with the passage in question
and (2) once a Targumic reading was itself accepted as traditional, the
opportunity to alter it would have been inversely proportional to its
acknowledged worth.[26] A corollary of the second principle is that
historical allusions to later periods are less likely to have been
incorporated than those from earlier periods, although allowances
must be made for local variation and the strength of popular opinion.[27]
But the simple fact is that the textual attestation for the Jonathan
Targum is medieval,[28] so that the eventual and nearly absolute
restriction of historical allusions seems established, and it is a
reasonable inference that this restriction grew quite inevitably out of
the increasingly conservative process of Targumic transmission. The
growth of the conservative tendency probably corresponds to the
decline of Targumic Aramaic as the popularly spoken Jewish language
and the resultant ascendancy of the rabbis in transmitting what were
after all more and more extensive traditions.[29] While the rabbis have
preserved much ancient material for us, their participation in targumic
transmission also makes it impossible to speak meaningfully of an
absolute terminus ad quem for any Targum.

   Research into the literary affinities of the Prophets Targum leads us
to draw a similar conclusion. Naphtali Wieder and William H.
Brownlee posit congruence with the Habakkuk Pesher. The latter also
draws attention to the use Josephus may possibly have made of
Targumic renderings, an observation already made by Ralph Marcus.[30]
On the other hand, Samsom H. Levey suggests that, at 2 Samuel 22.32,
'The Targum's phrase, *leth elaha ela Yahweh*, is an exact literal
translation of the Arabic, *la ilaha illa-ilahu*, "there is no God but
Allah . . .",' and that Tg Is 11.4b reflects an exegesis traceable to Saadia
Gaon.[31] Since Levey concludes 'that the *terminus ad quem* of Targum
Jonathan to the Prophets cannot be earlier than the Arab conquest of
Babylonia' (p. 194), consideration of his argument is in order.
Specifically, the former passage may be nothing more than a
'translation' of vital monotheistic faith in any period,[32] and the
importance of the latter passage is vitiated by the fact that it is a textual
variant.[33] More generally, everything we know about Targum formation
suggests that the latest (or earliest) passage in a given work need have
no substantive significance for the whole. Allusions to datable events
and circumstances help to fix an upper and lower limit for the
constituent readings of a Targum, but they tell us nothing about when

readings were so organized as to become recognizable as a Targum. Moreover, we may not assume that what we happen to be able to discern as the earliest or latest reading is in fact the earliest or latest— for the simple reason that the translation of most passages did not occasion any particular historical allusion. In a word, the nature of the Targums implies that it is impossible to fix their termini a quo and ad quem by this method, and the very attempt to do so may be misleading.

Research into the language of the Targums has proceeded at an intense level during this century, so that one might have hoped that by now it would have shed some light on their date and provenience. Unfortunately, this is not the case, as Charles Perrot's rather desperate comment indicates:

> Dans le domaine de l'araméen targumique, nous sommes toujours en pleine 'Tour de Babel,' pour une raison simple: nous ne savons pas encore exactement quel type d'araméen était parlé dans la Palestine du 1er s. (parler 'd'araméen moyen,' comme on le fait d'ordinaire, n'avance guère la situation). Selon P. Kahle, l'araméen de TgP s'imposait déjà partout au 1er s.; selon E.Y. Kutscher, la Judée parlait une langue proche de TgO, et la Galilée, celle de TgP. Suivant J.A. Fitzmyer, l'araméen du 1er s. est exactement celui des documents araméens de Qumrân (11QTgJob, l'*Apocryphe de la Genèse* et les lettres en araméen de Bar Kokeba) et des anciennes inscriptions araméenes. Au contraire, suivant A. Díez Macho surtout, l'araméen du 1er s. est celui de TgP et de TgN en particulier; l'araméen qumrânien serait plutôt un araméen littéraire des lettrés de Qumrân, et non pas un araméen populaire . . . [34]

The complexity of the discussion attests the complexity of the problem. The extant evidence suggests that Aramaic underwent a marked development, but that evidence consists of various writings composed in various times, in various places and for various purposes, and to fix a writing under any of the three aspects is often a matter of conjecture. This is why Fitzmyer and Díez Macho, to take prominent examples, disagree so comprehensively: their positions are contradictory in regard to both the provenience of the Targums and the development of the language in which they are written. Findings in respect of provenience and language have been coordinated, and while this is regarded as mutually supportive argumentation by partisans of a position, to the more sceptical it appears to evidence circular reasoning. Previous discussion does not therefore permit us to place the Prophets Targum linguistically in an agreed scheme of the development of Aramaic. As a result, the following survey of some major contributions to our understanding of the language of Targum Jonathan cannot be expected to bring us to any firm conclusions as to its date and provenience.

Since Zacharias Frankel, the linguistic position of Targum Jonathan as mediating between Onqelos and Pseudo-Jonathan, though nearer to the former, has been widely recognized. Frankel held that Onqelos represents an earlier form of Aramaic than Pseudo-Jonathan and the Hagiographic Targums do, with Jonathan representing an intermediate stage in the development of the language. He instanced the agreement of Jonathan with Onqelos against later Targumim (e.g., ארי for כי in the Masoretic Text, instead of ארום, and חזה for ראה, instead of חמא) and its agreement with later Targumim against Onqelos (e.g., כלי for קרא).[35] Gustav Dalman, while accepting that a Palestinian targum tradition has influenced Pseudo-Jonathan, argued from what he saw as 'der sprachlichen Anlehnung an das Onkelostargum' that we do not have here a 'vollständiges "palästinisches" Pentateuchtargum aus alter Zeit.'[36] He also agreed with Frankel in perceiving a linguistic link between the late Hagiographa Targums and Pseudo-Jonathan (pp. 37f.). Turning to Jonathan, Dalman observed that, since the Prophets were not read in worship in their entirety, 'ist indes (sc. Targum) anzunehmen, dass hier die Tradition weniger feststand als bei dem Thoratargum' (p. 15). Nonetheless, he held that Jonathan shared with Onqelos a proper handling of gutturals which 'zeigt hierin keinen galiläischen oder babylonischen Einfluss, während die *jer.Targume* durch ihre Behandlung besonders von ע, aber auch von ה beweisen, dass eine schlechte Aussprachetradition bei ihrer Entstehung wirksam gewesen ist' (pp. 60, 61).

Dalman's position involved the perception of two types of Aramaic, both of which were seen as preserved in the Targumim. First there was the 'hebraisiertes Aramäisch' of Onqelos and Jonathan, a characterization which Dalman borrowed from M. Friedmann's description of Mishnaic Aramaic (p. 10). Dalman admitted that this dialect was both 'scholarly' and 'artful' (pp. 13, 40),[37] and in this sense not representative of common speech. Common speech, he held, is represented in Galilean and Babylonian Aramaic, but it is far from the idiom of Jesus' day, since these dialects date from the fourth and seventh centuries

C.E. respectively (pp. 41, 42). These late, to his mind corrupted, dialects have influenced the so-called Jerusalem Targums (that is, Pseudo-Jonathan and the Fragment Targums).

Paul Kahle and his famous student, Matthew Black, offered an alternative reconstruction. Kahle's study of the Cairo Geniza targums, which are dated in the period between the seventh and the eleventh century, revealed a wealth of variety which in his opinion belied the authority of Onqelos. In the main, these various readings manifested a close relationship to Pseudo-Jonathan and the Fragment Targums. Kahle went so far as to suggest 'that Onkelos had been without importance in Palestine, indeed, that it had not even existed there till it was introduced from Babylonia, and then scarcely before 1000 A.D.'[38] Accepting the reconstruction of Gerard J. Kuiper, Black takes the more nuanced line that 'Onkelos, while admittedly showing traces of Babylonian influence, appears nevertheless to have been an authoritative redaction *of the same kind of Palestinian Targum tradition which is preserved, still in its fluid state, in the Fragment Targum, the Geniza Fragments, Pseudo-Jonathan and Targum Neofiti 1'* (p. 19). By analogy, Jonathan is held to represent the same process (p. 18), and Alejandro Díez Macho has accordingly explained alternative developments in the Prophetic targum tradition as Kahle did the Cairo Geniza material.[39]

Acceptance of the Kahle-Black model for the development of Targumic Aramaic necessitates inverting the order of the Frankel-Dalman model. Now Jonathan is earlier than a late Onqelos instead of later than an early Onqelos. But the more recent model must posit a cipher in order to account for the immense variety in the so-called Palestinian Targums: this is the 'Palestinian Targum' in what Black has called its 'fluid state.' With the possible exception of Neophyti I, the attestation for the cipher is late, viz. Pseudo-Jonathan (post-Islamic), Fragment Targums (medieval), Cairo Geniza material (from the seventh century and later).[40] Obviously, earlier evidence for the 'Palestinian Targum' was necessary to make the hypothesis viable. This was why the identification of Neophyti in 1956 has had such an impact, as Díez Macho has not been backward in pointing out:

> La publication, par P. Kahle, des fragments du TargP en 1930, la publication de son *The Cairo Geniza* (1re éd. London 1947, 2e éd. Oxford 1959) et la découverte du ms Neofiti 1 en 1956 marquent le tournat d'une nouvelle époque des études targumiques.[41]

Díez Macho claims that, while 'l'araméen des mss du VIIe—VIIIe siècle
ne diffère guère de celui de Neofiti' (p. 36), Neophyti is clearly pre-
mishnaic in content (pp. 38f.). This is enough to convince him that
Kahle was correct.

We have already seen that caution is appropriate in comparing the
Targums with rabbinic literature. Ch. Albeck long ago warned more
generally, but with considerable evidential support, that what seems to
be anti-mishnaic is not to be dated as pre-mishnaic[42]; further, Martin
McNamara, though substantively in agreement with Díez Macho,
argues that Neophyti is a recension of the Palestinian Targum from the
Talmudic period.[43] On the latter understanding, Neophyti no more
substantiates the cipher than do Pseudo-Jonathan and the Fragment
Targums. Doubt has also been cast on Díez Macho's claims linguistically,
in that the language of the Targum presents Greek influences,
apparently from a later period than he postulates,[44] and textually, in
that the manuscript is the victim of poor scribal handling.[45] In sum,
while the importance of this sixteenth century document is not to be
minimized, neither will it serve as the vindication of Kahle's thesis.

Moreover, Dead Sea discoveries have been hailed recently as
linguistically similar to Onqelos and Jonathan. Joseph A. Fitzmyer has
been principally responsible for stimulating the investigation of this
material from the point of view of Aramaic language and the Targums.
In his introduction to *The Genesis Apocryphon of Qumran Cave I*,
Biblica et Orientalia 18 (Rome: Pontifical Biblical Institute, 1966,
1971²), he dealt with 'The Language of the Scroll' (pp. 17-25, in the first
edition) and 'The *Genesis Apocryphon* and the Targums' (pp. 26-34).
While admitting that the 'extent to which this *literary* Aramaic actually
differed from the spoken, popular patois of the time is difficult to say'
(p. 20), he is adamant that the language it represents is older than that
found in the Targums (p. 25), and he buttresses this finding with his
literary analysis in respect of Neophyti, Pseudo-Jonathan and Onqelos
(see p. 32 especially). Díez Macho's response has been to resuscitate an
argument used by Kahle against Dalman,[46] namely that 'il y a des
raisons sérieuses pour considérer les formes "évoluées" de l'araméen de
Qumrân et de Murabba'ât comme un araméen d'Empire, littéraire,
contaminé par un araméen populaire parlé et *contemporain*, conservé
dans le TargP' (*art. cit.*, p. 27). But Fitzmyer's reference to the letters of
Murabba'ât, Seiyâl and Ḥabra (p. 24), to the other Qumran Aramaic
texts (p. 18) and to Megillat Ta'anît (p. 18) protects him from the claim
that he relies too heavily on an isolated literary text, which can more
truly be said of Dalman.

One linguistic element cited by Fitzmyer as distinguishing the *Genesis Apocryphon* from the Targums is the use of ל instead of ית as the sign of the accusative (pp. 23, 33). But the Job Targum from Qumran uses ית as well as ל, as Stephen A. Kaufman points out in his important review of the van der Ploeg/van der Woude edition (p. 325).[47] Kaufman builds on E.Y. Kutscher's case for the connection between the *Genesis Apocryphon* and Onqelos and Jonathan, and extends this to include the Job Targum on the basis of lexical evidence (p. 326). In regard to Neophyti and Palestinian Targums, he concludes (p. 327):

> On the other hand, western features common to 11QtgJob (and/or 1QapGen) and Targum Neofiti show only that the Qumran texts are of western origin, not that Neofiti is contemporaneous with them. True, many scholars ... still insist on an early dating of the Palestinian Targum tradition as represented by Targum Neofiti I, in spite of the opinions of Kutscher, Fitzmyer, Greenfield and others; but 11QtgJob should settle the matter in favor of a post-Bar Kochba dating for the Palestinian Targums.

On the same page, Onqelos and Jonathan are dated 'between 70 A.D. and the fall of Bar-Kochba,' that is, earlier than the Palestinian Targums, but later than the *Genesis Apocryphon* (which he dates in the first century).

The circular path of recent discussion of the Aramaic language reminds one, if not of the tower of Babel, then of a plateau of discordant opinions from which continued ascent is difficult. Nor should it be thought that this discussion, even were it conclusive, would definitely settle the literary question of the relationship between the Targumim. As Díez Macho reminds us, 'le contenu pourrait être plus ancien que la langue' (*art. cit.*, p. 35). And in the end, it would seem premature to base Targumic exegesis on any single theory of Aramaic evolution; there seem to be more variables than any of them can comfortably accommodate.

When, in the course of my research on Jesus' announcement of the kingdom of God, I discovered that the Prophetic Targums present striking parallels to dominical diction,[48] I looked to works cited in this introduction for guidance in regard to their date and provenience. But it did not seem appropriate in a work of New Testament exegesis to devote considerable space to a generally inconclusive discussion of Targumic origins, as the historical, literary and linguistic contributions seem in aggregate to be. It appeared moreover that a rather different approach was called for, one which focused on what I should like to call the exegetical framework of the Targums.

While historical and literary allusions might guide us to an understanding of the date and provenience of a given passage or motif, and language (if it were an established criterion) would help to establish the time and place of the final redaction of the whole, Targums as such are not farragos of tradition or de novo compositions, but specimens of extended exegesis. To discover the provenience and date of a Targum one must ask, first, what exegetical terms and phrases are so frequently used as to constitute characteristic conventions, and then, how do these conventions relate to historical circumstances, to the New Testament and early Jewish literature generally? Such conventions, when repeatedly used in a given work, would provide the ordering principle for traditional interpretations and for the inclusion of subsequent insights. This exegetical framework belongs to the *esse* of a Targum: without it, targumic readings are only a pot pourri, while with it even the addition of material does not constitute a recension, only an addendum.[49] If the analysis of individual passages is too atomistic to be pertinent for an entire Targum, and if linguistic criteria would say more about a copyist than his masters, perhaps the exegetical framework is a key to the understanding of Targums.

The compendious character of Targums also commended this method. Granted that they are the products of generations of comment, then the appropriate question for the student of an entire Targum is not, whence do its constituent readings derive, but, what are its constitutive principles of composition? Part II is a study of repeatedly used and evocative terms or phrases in the Isaiah Targum which manifest its exegetical framework. They have been chosen and tabulated simply on the basis of a reading of the text. This study seeks to establish that there is such a framework, i.e., that these various terms evince a coherent, ordering principle. It also suggests—on the strength of Targumic coherences with the Septuagint,[50] Intertestamental literature,[51] the New Testament,[52] and Rabbinica[53]—that the theology of an earlier framework reflects developments from just prior to the destruction of the Temple until the beginning of the Bar Kokhba revolt, while a later meturgeman who helped to shape the framework voices the concerns of the Amoraic period.

II

ANALYSIS OF CHARACTERISTIC TERMS OR PHRASES

A. 'Law' (אוריתא)

As one might have expected, 'law' in the Isaiah Targum is a central theologoumenon, indeed so central that it occurs in association with many of the other characteristic terms and phrases which are to be considered here. The meturgeman is so convinced that law is the means offered God's people for relating themselves to him that he frequently introduces the term when there is no analogue to it in the Hebrew text. The very opening of the Targum (vv. 2, 3) emphasizes that law is the revealed standard of behaviour from which Israel has fallen:

> Hear, heavens, which trembled when I gave my law to my people . . . they have rebelled against my memra . . . my people has not had the intelligence to return to my law.

In the same chapter, after the memra's abhorence at the cult (v. 14) and the removal of the Shekinah (v. 15) are mentioned, repentance to the law is called for (v. 16).[1] The reward for this repentance is, 'you will pray before me and I will enact your prayer' (v. 18), and those who do the law will return to Zion (v. 27), but, 'the rebellious and guilty will be destroyed together, and those who have forsaken the law of the LORD will perish' (v. 28). The very content of repentance, then, is law; law restores the prayerful relationship between God and his people and their restoration to Zion accrues from that righteousness which does the law. When we come to discuss 'Exile' and 'Repentance' we will be able to describe in more detail the meturgeman's understanding of how such restoration comes about; our concern for the present is merely to stress that law is Israel's only way of putting herself on the path to restoration. To forsake the law is to forsake life, to turn away from a messianic vindication which can be described in the most positive of terms (53.10b):

> They will gaze upon the kingdom of the messiah; they will
> increase sons and daughters; they will prolong days, and the
> servants of the law of the LORD will prosper in his pleasure.

The messiah can be said to act 'to subject many' (v. 11) or to subject
'the rebellious' (v. 12) to the law; as the means of Israel's vindication,
law is the messianic programme.

This vindication, as we will see again and again in the Targum, is
associated with 'sanctuary,' as the place of the 'Shekinah,' in
Jerusalem (2.3):

> And many peoples will go and say, Come, and we will go up to
> the mount of the sanctuary house of the LORD, to the
> Shekinah house of the God of Jacob, and he will teach us
> from the ways that are established before him and we will go
> in the teaching of his law ... [2]

Keepers of the law join in the messiah's glory (4.2),[3] and 'he that does
the law will be established in Jerusalem' (v. 3). But the meturgeman's
doctrine of law is double-edged, in that the failure to keep it results in
punishment (5.20c):

> Tg   and the words of the law are sweet to the ones who do
>   them, and bitterness will come to the wicked, and they
>   will know that in the end sin is bitter to the one doing it.
> MT   who put bitter for sweet and sweet for bitter.

The meturgeman had God say of Assyria, 'against the people who
transgressed my law I will appoint him' (10.6)[4]; this rebellious group
serves as the foil to those 'who keep the law with a perfect heart'
(26.2).[5] But the ultimate efficacy of the law is expressed at 26.19:

> Tg   You are he that quickens the dead and raises the bones of
>   their corpses ... for your dew is a dew of light to the
>   servants of your law, and the wicked to whom you gave
>   might and they transgressed your memra to Gehinnam
>   you will deliver.
> MT   Your dead will live, my corpses will rise ... for your dew
>   is a dew of light, and you will make it fall on the land of
>   the ghosts.

Several comments seem appropriate in the light of the interpretation
of this text. First, it is striking that the meturgeman's conviction that
law is the engine of vindication causes him to understand resurrection
as the proper possession of 'servants of the law.' Second, the double-

edged nature of the meturgeman's law doctrine results in, or at least contributes to, an understanding of resurrection as both to praise and blame (cf. Daniel 12.2). Third, the antithesis to serving the law is transgressing God's memra; as our discussion of the latter term will explain, this amounts to saying that the failure to observe the law is a personal affront to the LORD.

Chapter twenty-eight in the Targum will figure prominently in our discussions of several of the characteristic terms and phrases. In it, the meturgeman expresses his hope for Israel's vindication even as he bitterly laments her apostasy (especially in respect of Temple service). The ground of both his expectation and his bitterness is his assurance that Israel has been chosen by God and that law is the seal of her election (vv. 9, 10):

> Tg   To whom was the law given . . . was it not to the house of
>   Israel that were cherished more than all the nations . . . ?
>   They were commanded to do the law . . .
> MT Who will teach knowledge . . . those weaned from milk . . . ?
>   Because it is precept upon precept . . .

References to the prophetic preaching of repentance and the consequent forgiveness, and to the sanctuary and the Shekinah follow. In v. 13, 'Precept upon precept' is also rendered with the statement that they were commanded to do the law, and their failure to do so (and their contempt for the sanctuary) is held to result in exile. But the severity of the punishment serves to heighten the promise, 'If the house of Israel set their faces to do the law, would he not turn and gather them . . . ?' (v. 25).[6]

The frequent association of 'teaching' and 'law' reminds us that the meturgeman saw the law as a living tradition. It was given on Sinai[7] to Israel alone,[8] but it can only be apprehended and handed on by those who seek the LORD.[9] The law can be so perverted by human exposition[10] that a worthy scribe is not to be found.[11] As a divine gift, law distinguishes Israel as Israel; the messiah's programme is also conditioned by law, since only through law can Israel know her restoration. But Israel's responsibility is to appropriate the law, in action and teaching, and the failure to act on her responsibility can only result in the terrible consequences which inevitably follow transgression.

The Targumic rendering of Is. 26.19 is quite consistent with the rabbinic understanding of the verse, in which, apparently from the time of Rabban Gamaliel (cf. Sanhedrin 90b), the resurrection was seen to be at issue. Already in the Palestinian recension of the Shemoneh Esreh, God is praised (in the second benediction) as he who 'quickens the dead,' and 'dew' is used as an image of the resurrection. Moreover, God's action in raising Israel is seen as salvific, and is associated with the punishment of the arrogant.[12] Interestingly, the corresponding benediction in the Babylonian recension so stresses the positive aspect of the resurrection that God's punitive action is not mentioned.[13] A similar distinction in emphasis is evident in the rabbinic opinions expressed about this verse. R. Eleazar (the Amora), referring to 'for thy dew is a dew of light,' commented, 'him who makes use of the light of the Torah will the light of the Torah revive, but him who makes no use of the light of the Torah the light of the Torah will not revive' (Kethuboth 111b).[14] Taking a different view, R. Abba b. Memel, a Palestinian Amora of the same period,[15] referred 'thy dead will live' to 'the dead of the land of Israel' and 'my dead bodies will arise' to the dead of the diaspora (Kethuboth 111a). Naturally, none of this evidence demonstrates that the Targum to Isaiah was extant at the time the prayers were formulated and the statements cited made, but we can say that the connection between resurrection, judgement and Is. 26.19 was made from around the end of the first century, and that the legal implications of the same verse seemed secure to R. Eleazar, even though the emphasis of the Targum does diverge somewhat from another stream of Amoraic opinion (represented by R. Abba b. Memel).

R. Eleazar's view seems to be an exegetically refined expression of the sort of belief found in the Targum, and it is of note that R. Eleazar also comments on Is. 2.3 in a way which permits of the suspicion that there is some connection between his thought and that of the Isaiah meturgeman. The Targum, we recall, refers to the 'sanctuary house of the LORD' as 'the Shekinah house of the God of Jacob.' Eleazar exegetes 'the God of Jacob' in the Hebrew text as Beth-el, i.e., God is home (Pesahim 88a). In his index (cf. n.15), Slotki ascribes the latter opinion to R. Eleazar the Tanna, but we may wonder whether two exegetically refined arguments, both with a certain affinity with the Targum, derived from different people in quite different times. There are so many rabbis named as Eleazar in Babli, however, that we are in no position to select one of them as having had some characteristic affinity with Targumic interpretations. In Jerushalmi, R. Nathan emphatically cites Is. 2.3 by way of asserting the provenience of the

law from Zion, not Babylon (Nedarim 6.9; cf. the view of R. Levi in
Leviticus Rabbah 24.4, that of R. Judah b. R. Ḥiyya in Pesiqta
Rabbati 39.2, and the unascribed opinion in Pesiqta Rabbati 41.1),
and R. Judah b. Pazzi tells a delightful parable in which the 'dew' of
the resurrection is compared to a physician's bag (Berakhoth 5.2).
Such passages show only the continued interest in the Isaian verses
in the Amoraic period; they seem neither prior to nor dependent on
the Targum. Even such affinities as are manifest in Babli are more
illuminating of the general coherence between rabbinic and Targumic
theology and exegesis than of the provenience of the Targum.

The emphatic assertion in Tg Is. 28.9, 10 that the law is Israel's
communal possession is reminiscent of the similar statement of R.
Aqiba in Aboth 3.15; it is worth recalling (although the fact may be
merely coincidental) that this rabbi was peculiarly concerned with the
tangible restoration of Israel, a motif in the Targum to Isaiah which we
have already seen to be central. Other Prophetic Targumim would
appear to share a similar outlook. Twice in Targum Jeremiah, the
messiah is said to 'enact true judgment and righteousness in the land'
(23.5; 33.15), and Israel as a whole is addressed in Targum Hosea
(10.12) with an imperative (' . . . establish for yourselves the teaching
of the law, behold in every time the prophets were saying to you,
repent to the service of the LORD . . . ') which presents the law as the
content of repentance. In his study of Jewish eschatology in the New
Testament period, Paul Volz observed that in 2 Baruch the law and
the cult are associated,[16] and the mention of the LORD's 'service' in
the Hosea Targum (as in the fifth of the Shemoneh Esreh in the
Babylonian recension) may imply such an assocation. In any case, the
Isaiah Targum explicitly associates the law and the sanctuary, as we
have seen: one is reminded also of the image in the Sibylline Oracles of
men turning to the Temple and the law (cf. Is. 2.3).[17] Moreover, Volz
explains that Baruch sees the law and right teaching as means of
restoration:

> Wenn die Juden geduldig ausharren und sich dem Gesetz
> und dem Weisen unterwerfen, so werden sie die Tröstung
> Zions schauen 44.7; 46.6, Jerusalems Neubau für immer 6.9;
> 32.4 und die Sammlung der Zerstreuten 78.7.[18]

Law is of perennial interest as the quintessential divine gift to Israel,
but when the emphasis falls so squarely — as it does in the Isaiah
Targum — on the messianic restoration in Zion of God's people, who

attend to the teaching which comes from the Temple, then this emphatically eschatological faith in the efficacy of law would seem to be most consistent with the theology of the early documents discussed by Volz. As we shall see, however, and as the Amoraic views adduced already indicate, the Targumic theologoumena — 'law' included— were certainly seen to be relevant by rabbis who lived long after the period to which Volz limits himself. For this reason we cannot conclude, but only tentatively suggest, that the understanding of law in the Targum reflects an expectation of restoration among the rabbis such as resulted in the Bar Kokhba movement.

B. 'Sanctuary' (מקדשא)

In the Targum to Isaiah, the term 'sanctuary' is used with greater precision, to refer specifically to the holy place appointed by God in Jerusalem, than is the case in the usage of the corresponding Hebrew term (מקדש) in the Masoretic Text. This becomes immediately apparent when we consider the Targumic parallels to the occurrences of מקדש in the MT. On two occasions (8.14; 16.12), the meturgeman does not use מקדשא when מקדש appears in the Hebrew text, although in a third instance (60.13) he does so. Only in the third case is the place of God the reference of מקדשא[1]; in the other two, the term is used more loosely. At 8.14, the Hebrew 'sanctuary' is used along with 'stone of offence,' 'rock of stumbling,' 'trap,' and 'snare' to describe the LORD's dread presence. It would appear that is used here because אתו תקדישו ('you shall count him holy') appears in the previous verse; it is not the holy place, but God's holy nature which is at issue.[2] Accordingly, the meturgeman renders the term with 'vengeance' (פורען) and avoids confusion with the Temple. At 16.12, the meturgeman refuses to use מקדשא of Moab's idol temple, and so again does not follow the looser usage of the MT. There are occasions in the Targum when the plural of the noun is apparently used to refer to additional Jewish sanctuaries (5.5; 37.24: מקדשיהון in both cases). In each, a singular usage precedes (5.2; 37.14), so that we are encouraged to think of such places (presumably synagogues) as distinct from the Jerusalem Temple, but as related to it in some way.

Such precision of usage is also manifest in the meturgeman's introduction of the term into passages which speak of the Temple in the MT, but which do not have the term מקדש. So we find that 'sanctuary' frequently refers to the Temple which the MT knows as God's 'house' (2.2; 6.4; 37.1, 14; 38.20, 22; 56.5, 7). But the term is also used to render other Hebrew words, such as 'site' (מכון, 4.5) and 'watchtower' (מגדל, 5.2), and this suggests that the meturgeman had the Temple on his mind more than the author or editor of Isaiah did.[3] In some cases, the meturgeman speaks of the sanctuary without full linguistic warrant from the Hebrew text, but because it seemed to him appropriate (10.32[4]; 22.8[5]; 38.2; 52.11). Such instances are readily explicable on the basis of the contextual sensitivity of the meturgeman.[6] One other innovation is far more dramatic, and suggests that the meturgeman is guided by more than common sense in his understanding that the Hebrew text refers to the Temple more often than the term מקדש appears. At issue is 22.22, which departs markedly from the MT:

> Tg   And I will place the key of the sanctuary house and the government of David's house in his hand . . .
> MT   And I will place on his shoulder the key of the house of David . . .

It may appear extravagant to so honour Eliakim, but that this addition is deliberate is shown by v. 24, where the meturgeman promises him a specifically priestly progeny. The meturgeman uses מקדשא more precisely than the Hebrew writers of Isaiah used מקדש, but he also used it more frequently; it is the place of God, and as such it figures prominently in the relationship between man and God.

This prominence obtains in the case of both the personal and the communal relationship with God. At 30.29, the meturgeman introduces the term (with 'mount of the LORD,' as in the MT) into the festal imagery which describes the joy of God's people at his coming. The righteous man, who is to dwell in 'fortresses of rocks' in the MT, is understood by the meturgeman to inhabit the sanctuary (33.16). The theme of the joy for the righteous[7] which is to spring from the sanctuary is expressed by a slogan in the Targum, first at 24.16:

> Tg   From *the sanctuary house, whence joy is about to come forth to all the inhabitants of the earth* . . .
> MT   From the end(s)[8] of the earth . . .

In the thanksgiving of Hezekiah (38.11), the italicized phrase is repeated (with orthographic variants), so that we might say it is a firm conviction of the meturgeman.[9] For him the sanctuary is not merely the place where important events occurred, nor only a place appointed by God in connection with which his authority is manifest: it is also to be the locus of a fresh and fulfilled existence inaugurated by God himself.

It is therefore a matter for sorrow and anger that Temple service is improperly conducted. The meturgeman rages against the (philo-Roman, perhaps Herodian) ruler who 'gives the turban to the wicked one of the sanctuary house of his praise' (28.1; cf. v. 4 MT: 'the fading flower of its glorious beauty'). Under the high priest, the proper service of the sanctuary which the prophets enjoined has been so perverted that idolatrous worship is practised, and for this, exile will be the punishment (28.10-13). Comparison with the MT will immediately show what an innovative interpretation this is: the meturgeman here paraphrases a rather abstract oracle so that it directly pertains to his own experience. But is is striking that his experience is of perversion in the Temple cult, and not of the destruction of the Temple. A reference to destruction, rather than exile, would have been appropriate in v. 13, had it been possible.[10] It apparently was not.

Other readings in the Targum, however, do presuppose that the Temple has been destroyed and the divine presence taken up:

30.20
Tg ... and he will not again take up his Shekinah from the sanctuary house ...
MT ... and your teacher will not hide himself again ...
32.14
Tg For the sanctuary house is desolate ...
MT For the palace has been forsaken ...

Both of these references occur in contexts in which the renewed presence of God is promised. This is evident in 30.20 itself, and the verse following the second passage speaks of a refreshing spirit from on high (to which the meturgeman adds the term Shekinah). The terrible events involved with the war of 66-70 therefore did not shake the conviction of the meturgeman that the divine act on behalf of the righteous (cf. Tg Is. 30.18; 32.16) would be effected in association with the Temple. Where the MT reads, 'he was wounded for our transgressions and he was bruised for our iniquities' (53.5), the meturgeman asserts, 'he [viz. the messiah, 52.13] will build the sanctuary house that was profaned for our transgressions and delivered over for our iniquities.' The confidence which could endure what was seen as the profanation of the Temple cult also found the resources to declare a divinely appointed renewal of the sanctuary after 70 C.E.[11]

If we were dealing with a composition which was a literary document *de novo*, one might be inclined to infer that a pre-Temple destruction source has been conflated with a post-Temple destruction source. There are two reasons for which this sort of analysis is inappropriate. In the first place, our Targum was always oral in principle, if not in practice: in a synagogue it would have had to be spoken from memory even after written notes existed.[12] Such a process, which must have influenced the literary production of the Targum as a document, would have tended to blur the lines between one 'source' and another. In the second place, we have seen a consistent theological motif associated with the term מקדשא which maintained its identity even as its exponent(s) faced different circumstances. Whether we are dealing with an individual or a group, the extant evidence presents itself as a single thought expressed under various exigencies. The theme speaks to situations which obtained from the woeful denigration of the high priestly office, probably under the Romans (in the period leading up to, and perhaps including, the siege of Jerusalem), until the definitive destruction of Jewish hopes for a restored Temple, again by the Romans, in 135.[13] Because we are not dealing with a single author, we must learn to rest content with identifying the shape and likely provenience of a motif; speculation about the particular occasion of composition is even less likely to prove adequate than is usually the case when dealing with ancient documents. Nonetheless, we do have clear evidence in the present instance that the theologoumenon in question was used before and after the destruction of the Temple, so that we may speak of distinct interpretative strata or layers.

An early, sanctuary-centered theology of restoration which is cognate with that of the Isaiah Targum was current from the first century B.C., as Volz described:

> Das Buch Tobit (ca. 100 v. Chr.) erhofft in c. 13f. die Umkehr und Wiederbegnadigung des Volkes 13.6, die Sammlung der Zerstreuten aus den Heiden 13.5, 13, die Rückkehr ins Land 14.5; die Erhöhung Israels 14.7, den Wiederaufbau Jerusalems 14.5 in farbig ausgemaltem Glanz 13.6, den Wiederbau des Tempels in Herrlichkeit 13.10; 14.5; es ist Freude über das Glück Jerusalems 13.14, und die Völker eilen herbei zum

Namen Gottes (codex א zu dem heiligen Namen Jerusalem,
Name = Tempel?); alle Götzendiener bekehren sich 13.11;
14.6f., sie haben auch ihre Freude am Heil 14.7; 13.6, 12.[14]

The sanctuary (or Temple) occupies a similar place in the Sibylline
Oracles and in the Shemoneh Esreh,[15] and Volz dates to the period of
Johanan ben Zakkai the hope for the speedy rebuilding of the Temple
expressed in Rosh Hashanah 30a.[16] He assigns a more developed form
of this hope (found in Pesahim 5a) to the school of Ishmael; here the
rooting out of the children of Esau (i.e., Rome), the building of the
Temple and the name of the messiah are specified as the rewards
allotted the children of Israel.[17] Moreover, the Psalms of Solomon 2.3;
8.12f., 26 show clearly that, from an early period, the conviction of the
Temple's importance expressed itself as a vigorous attack on lax cultic
practice.

When we turn to the later rabbinic exegeses of a passage which, in
the Targum, focuses on the sanctuary, such an acute concern for the
Temple is notably lacking. The Amoraic discussion in Kethuboth
112b refers Is. 24.16 (end) to the persecution of scholars, without
connecting their function to the Temple. The song of praise in Isaiah is
understood in the Pirqe de R. Eliezer (37, Friedlander, p. 282) to extol
Jacob in his encounter with the angel, not the righteous in their
adherence to a re-established sanctuary. Obviously, such evidence
does not prove that the rabbis ceased to be interested in the Temple
and its service; the continued use of the Shemoneh Esreh and the
prominence of cultically oriented tractates in the Talmud absolutely
militate against any suggestion to that effect. The fact does remain,
however, that a passage which is seen to refer to the sanctuary in the
Targum is not so taken by the later rabbis, even when they read the
same verse as relating to persecution and vindication.[18]

By contrast, the other Prophetic Targumim also emphasize the
place of the sanctuary. Praise from the mount of the sanctuary house is
forecast in Tg Jeremiah 31.12, and in Tg Jer. 30.18; in Tg Zechariah
1.16 God's restoration of Jerusalem and the rebuilding of the
sanctuary house are specifically promised. More generally, one
repeatedly finds the sanctuary and the sacrifices therein mentioned in
association with individual (Tg Joel 2.14, discussed more fully in the
'Repentance' section) or corporate (Tg Ezekiel 34.26; Tg Hosea 14.8)
blessings. But the specific expectation that the messiah will build the
Temple is shared with the Targum to Isaiah by the Targum to

Zechariah (6.12, 13). The Targum to Jeremiah, like the Isaiah Targum, has specific references to the Gentile defilement (51.51) and destruction (26.18) of the sanctuary. In comparison with these passages in other Prophetic Targumim, the Isaiah Targum presents a consistent theology of sanctuary restoration, but its particular interest seems to centre on the lax practice of Israel, which occasioned the need for restoration.

One might argue that the general pattern of laxity—destruction—restoration might as well apply to the period of Antiochus IV as to that of Titus. (The charge of complicity in Tg Is. 28.1 between 'the prince of Israel' and 'the wicked one of the sanctuary' would seem inappropriate to the time of Hadrian.) Indeed, the complaint voiced in Tg Is. 28.10 ('They hoped that idol service would establish them, and did not hope in the service of my sanctuary house') might be thought better to apply to the earlier period, when the Hellenization of the cult was pursued.[19] On the other hand, the charge of idolatry might be hyperbolic, referring to cooperation with Gentile power, and the reference in 29.1 to 'the gathering of the armies which shall gather together against it (sc. the city) in the year the feasts shall cease in you (sc. the altar)' is reminiscent of the later siege of Jerusalem.[20] Moreover, the meturgeman expresses the confidence in 25.2 that 'a worship house of the nations will never be built in the city of Jerusalem.' Such confidence, even in the face of the destruction of the Temple, was appropriate and pertinent from 70 C.E. until the Bar Kokhba disaster, but the innovations in the cult perpetrated by Menelaus and his Tobiad supporters were perilously close to the establishment of a heathen temple, or so at least it seemed to those who opposed the reform (cf. Daniel 11.31). An interpreter who had the circumstances of the first half of the second century B.C. freshly imprinted on his mind would not, perhaps, have written so sanguinely that Jerusalem would never house an idolatrous cult. More important, the distinction between the secular and cultic authorities in 28.1 better corresponds to the situation in the Herodian (taking this adjective to refer generally to the time of Herod until the destruction of the Temple) than to the Maccabean or Hasmonean periods.

The experience of high priestly corruption led the Prophetic interpreters vividly to portray the cultic integrity of the messianic period:

> He will build the Temple of the LORD . . . and there will be
> a high priest on his throne, and there will be a counsel of peace

between them (Tg Zechariah 6.13).

I will raise up before me a trustworthy priest, who will
minister according to my word, my will, and I will establish
for him an enduring reign and he will serve my messiah all the
days (Tg I Samuel 2.35).

Against the background of the pairing of the messiah and the priest—
which we also know from Qumran, the Testaments of the Twelve
Patriarchs and the coins of Bar Kokhba—the exaltation of Eliakim in
Tg Is. 22.22 is explicable.[21] That he is a priestly figure is established in
v. 24, and his assocation with the messiah (who is, for our interpreter,
the son of David; cf. the section on the messiah) is established by the
reference to David's house in v. 22 itself. The historical reference in
the Isaiah text, it would seem, has triggered the meturgeman's hopes
for his own day.

The sanctuary theologoumenon of the Isaiah Targum—especially
when seen against the background of the usages in other Prophetic
Targums, Rabbinica and the Intertestamental literature discussed
above—expresses a theology of hope in righteous Israel's vindication
which is perfectly consistent with the meturgeman's use of the term
'law' (cf. the last section). The failure to maintain the integrity of the
cult, which is coherent with refusal to attend to the law, strains Israel's
relationship with God. With the events of 68-70, the strain could be
portrayed as reaching to the breaking point, and the removal of the
Shekinah was seen as terribly tangible in its consequences. Even these
events, however, did not crush the hope of God's act through his
messiah and the priest on behalf of the righteous, and God's act was
seen to be on his own initiative and focused on the sanctuary. The
expectation of a divine initiative, despite Israel's cultic impropriety, is
implicit in the sanctuary theology, and this emphasis distinguishes it
from the law usage, which is rather more concerned with Israel's
response to God. The durability of the meturgeman's sanctuary-based
hope is attested by its presence in contexts in which the destruction of
the Temple, not only laxity in Temple service, is presupposed. This
contextual distinction forces us to speak of distinct interpretative
layers, layed down before and after 70; but the theological congruence
of these layers prevents us from styling them as 'sources' (as does the
consideration that the term 'source' is generally reserved for reference
to a specifically literary antecedent to a given work).

C. 'Jerusalem'

The first use of this name in the Targum (1.24) is in an innovative assertion. The second part of the verse speaks of God's just punishment of the wicked, as in the MT, but we find in the first part, 'I am about to comfort the city, Jerusalem.' It may seem odd to speak of Jerusalem's consolation in the same breath in which woes are pronounced, but in fact the theme of consoling vengeance for the holy city recurs. At 66.6, the reference to Jerusalem in a passage which speaks of recompense in the MT is hardly surprising, since the Hebrew text already mentions 'the city' in which the Temple is located.[1] But on two other occasions, the meturgeman introduces a striking slogan:

> 54.15b
> Tg   the kings of the peoples that gather to oppress you, Jerusalem, will be cast down in your midst.
> MT   who provokes you will fall because of[2] you.
> 56.9
> Tg   All the kings of the peoples that gather to oppress you, Jerusalem, will be cast down in your midst. They will be food for the beasts of the field; the beasts of the forest will be sated with them.
> MT   All[3] the beasts of the field, come to devour, all beasts of the forest.

In both instances, a positive promise is associated with the retribution (54.15a, where the Targum mentions the return of exiles; 56.8). The meturgeman quite clearly longs for an end to Jerusalem's oppression, and for suitable treatment for those who have done the oppressing.

The longing for what is seen as justice stems from the conviction that God himself is intimately associated with Jerusalem. Before referring to Jerusalem at 4.6 (see n.1), the meturgeman twice uses the term 'Shekinah' in the previous verse. It is therefore to be expected when the sanctuary is mentioned in the same passage. The same association between Shekinah, Jerusalem and sanctuary is expressed at 33.14, 16 and at 38.11. Jerusalem belongs to God, 'therein are the wicked to be judged, and to be delivered to Gehinnam for eternal burning' (33.14c). Precisely because Jerusalem is the seat of the majesty, it is to be the locus of judgment and consolation. For the same reason, the meturgeman is confident that 'a worship house of the Gentiles will never be built in the city of Jerusalem' (25.2, instead of 'palace of aliens' in the MT). It is unlikely that such an interpretation arose after Hadrian renamed Jerusalem Aelia Capitolina and dedicated the temple of Jupiter Capitolinus therein.

The root of the meturgeman's confidence is not any momentary improvement in the fortunes of the city. On the contrary, he alludes to dire circumstances. Where the MT speaks of an army (using the metaphor of 'the river') reaching 'to the neck,' the Targum reads 'to Jerusalem' (8.8). The interpreter chose to make his insertion in 25.2 (cited above) into a passage which refers (in both the Aramaic and Hebrew versions) to urban destruction. Why does he refer to Jerusalem in such contexts? Prima facie, the city is near to enduring and/or has endured, a catastrophe. We have seen the same confidence in the face of adversity expressed by 'sanctuary' usage, with which the present diction seems to cohere. As in the case of the sanctuary theologoumenon, the present usage makes very good sense on the understanding that it was in circulation around 70 C.E.: it is a period of crisis, in which a dispersion may even have occurred,[4] but in which fervent hope is still possible and the integrity of the Temple site has not been so definitively compromised as it was by Antiochus Epiphanes (25.2). Nor is the meturgeman reticent about naming the oppressor:

> 54.1b
> Tg for more shall be the sons of desolate Jerusalem than the sons of inhabited Rome, says the LORD.[5]
> MT for more shall be the sons of the desolate (woman) than the sons of the married (woman), says the LORD.

Even confrontation with such an enemy does not shake the faith of the meturgeman; the Shekinah may be removed momentarily (so 54.8), but Jerusalem is named as the recipient of 'my covenant of peace' (as in the MT) in v. 10, and as the one to whom it is promised that 'no weapon formed against you will avail' (v. 17). Whatever may happen, the glory of the LORD 'shall be revealed' (not 'has risen,' as in the MT) upon Jerusalem (60.1, and note the addition of the name in vv. 4, 12, 17). The praise of Jerusalem is what is prophesied in 61.11d (for 'praise' in the MT), and it is Jerusalem that proleptically rejoices in v. 10.

The pattern of Jerusalem's exaltation and Rome's destruction is also evident in book five of the Sibylline Oracles. Babylon (that is, Rome) and the land of Italy are to be burned by the great star from heaven because they killed the righteous of Israel (158-161) and utter desolation will be the lot of the unclean city (163, 168; cf. 342, 434–446). This picture serves to heighten the vision of Jerusalem's prosperity: even Gentiles will conform to the law, and sacrifices will again be offered to God (260-268; cf. 415-433). In his recent monograph, J.J. Collins observes the similarity between the great star of 155-161 and Revelation 8.10[6]; 9.1f, and it is notable that in the same book (21.2, 10) Jerusalem, albeit a new Jerusalem, is the outcome of destruction on a cosmic scale. Collins also cites the references to the desolation of the Temple and the favourable mentions of Hadrian (p. 75) as evidence for dating the fifth book between 117 and 132 C.E. The theological similarity of this Sibylline book to some aspects of the meturgeman's thought, and its chronological proximity to the period we are increasingly seeing as the time of the meturgeman, encourage us to think that it may help us to catch a glimpse of the sort of hope which finds exegetical articulation in the Targum (cf. 4 Ezra 10.41f).[7]

The motif of Jerusalem as the locus of vindication is obviously the common property of Jewish hope, and is to be found in Enoch (already with reference to the punishment of the wicked),[8] Tobit,[9] the Psalms of Solomon,[10] the Testaments of the Twelve Patriarchs,[11] 4 Ezra (as cited above), and 2 Baruch.[12] The time spanned by these documents is so extensive that it would be fruitless to pretend that the eschatological hope for Jerusalem belonged to any particular period within it. The meturgeman seems to have expressed the hope of his age generally in the particular circumstances of Roman action against Jerusalem.

The rabbis were possessed of a similar hope, as Piska 41 of Pesiqta Rabati clearly indicates. More specifically, the Amora R. Levi, citing Is. 54.1, applied the rule, 'Whenever scripture says "there is not," it is implied that the alternative will be'; hence the statement that barren Zion did not travail implies that she will do so (32.2). The fourteenth of the Shemoneh Esreh in both the Palestinian and Babylonian recensions pleads for the rebuilding of 'your city' and praises the 'God of David, builder of Jerusalem.'[13] In Berakhoth 48b, R. Eliezer asserts that whoever fails to mention the kingdom of the house of David in the blessing 'builder of Jerusalem' has not done his duty[14]; the concrete restoration seems to have been a carefully preserved tenet of rabbinic faith. At the same time, however, rabbinic exegesis of Is. 54.1 was strongly inclined to take an ethical turn: Israel's blessing lies in not bearing children for Gehenna,[15] but rather righteous men.[16] While such interpretations are quite consistent with the hope of Jerusalem's restoration (which is, after all, largely a function of her righteousness), we miss in the last rabbinic passages cited the passionate sorrow for Jerusalem's plight and the equally passionate hope for her future which is a characteristic feature of the Isaiah Targum.

Both aspects of the Isaian meturgeman's concern for Jerusalem are paralleled in the Targum to Jeremiah. Here, 8.21 is prefaced with the statement, 'Jerusalem said,' so that the emotive language of that verse is made to characterize Jerusalem's anguish 'over the wound of the congregation of my people.' A certain restraint prevents the Jeremian meturgeman from referring to Jerusalem directly when describing the destruction of 'this city' (which normally stands without explicit identification in this context); the name to his mind is more appropriately reserved for such occasions as 30.18 (where it does not appear in the MT), because here the building of Jerusalem and the sanctuary, and the return of the exiles of Jacob are declared as the intentions of the LORD. Here—as in the Isaiah Targum and the Sibylline Oracles—we have the same sort of hope which characterized ancient Jewish religion generally, but which seems to have been articulated in the context of a recent and definite challenge to Jerusalem's existence, not in the context of a comparatively undisturbed prosperity (as under Herod and the Roman governors) or of the definitive expurgation of the cult (as under Hadrian).

D. 'Exile' (גלותא)

It has already been noted in the discussion of 'Jerusalem' in the Isaiah Targum that the meturgeman is confident that those dispersed in the conflict with Rome will return.[1] This confidence is reflected in the insertion of phrases which include the term 'exile.' We first meet this diction at 6.13; where the MT appears to have a remnant in view,[2] the Targum announces that 'the exiles of Israel will be gathered and return to their land.'[3] Similarly, the meturgeman understood the growth imagery of 27.6 to refer to a gathering 'from among their exiles.'[4] The same phrase is present—quite understandably, given the sense of the Hebrew text—at 35.10 (cf. 51.11), and, because the meturgeman took this motif to be the burden of the passage as a whole, he interpreted the lame man of v. 6 as referring to the gathering of 'the exiles of Israel.' The tendency, manifest in the last passage, to reduce a metaphor to an explicit entity[5] can also be illustrated at 42.7, where 'to bring forth the prisoner from the dungeon' (MT) becomes: 'to bring forth their exiles from among the Gentiles,[6] where they are like prisoners.' The use of 'exiles of my people' at 43.6c for 'my daughters' is quite natural,[7] in view of the meaning of the verse in both Hebrew and Aramaic, but when the meturgeman recalled that God is 'he that brought the people from Egypt' in v. 8 (for MT: 'bring forth the people'), he was innovatively using the Exodus motif to express his certainty that God would act. The same motif can be applied to suggest a militarily triumphal return: where the MT refers to God's cutting up Rahab and piercing the dragon, the Targum reads, 'Did I not, for your sake, congregation of Israel, break the mighty men and destroy Pharaoh and his armies, which were strong as a dragon?' (51.9).[8] In an analogous fashion, the interpreter may have implied, 'the redeemed of the LORD will be gathered from among their exiles and enter Zion' (51.11).[9] By a comparable use of typology, a Masoretic oracle about Cyrus becomes a promise to the exiles, sworn to them as descendants of the greatest patriarch:

46.11a

Tg   (I am he) that says to gather exiles from the east, to bring openly as a swift bird from a far land the sons of Abraham my chosen.

MT   calling from the east a bird of prey, from a distant land a man of my (*ketib:* his) counsel.

The return of the exiles, carefully purposed by God, is also to be sudden, swift and public.[10]

Nor should we imagine that the exile itself occurs outside of the divine will in the Targum. As early as 8.18, the meturgeman specifies in an innovative phrase that it is a 'decree that he decreed upon them, that they should go into exile (דיגלון) so as not to appear before the LORD of hosts whose Shekinah is in Mount Zion.'[11] The reason for the decree is made explicit in v. 23, where the verb is also introduced (and quite reasonably,[12] for הקל in the MT), 'because they did not remember the miracle of the sea, the wonders of Jordan, the war of Gentile cities.' That is, the failure to keep in mind the mighty acts of God, recorded in Torah and in the Former Prophets,[13] has compromised the identity of God's people, and he has acted appropriately. His action is described in chapter 28, which we have already seen to be of crucial importance to an understanding of the meturgeman's attitude to the

sanctuary. In that chapter גלא is used in verses 2, 13, 19. In v. 13, an
innovative passage, as we have already seen (in our discussion of
'sanctuary' in the Targum), a twofold reason is given for the
punishment: they do not observe the law[14] and they fail to respect the
sanctuary. This association of 'exile' with 'sanctuary' is consistent
with its coherence with 'Jerusalem' diction (54.15; cf. n.9), and
suggests that all three dictional patterns are the work of a single
(individual or collective) mind. References to the Shekinah may also
suggest a date for 'exile' usage shortly before and after 70.[15] At 8.18, as
we have observed, the Shekinah is understood to be in Zion, even
though the displacement of the populace is threatened, and at 57.17b,
the Roman action against the Temple seems presupposed:

> Tg   I took up my Shekinah from them and cast them away, I
>   scattered their exiles
> MT   I hid my face and was angry.

We are to treat of 'Shekinah' usage in a separate section, but that God
has justly exiled his people is clearly a dominant theme in the Targum.
It is therefore understandable that a later interpreter should apply this
belief to his own situation (43.14):

> Tg   ... because of your sins you were exiled (איתגליתון) to
>   Babylon ...
> MT   ... for your sake I sent to Babylon ...

The reference to 'Babylon,' of course, makes one think of a later
period, when the Rabbinic academies were forced to move there.[16] But
there are also other indications that we are dealing here with the use of
an earlier motif to address a later situation: two features of this
statement are unusual when compared to those we have already seen.
First, the use of גלא in the reflexive is not the norm in 'exile'
statements; second, 'sins' in general are here the cause of the exile,[17]
instead of the more specific reasons which we have come to expect.
This later passage, in its departure from the language of the more
primitive theologoumenon, permits us to see a distinctive, subsequent
level (cf. n.4) in the development of the Isaiah Targum in a way which
highlights the characteristics of the earlier strata.

If we may return to the import of the theologoumenon, it asserts that
God is master of Israel's fate, be it in respect of her punishment or of
her consolation. In several passages, both aspects of the LORD's
control are spoken of in a single breath. It is to be observed that these

readings occur towards the end of the Targum, as if providing a deliberate coda to what has gone before:

53.8
Tg From chastisements and punishment he will bring our exiles near . . . [18]
MT From oppression and judgment he was taken . . .
54.7
Tg With a little anger I put you away, and with great mercies I will bring near your exiles.
MT For a brief moment I forsook, and with great mercies I will gather you.

It is, then, quite natural that our term should appear at 54.15 in connection with the consoling vengeance promised to Jerusalem. After all, the agent of the exile is inclined to boast that his own ability ensures the success of the action (10.13; גלא occurs in the Targum, for סור in the MT). Retribution alone can put matters into the proper perspective. But there is not the emotional thrill in this prospect which there is manifestly in the case of 'Jerusalem' usage. Rather, the 'exile' motif is more concerned with an almost theoretical expression of God's sovereignty than it is with vindication:

66.9
Tg I, God, created the world from the beginning, says the LORD. I created all men; I scattered them among the nations.[19] I am also about to gather your exiles . . .
MT Will I cause to break, and not bring forth, says the LORD. Will I, bringing forth, shut up?

In the MT, God's just recompense (v. 6) is as sure as the process of birth; the meturgeman believes it is as certain as the very foundation of the world. The creator says it is so.

The motif of Israel's return, inherited from the biblical Prophets, is prominent in the literature of our period (Tobit 13.5, 13; 14.5[20]; Psalms of Solomon 8.28; 11; 17.26f.[21]; Enoch 90[22]; II Baruch 78.7[23]), and it is notable that, as Volz observes, in these sources Israel's desertion of God occasions exile in the first place.[24] The defection is not God's, who in the tenth benediction in the Shemoneh Esreh (both recensions) is praised as the gatherer of Israel's outcasts even as he is asked to return the exiles.[25] In fact during the rabbinic period God was thought of as going into exile with his people. From the time of the second century Tanna R. Simeon b. Yoḥai, such an understanding was associated with Is. 43.14 (Megillah 29a): 'They were exiled to Babylon, and the Shekinah was with them, as it says, For your sake I was sent to Babylon.' Later in the same passage Abaye, a Babylonian Amora, attempts to specify the synagogues in which the Shekinah abides.[26] Exile here is not something which is shortly to be ended, but an obstacle in the way of Israel's relationship to God which God himself— through his Shekinah—undertakes to overcome; the conditions of exile are tacitly accepted as the *status quo*. The possibility emerges that the rabbis, in their retention of the hope for the restoration of Israel on the one hand and their acceptance of exile as their lot on the other, came to see the return from exile in a metaphorical way. We have already seen (in the 'Jerusalem' section) that the hope of the rabbis emphasized the ethical, as distinct from the tangible, restoration of Jerusalem, and in fact the rabbinic view that the Shekinah is with Israel in Babylon, which may be described as a metaphorical statement that God wills the exile as the *status quo* of Israel, is repeated so often in Midrash Rabbah, and in the names of so many rabbis, that we may speak of it as insistent teaching.[27] It appears three times (in each case unascribed) in Pesiqta Rabbati (8.4; 29/30.1; 30.2), and the third case is particularly interesting from the point of view of the Isaiah Targum:

> Because of your sins you made me take up the burden of Babylon, as is said, 'Because of you I had myself sent to Babylon' . . .

The coherence of Tg Is. 43.14 with this view (whose attestation is late) supports our observation above (made purely on internal grounds) that the meturgeman here expresses a distinctive point of view from that found in such passages as 53.8, where the emphasis falls on concrete vindication.

The evidence considered cannot reasonably be construed to suggest that there is a dichotomy between the exilic theology of the c.70 period and that of the Tannaitic and later eras, but that there is a development from a literal hope for immediate return to the land to a more nuanced theology of God's presence with his people, even in their exile, seems patent. We were led in the 'Sanctuary' section to discern distinct interpretative strata or layers in the work of the c.70 meturgeman; the phenomenon to be accounted for involved the application to different situations (i.e., the laxity in Temple praxis and the destruction of the Temple) of a theologoumenon with a single meaning. In the present case, however, the usages of the theologoumenon are distinctive from the point of view of meaning. 'Exile' in one circle of Isaian Targumic usage evokes the expectation that the dispersed children of Israel are soon to be vindicated and returned if they but return to the law and proper cultic practice, while in another circle 'exile' is an enduring condition caused by Israel's general sinfulness (and alleviated by the Shekinah). In these emphases there is a certain congruence: exile is a condition suffered justly by Israel which God seeks to rectify. But the distinction in emphasis and the Intertestamental and Rabbinic evidence considered leads us to speak of a c.70 meturgeman and a post-Tannaitic successor.

The theologoumena so far discussed seem better to cohere with the work of the former (although the 'law' usage would also be consistent with that of the latter), and it must be admitted that almost all of the 'exile' usages discussed seem to derive from his interpretation. Moreover, usages in the other Prophetic Targumim are more coherent with the work of the earlier interpreter.[28] The Amoraic (cf. the lateness of Pesiqta Rabbati and its lack of coherence with the statement in the Mekhilta) interpreter may not have been a framework meturgeman, but merely a later, non-systematic contributor. Nonetheless, he contributed a new interpretative level (not merely a distinctive stratum within the same level) to the Isaiah Targum. Even as he passed on the work of his predecessor(s), he adapted their message, in which the exile was to be speedily terminated, to his own circumstances, in which exile seemed more a permanent result of Israel's sins, but a situation in which she could maintain her identity as Israel.

E. 'House of Israel' (בית ישראל)

This phrase is consistently used[1] as a collective for God's chosen, whether obedient to God or not. Israel is Israel in exile and in prosperity. She may forget herself in her apathetic attitude to law and worship (see below, on 5.3; 27.4; 28.9, 25; 48.19; 65.11), but God is faithful as he rewards and rebukes her. At 5.3a, the house of Israel is described as rebelling against the law; this innovative phrase presents the meturgeman's explanation for God's attitude in the song of the vineyard. The people walking in darkness of 9.1, 2 in the MT are identified by the meturgeman as the house of Israel in Egypt. The fact that these first uses of the phrase as a collective are associated with the foundational importance of the law may be taken to suggest that a consciously shaped pattern of usage is in effect.[2] The association between Israel's fortunes and her attitude to law is explicitly (and rather unusually, given the MT reading) expressed at 27.4:

> Tg ... if the house of Israel set their face to do the law, would
>   I not send my anger and wrath against the nations ... ?[3]

The vineyard of v. 2 is already associated with 'the congregation (כנשתא)[4] of Israel,' and v. 3 contains an eloquent statement of Israel's covenantal identity:

> Tg I, the LORD, keep for them the covenant of their fathers,
>   and I will not destroy them. But in the time that they
>   anger me, I give them to drink the cup of their punishment ...
> MT I, the LORD, keep it. Regularly, I water it ...

By analogy to this interpretation, it is hardly astounding that we read in 28.9, 'To whom is the law given?' (for MT: 'whom will he teach knowledge') and, 'Was it not to the house of Israel?' (an innovative reference). To the agricultural imagery of 28.25, the question is prefixed:

> If the house of Israel set their faces to do the law, would he not
> turn and gather them?[5]

In this case, again, the rendering—while intelligently related to the Hebrew text—is better understood on the basis of the meturgeman's preoccupations than as exegesis. It would appear that the question of Israel is such a burning one that the interpreter is somewhat less circumspect in the introduction of this theologoumenon than he is with that of others.

Given that everything depends on Israel's attentiveness to the law, it is understandable that the meturgeman hopes for someone who will bring about a change in the prevailing attitude. In an interpretation of a servant passage which, as we have seen, relates prisoners to exiles, 'the blind' also receives a more specific referent (42.7):

> to open the eyes of the house of Israel, who are as if blind to the
> law ...

The servant—explicitly named as the messiah (v. 13)—is the object of Israel's hope for deliverance (52.14):

Tg As the house of Israel waited for him many days . . .
MT As many were horrified at him . . .

The prospective triumph of Israel over her enemies, which is to be achieved by a divine victory, is celebrated by the meturgeman in anticipation: 'The house of Israel shall sing praise concerning the great battle which will be waged for them with the nations' (30.32b).[6] He also anticipates that Israel will gather the victor's spoil (33.4; 33.23), but the dominant expectation is for the joy of a people gathered together again (33.24; 35.2, 10), as the rendering at 51.11 exemplifies:

And the redeemed of the LORD will be gathered from among their exile and will enter Zion with a song of praise, and eternal joy will be theirs, that does not cease, and a cloud of glory will cover their heads. They will find gladness and joy; sorrow and sighing will cease from them, from the house of Israel.

In this new dispensation, 'the eyes of the house of Israel, which were as if blind to the law, will be opened' (35.5a; cf. 42.7a); this is the matrix of Israel's prospective ascendancy. The basic congruence with the theodicy of exile in the Targum is obvious, though perhaps here the emotional engagement of the meturgeman is more manifest. The expectation is also, on the whole, more positively stated than it is in the case of 'Jerusalem' diction. But there is also a threat against the house of Israel as those who 'have forsaken the service of the LORD' (65.11); the theologoumenon therefore coheres with 'Sanctuary' as well as with 'Exile'.

God's discipline of Israel (normally by exile), which is seen as a prelude to messianic vindication, belongs to the topoi of Intertestamental Judaism (cf. Psalms of Solomon 18.6 and, more generally, chapter 9; Testament of Levi 15-18; Testament of Zebulun 9),[7] and this vindication could be seen as having a military aspect (Psalms of Solomon 17.23-end; Sibylline Oracles 5; Revelation 18-19). The redemption of Israel is expressed as an article of faith in the Shemoneh Esreh (both Palestinian, in the seventh, eighth, tenth, fourteenth, and eighteenth benedictions, and Babylonian, in the seventh, eighth, tenth, seventeenth, nineteenth), and Midrash Rabbah shows that Is. 27.2 (as in the Targum) was used as an image of God's protection of

Israel.[8] Similarly, in Pesiqta Rabbati (37.3), Is. 51.11 is referred to Israel's return (with the imagery of a bridal procession). Interestingly, the Pesiqta mentions the *congregation* of Israel (cf. the Targum; have we here another instance of coincidence between this late compilation and the Amoraic meturgeman [cf. 'Exile' and n.4 above, and the use of the term 'congregation' in Tg Hosea 3.3, cited in n.28 of the previous section]?). But of more particular interest to us, the Mekhilta de R. Ishmael (Shirata 5.62) makes a statement in respect of Is. 27.4 which is inconsistent with the (earlier) meturgeman's rendering:

> But when the Israelites do the will of God, there is no anger in him . . .

'Anger' here is to be avoided (lest it be directed against Israel); in the Targum it is desired as righteous wrath against the nations. The understanding of the Mekhilta is presupposed by R. Hama b. Hanina, a second century Amora, but in the same passage (Abodah Zarah 4a) R. Hinena b. Papa, a later Amora, has God regret the vow 'Fury is not in me,' because otherwise God would act as the thorns and briars burning. A. Cohen, the Soncino translator, takes the latter opinion also to refer to Israel (p. 13, n.2), so that Hinena (or, as some mss. would have it, R. Aha b. Hanina) is in line with the Mekhilta. But the following opinion of R. Alexandri—another Amora from Palestine, commenting on a different passage—is cited in Babli as according with that of Hinena, and Alexandri speaks of God's destruction of the nations. Babli would therefore seem to understand Hinena to offer an alternative exegesis to Hama's, in which anger against the nations is desired. The Targumic theologoumenon is therefore consistent with Amoraic as well as with Intertestamental teaching; one cannot speak of its provenience more precisely without running the risk of subdividing arbitrarily the Israel motif, whose consistent application in different periods is its most striking feature. Its coherent usage within the Targum, however, with such central theologoumena as 'Sanctuary' and 'Exile' justifies its inclusion as an element of the early framework meturgeman's work.

The above suggestion is reinforced when we consider usages in the other Prophetic Targumim. We find instances of a general expression of hope for Israel's vindication (Tg Jeremiah 31.11, the phrase here is 'house of Jacob'), and also laments (cf. Tg Jer. 8.20) that Israel has deserted the sanctuary service (Tg Hosea 2.15) and the law (Tg Hos. 13.14), with the consequence that the Shekinah is taken from her (Tg

Hos. 13.14). An example of a late 'congregation' (rather than 'house'; cf. the above paragraph) usage appears in Tg Micah 4.8, where the messiah of Israel is said to be hidden from before the sins of the congregation of Zion. This is consistent with the later messianology of R. Aḥa and R. Tanḥum b. Ḥiyya, cited in Jerushalmi (Taanith 1.1), to the effect that one day of Israelite repentance would bring the messiah.[9] The use of 'daughter' in the MT made the interpreter remember Israel's loss of national status (as more than a momentary setback), so that 'congregation' seemed a more natural rendering to him than 'house.'[10] In this case (cf. the 'Exile' section), the number of 'congregation of Israel' usages in the Prophetic Targums, and their distribution, make us speak of a meturgeman (not merely isolated readings) at the Amoraic level. For him Israel is a synagogue-people awaiting the messiah, less a nation which expected immediate vindication. The latter perspective belonged to the c.70 meturgeman, for whom the tangible restoration of the house of Israel was so vivid an expectation. The distinction is certainly no dichotomy, but a matter of emphasis. Moreover, within the Isaiah Targum the Amoraic meturgeman seems to have been content largely to accept the framework and vocabulary of the c.70 meturgeman; the work of the earlier interpreter was apparently foundational for his successor.

F. 'Repentance' (תיובתא)

Given that Israel's fortunes hang on her attitude to the law, the call for a radical change in this regard is logical and necessary. The meturgeman makes such a call unequivocally, and the verb form תוב correspondingly predominates over that of the noun. The term basically means 'to (re)turn' (not 'to be sorry,' as in Hebrew נחם), and the repentance demanded in the Targum is both *to* the law and *from* iniquity. Usages appear in the first chapter, in the opening paraenesis in the name of the LORD (vv. 16, 18):

    Tg Return to the law . . .
    MT Wash yourselves . . .

Tg Then, when you return to the law, you will pray to me,
and I will do your prayer, says the LORD . . .

MT Come, now, and we shall dispute together, says the
LORD . . .

Once the content of repentance is so explicitly defined (viz. as
adherence to the law), the term can be used without qualification.
Reference has already been made (in the 'Exile' section) to the divine
decree mentioned in 8.18: the point of calling attention to the decree is
that Israel might repent, and the sentence be annulled (תבטל). God's
attitude to Israel is not immutable, but responsive, and repentance (or
its lack) is what determines his response.

In a reading occasioned by word play, the meturgeman makes it
clear that repentance necessarily involves turning from sin (10.21):

Tg The remnant that have not sinned and that have turned
(דתבו) from sin,[1] the remnant of the house of Jacob, shall
return (יתובון) . . .

MT A remnant will return . . .

Quite clearly, the repentance here demanded is of a communal nature,
and coheres with the motif of national vindication. But other
renderings manifest a less national, more individualistic, notion of
repentance. In a striking interpretation, the meturgeman warns the
reader of the failure to repent from wickedness (21.12):

Tg The prophet said, there is reward for the righteous and
there is retribution for the wicked. If you are penitent
(תיבין), repent while you can repent.

MT The watchman said, morning comes, and night also. If
you will inquire, inquire; return, come.

The introductory phrase, 'The prophet said,' is also found in v. 8,
where the prophet is identified as the one appointed to stand watch.
What he reports is the fall of Babylon (v. 9); the meturgeman adds that
Babylon 'is about to fall.' As Pinkhos Churgin has pointed out, 'the fall
of Babylonia is with the author still a desire,'[2] so that this particular
reading would appear to derive from the period of the Babylonian
Amoraim (cf. the discussion below). The fact that the repentance
required is associated here more with the eschatological judgment of
the individual than with the fate of the nation might also be taken to
suggest that the reading comes from a situation in which the
communal, ethnocentric hope of restoration is no longer literally held.

Repeatedly (in respect of the theologoumena 'Sanctuary,' 'Exile,' 'House of Israel'), we have observed that a coherent and primitive paraenesis is reflected in chapter 28 of the Targum. In this context, reference is made to repentance in association with law as the message of the prophets (v. 10):

> Tg   They were commanded to do the law, and what they were commanded they did not wish to do. The prophets prophesied to them, that if they repented it would be forgiven them...

The latter part of this verse, as has already been stated, contains uses of 'Sanctuary' and 'Shekinah,' and the whole is a free interpretation of what is a difficult passage in the MT.[3] The usage of a repentance-to-law phrase in this paraenetic section, particularly where such crucial terms for the understanding of its theology are also found, suggests that this motif is part of the early framework to which we have called attention. The meturgeman has used some of his favourite language to render what he apparently felt was an obscure sentence and it would appear that repentance was an element in that characteristic diction.[4]

It is quite consistent with this diction that repentance is a positive option for those who are now apostate (42.19):

> Tg   If the wicked repent, will they not be called my servants ...?[5]
> MT   Who is blind but my servant...?

Such a promise is implicit in a call to repentance, since it is presupposed that obedience will have a good issue. In fact, the meturgeman can view repentance as proleptically accomplished, just as he can envisage the anticipated restoration of the sanctuary, Jerusalem, and the exiles of the house of Israel (57.18):

> Tg   The way of their repentance is revealed before me, and I will forgive them...
> MT   I see his ways, and I will heal him...

Such confidence, one might fairly suggest, is not quite in accord with the conditional statement: 'If you repent, it will be forgiven you.' In the paraenetic usages, repentance is demanded; in 57.18 it is as if it were a *fait accompli*. This might be taken to reflect the irrepressible hope of the meturgeman, as stated above. On the other hand, one might argue that 57.18 in the Targum presupposes that a call to repentance such as we meet elsewhere in the paraphrase has been voiced and that it has met a positive response. This impression could be strengthened by reference to 57.19:

> Tg ... and peace will be done to the penitent who have
> repented to my law recently (קריב)[6] ...
> MT ... peace ... to the near (קרוב) ...

In this connection, it might also be noted that a linguistic innovation, in comparison to תוב usage elsewhere in the Targum (i.e., the use of תביא, 'penitent'; cf. 21.12 and our comments above), accompanies the slight shift in meaning from what appears to be the more primitive idea.[7] In the absence of some references to a datable event or circumstances, one is left to such a comparison of passages within the document as the only possible means of distinguishing one interpretative layer from another. But it could be argued that individual and proleptic repentance do not exclude the demand for repentance in view of national restoration, and can be seen as variants of a coherent conception. For the moment, however, it is enough to say the Targum presents a repentance motif which is quite consistent with the usage of other important theologoumena and of which other repentance motives appear to be more recent variants.

The Palestinian recension of the Shemoneh Esreh asks God to grant Israel repentance, that it might return to him (in the fifth benediction), and the content of repentance, as attendance to law and service, is spelled out in the Babylonian recension (also in the fifth benediction; cf. Petuchowski, *art. cit.*; see 'Law,' n.12). The necessity of repentance for salvation is obvious in such passages from Intertestamental literature as II Baruch 85.12, and law appears as the content of repentance in IV Ezra 7.133 and in the Damascus Document (CD 20.2). The Testaments of Judah (25.5) and of Dan (6.4) clearly show that the motif of national repentance would appropriately have figured in the work of a c.70 meturgeman. Cognate interpretations are available in the other Prophetic Targumim, as well. 'Law,' more specifically the teaching of correct service, is what Israel is called to (Tg Jeremiah 3.1, 7, 12, 22; 24.7; Tg Hosea 6.1; 10.12; Tg Malachi 3.7), and such repentance can annul the sentence decreed against her (Tg Jer. 4.1); the consequences of failure to repent (Tg Hosea 7.10; Tg Amos 4.6, 8, 9, 10, 11) serve to highlight the interpreter's paraenesis. Indeed, this is such a prominent theme in the Isaiah Targum itself that we might now turn to passages in which it is articulated.

The passage from Targum Isaiah 28.10 cited above voices the complaint that 'what they were commanded they did not wish to do'; the early, paraenetic repentance theologoumenon was associated with a motif of the persistent refusal to repent, and this served to highlight the urgency of the imperative. The refusal motif is so prominent as to demand attention as a characteristic theme in the Targum, although the terminology of the motif is not so stereotyped that it could be styled a theologoumenon. Obviously, it is more consistent with the call to repentance than with the assurance that the way of repentance is already being followed.[8]

The theme is first sounded very early in the Targum (1.3c; 1.6c):

   Tg my people have not considered repenting to my law.
   MT my people do not understand.
   Tg ... they do not desire to repent ...
   MT ... they are not bound (viz. because of their wounds) ...

With both of these renderings, especially the first, the meturgeman showed the extent to which he saw repentance as the primary means of access to God. Indeed to understand God is to undertake repentance; it is the treatment which would lead Israel to recovery, if only it were applied. On three occasions in the ninth chapter (vv. 11, 16, 20) and at 10.4, the meturgeman used the formulation, 'For all this they have not repented (תבו) of their transgressions, that his anger might turn (יתוב) from them, and they still continue their rebellion,' in order to render 'For all this his anger has not returned' in the MT. At first glance, this interpretation may seem arbitrary, but we have seen already that the meturgeman understood God's attitude to Israel to be responsive (cf. on 8.18 in particular). He therefore avoided any suggestion that the divine anger is inevitable or unwarranted: God's rage at impenitence is the dark side of the statement that repentance occasions forgiveness.

The desperate condition that Israel leaves herself in by the refusal to repent is emphasized at 17.11[9]:

   Tg ... you put away the day of repentance until the day of
        your destruction ...
   MT ... the harvest a heap in the day of inheritance.[10]

That our interpreter saw repentance in the image of a harvest shows the urgency of his message, and the refusal theme is used to underline this urgency. Such an emphasis is achieved in a different way at 26.10a. Here it is asserted that the wicked have been given respite, that if they repented they might do righteousness. Into this statement, which is a reasonable paraphrase of the Hebrew text, the innovative clause is inserted, 'and they did not repent all the days they were alive.' Again, the meturgeman managed to suggest that repentance is not an option which can be deferred; one either takes advantage when the time is ripe, or falls into the self-destructive trap of the consistent refusal to repent. A very similar form of words is introduced at 42.14a:

> Tg   I gave to them respite from of old that if they repented to the law, and they repented not . . .
>
> MT   I was silent from of old; I will be quiet and restrain myself . . .

The Hebrew text already understands God's patience to be at an end; in the Targum his patience is explicated in terms of the opportunity he gives for repentance. Our motif is also brought into the divine frustration expressed in 50.2a:

> Tg   Why, when I sent my prophets, did they not repent? They prophesied, and they received not.
>
> MT   Why, when I came, was there no man? When I called, was there no one answering?

The point again is that the previous refusal to repent has brought Israel to a critical juncture in her relations with God, as is affirmed at 57.11b in terms reminiscent of those seen above in 42.14a:

> Tg   Did I not give you a respite from of old, that if you repented to my law,[11] and you have not returned to me?
>
> MT   Have I not been silent from of old, and you do not fear me?

The sense of crisis is enhanced by the rendering of the preceding verse, where 'you thought not to repent' appears for 'you did not faint.' Finally, in two passages near the end of the Targum (65.12; 66.4), God is made to give the reason for which he brings on Israel's destruction: 'because I sent my prophets, and you (or 'they' in the latter passage) repented not' (for 'because I called and you did not answer' or 'and there was no one answering'). It is also striking that both passages refer contextually to abuse of the Temple service, so that the coherence of the present motif with the theology of the early Targumic framework is again indicated.[12]

Certain passages from the other Prophetic Targumim also evidence the more individualistic repentance motif apparent in the Isaiah Targum (cf. above, on 21.12 and 57.18, 19 and n.7) in which the positive response of the righteous in the congregation of Israel is presupposed. In Tg Joel 2.14, the man who repents is said to receive 'blessing and consolation and his prayers are as a man who offers offerings and libations in the sanctuary house of the LORD your God.' Such an individual understanding of repentance would, of course, have been possible at an early period (cf. CD 20.2, cited above), but in the present instance it is articulated in the context of a 'sanctuary' usage which is markedly less expressive of the theology of messianic vindication than the usage which we have seen to be characteristic of the c.70 Isaian meturgeman. The Temple is here replaced by individual piety, rather than serving as the focus of Israel's communal restoration. Tg Malachi 3.18 provides a rather close parallel to the theme of Tg Is. 21.12: 'And you will repent and see the difference between the righteous and the wicked . . . .' Is. 21.12 formed the basis of an assertion in an unascribed statement from Jerushalmi (Taanith 1.1), cited by Strack-Billerbeck ('der Morgen kommt für die Gerechten und die Nacht für die Gottlosen, der Morgen für Israel und die Nacht für die Völker der Welt'),[13] in which the individual and communal aspects of repentance (which Isaiah is held to have demanded of the Israelites) are coordinated. In Exodus Rabbah 18.12, Is. 21.12 is explained (in an unascribed statement) by the parable of 'a woman eagerly awaiting her husband who went abroad and said to her, "Let this be a sign to you, and whenever you see this sign, know I will soon come back." So Israel has eagerly awaited salvation since the rising of Edom.' The nationalistic expression of hope, all the stronger when Edom is recognized—as by S.M. Lehrman (the Soncino translator)— as a cipher for Rome, is evident. Why should the meturgeman be less nationalistic than the commentator on Exodus, when elsewhere he is far from backward in this regard? Nor can the phenomenon be written off as a matter of happenstance: in Numbers Rabbah (16.23), Mal. 3.18 (which, as we have seen, is rendered in Jonathan to accord thematically with Is. 21.12) is cited along with Is. 21.12 to show 'when the time of the world to come arrives . . . we shall know in whom he delights.' The choice is between Israel and the nations, and the explication of the texts is parabolic (relating the jealousy between a wife and an Ethiopian maid). The individualistic, non-national repentance motif of the Amoraic meturgeman of Is. 21.12 and Mal. 3.18 is, then, to be contrasted with the nationalistic, parabolic exposition found in Midrash Rabbah (cf. also Pesiqta Rabbati 33.4). The material contained in the latter sources, may, of course, be more primitive than that presented by the meturgeman whose work we are now considering, but this conclusion is as shaky as the dating of the passages in Midrash Rabbah; it may be safer simply to observe that our meturgeman represents a distinctive stream in Amoraic opinion.

The exposition of the Amora R. Johanan on Is. 57.19, presented in Berakhoth 34b, accords well with the rendering of our meturgeman:

> What is meant by 'far'? One who from the beginning was far from transgression. And what is meant by 'near'? That he was once near to transgression and now has gone far from it.

R. Johanan conceives of repentance negatively (as from sin) rather than positively (as to law; cf. Tg Is. 57.19), but he agrees that the 'near' are recent penitents (cf. the unascribed comment in Numbers Rabbah 11.7). For R. Abbahu (commenting in the same passage), however, the 'near' are those who were always near to, the 'far' those who were once distant from, God (so also Sanhedrin 99a, and cf. the equally individualistic comments of R. Joshua b. Levi and R. Hiyya b. Abba in Berakhoth 34b; Joshua's comment is more substantively to be found in Leviticus Rabbah 16.9; cf. also the unascribed statement in Numbers Rabbah 8.4 in respect of proselytes, Deuteronomy Rabbah 5.15 and Pesiqta Rabbati 44.8). While the Amoraic discussion of Is. 57.19 was lively, and is well represented in our sources, a characteristically individualistic orientation is evident throughout. It would appear, therefore, that the Amoraic meturgeman was so influenced by discussions of this kind that he rendered Is. 21.12 as he did, even though some of his contemporaries continued to understand that verse within a nationalistic perspective.

For what reason did the Amoraic meturgeman behave in this way? There can be no question of his wishing to expunge a nationalistic understanding of repentance and its consequences; he accepted and incorporated the work of the c.70 meturgeman in his interpretation, just as his colleagues continued to believe that national restoration would follow upon repentance at the same time as they developed a paraenesis aimed at individuals. But his desire to present a balance in these emphases is apparent in his decision to render Is. 21.12 in a less nationalistic way than he might have done if he had not had the strongly nationalistic framework of the c.70 meturgeman to compensate for. Even so, we must recall that v. 9 makes it quite plain that, for the Amoraic meturgeman, national and individual restoration were complementary aspects of the same hope. In this recognition, he showed the reflective insight of a settled theologian more than his c. 70 predecessor, who was more concerned to address an Israel whose very existence was threatened by a refusal to repent.

In a recent article,[14] Moses Aberbach has claimed that Babylon in Tg Is. 21.9 should be understood as a cipher for Rome, *pace* Pinkhos Churgin. Aberbach bases his opinion on the use of such a cipher in the Talmudic period and on the fact that ancient Babylon no longer existed at the time the Targum was produced. The possibility he raises cannot be discounted, but there are several considerations in the light of which it appears improbable. We have already seen that, at Tg Is. 54.1, Rome is explicitly mentioned, and this is also the case (in a prediction of military defeat) at Tg Ezekiel 39.16. This is to be contrasted with the Babylon cipher for Rome in I Peter 5.13, or for that matter the Esau cipher (IV Ezra 6.8, 9; Pesaḥim 5a) or the Edom cipher (jTaanith 1.1; Exodus Rabbah 18.12) or the Se'ir cipher (jTaanith 1.1). Once Rome is openly identified, one must consider the possibility that what might once have been seen as a cipher now has a more straightforward referent, which is precisely Churgin's programme.[15] (In any case, we can say that the failure to use a cipher for Rome is more consistent with non-Roman than with Roman provenience.) Moreover, Tg Habakkuk 3.17 clearly shows that at least one Prophetic meturgeman did not see Babylon as a self-evident cipher for Rome:

> For the kingdom of Babylon will not endure, nor will it exercise dominion over Israel. The kings of Media will be slain, and the mighty ones of Greece will not succeed. The Romans will be destroyed, and will not levy the tax from Jerusalem.[16]

Here, a reference to Babylon (which is not even demanded by the Hebrew text) is not thought sufficient to make the hearer call Rome to mind; indeed, he would miss the point of the interpretation if it did. A similar situation obtains in Pesiqta Rabbati 30.2, where, following a citation of Is. 43.14 (in respect of Babylon), Rome is mentioned under a cipher (via Jeremiah 49.38). The claim, therefore, that 'Babylon' in rabbinic literature consistently refers to Rome simply does not accord with the evidence. In any case, the Prophetic Targumim do not reflect such a practice. We would therefore follow Churgin in inferring that the later meturgeman was a Babylonian Amora.

G. 'Abraham'

In the section on 'Exile' in the Isaiah Targum, we had occasion to observe that, at 46.11a, God promises restoration to his people as descendants of Abraham. This patriarch is mentioned in several passages; he serves as the reminder that God keeps covenant and that it is up to Israel to respond appropriately (cf. 27.3, in the 'House of Israel' section). That is to say that Abraham is the symbol of Israel as God's chosen. So it is that the vineyard of 5.1 is explicitly identified as Israel, 'the seed of Abraham my friend.' The following verse refers to the sanctuary, and in the next the refusal to repent theme appears; the mention of Abraham makes the spectacle of Israel's obduracy despite the divine favour she enjoys all the more affective. Abraham is the paradigm of obedient trust in God. To call Israel Abraham's seed is to call her back to her identity, and the implication is that she has strayed from it.

We may even speak of a specific vocation to Temple service which Abrahamic descent lays on Israel (48.15, 16):

> Tg I, even I, by my word did make a covenant with Abraham your father. Indeed, I appointed him. I brought him up to the land of my Shekinah's house . . .
>
> MT I, even I, have spoken. Indeed, I called him. I brought him in . . .
>
> Tg . . . from the time the nations separated from my fear, from then I brought Abraham near to my service . . . [1]
>
> MT . . . from the time it was I am there . . .

The cultic integrity of Israel, as distinct from the waywardness of the nations, is therefore realized in Abraham. At 51.2, where the Targum follows the mention of the patriarch in the Hebrew text, the meturgeman added, 'I brought him near to my service,' so that what the reader is called to consider is Abraham's example in respect of his adherence to God.

Abraham is such a paradigmatic figure that God's act on behalf of his seed can be called 'benefits of Abraham' (29.23b, an innovative phrase), and the meturgeman could claim that God declared 'to Abraham your father what was about to come' (43.12a, again innovative). These statements are not in the least unusual once one takes seriously that Abraham is the supreme example for Israel's behaviour vis-à-vis God: to stand as such, enjoying God's favour, she must also embody the virtue of God's chosen. One of God's blessings was to bring 'Abraham quickly' (41.2, innovative) from the east, and this is what the meturgeman had God promise the exiles, the 'sons of Abraham my chosen' (46.11). The diction manifest in the Targum is perfectly comprehensible once one understands that 'Abraham' is a figure which points imperatively, to Israel's vocation, and indicatively, to Israel's τέλος.[2]

The meturgeman's Abraham theology is perfectly consistent with that expressed in the Liber Antiquitatum Biblicarum (33.5):

> Hope not in your fathers; they are of no use to you, unless you become like them.[3]

Such a critical understanding of God's blessing of the fathers, rather than a more purely optimistic emphasis on God's promise to them,[4] seems to be reflected in the work of the early framework meturgeman. In contrast, the Amoraim appear generally to have understood God's address in Is. 48.15, 16 to be directed, not to Abraham,[5] but to Moses on Sinai.[6] On this basis, two fourth century teachers (R. Berekiah in the name of R. Ḥelbo) could insist that Isaiah in the two verses cited rebuked the people for not recognizing that 'if you have heard Torah from the mouth of a scholar, it should be in your estimation as if your ears had heard it from Mount Sinai' (Ecclesiastes Rabbah 10§1). The same position, expressed in different words, is ascribed to R. Isaac in Exodus Rabbah 28.6. The distinction between the vocational Abraham motif of the meturgeman, calling Israel back to her cultic identity, and the academic Sinai motif of the Amoraim, calling Israel to attend to the correct exposition of Torah, seems manifest.

The Isaiah Targum is also notable for its failure to mention the Aqedah in any way. If, as has been recently argued,[7] the Aqedah is an Amoraic doctrine, then this silence of the early meturgeman is quite explicable. In the Micah Targum (7.20), on the other hand, the Aqedah is mentioned by name in association with God's covenant with Abraham 'between the pieces' (cf. Genesis 15.17). This connection is

made in some of the so-called Palestinian Targums (namely, Neophyti
I and the Fragment Targum, but not Pseudo-Jonathan) in their 'Poem
of the Four Nights' (at Exodus 12.42). In a recent study of the Poem, I
have argued that the Aqedah reference therein is an Amoraic
expansion of an earlier text.[8] This would suggest that the later
meturgeman is not represented in the Abraham material included in
the Isaiah Targum, but that his knowledge of the Palestinian Targum
tradition caused him or a colleague to include a reminiscence of the
Poem (particularly as found in Neophyti I, where 'between the pieces'
is explicitly used) in his rendering of Micah 7.20.

H. 'Holy Spirit' (רוח קודשא)

In all of the theologoumena which we have so far surveyed, the
meturgeman's confidence that the LORD is steadfast and responsive in
respect of Israel has been manifest. At the same time, however, the
desire to avoid anthropomorphism is a well-known trait of this
Targum. J.F. Stenning listed the following 'principal expedients' of
this tendency:

> (a) the insertion of 'Word' or 'Memra' (מימרא), 'Glory' (יקרא),
> or 'Presence' (Shekina, שכינא) when God is described as
> coming into relation with man; (b) the insertion of the
> preposition 'before,' or 'from before' after verbs denoting
> anger, hate, fear, etc., in place of the genitive case; (c) the
> substitution of the active for the passive when God is the
> subject of verbs such as seeing, hearing, knowing, remembering,
> etc.: verbs denoting physical activity, e.g., go down, go forth,
> come, etc., are translated 'revealed himself' or 'was revealed';
> (d) parts of the body, hands, eyes, face, are rendered by
> 'might,' 'presence,' 'memra,' e.g. 'hide the face,' 1^{15}, 8^{17}, 57^{17},
> 59^2, 64^6 by 'remove the presence.'[1]

The purpose of such usages (and we will consider the terms listed in
'(a)' under their own headings) is, as Stenning also observed, 'to
prevent any possible misconception.' Generally speaking, this characterization of the tendency is correct so far as it goes. But the meturgeman
had several terms at his disposal with which to speak of God in relation

to man, and he is by no means indiscriminate in his use of them. We will see the same sort of pattern and purpose in this diction as we have seen elsewhere, with the result that the Targum must be described as expressing a positive theology of divine revelation as well as having an anti-anthropomorphic tendency.

'Holy spirit' is one of the theologoumena in question. Its first usage appears in association with the prophets (40.13a):

> Tg Who has established the holy spirit in the mouth of all the
>   prophets, is it not the LORD?
> MT Who has established the spirit of the LORD?

Here, the meturgeman avoided the suggestion, even in question form, that someone could influence God's disposition, and instead spoke of God's spirit as the source of prophecy. Terms related to 'prophet' will be dealt with separately, but passages have already been considered (such as 28.10; 50.2a; cf. the 'Repentance' section), in which prophecy figures in interpretations which appear to date from before the destruction of the Temple and which address what is seen as a critical decay in Israel's relations with God. The present passage may be held to explain the reason for which prophecy was held in such high esteem: after all, prophets speak by virtue of the holy spirit at the direction of the LORD.

'Holy spirit' is always that which permits a person to act or speak in the LORD's name. The rendering at 42.1b is altogether natural, given the Hebrew text, but it also fits this pattern[2]:

> Tg I will place my holy spirit upon him; my judgment to the
>   nations he will reveal.
> MT I will place my spirit upon him; judgment to the nations
>   he will bring forth.

The meturgeman also had God say, 'I will pour my holy spirit upon your sons,' for the statement in the MT, 'I will pour my spirit on your seed' (44.3b). This rendering shows a sensitivity to the context of the passage, which in isolation might be taken to refer to a blessing bestowed on a passive Israel (cf. v. 4). But Israel (Jacob) is called 'my servant' in vv. 1, 2 (both in the MT and the Targum), and v. 5 speaks expressly of an active association with the LORD, so that it was well within reason for the meturgeman to invoke his prophetic theologoumenon (i.e., '*holy* spirit' and cf. 'sons') in translating 'my spirit.'[3]

Finally, the link of this phrase with prophecy, which we observed at 40.13, is tightened at 59.21:

> Tg   And as for me, this is my covenant with them, says the LORD, my holy spirit which is upon you, and the words of my prophecy which I put in your mouth . . . [4]

> MT   And as for me, this is my covenant with them, says the LORD, my spirit which is upon you, and my words which I put in your mouth . . .

'Holy spirit' is the normal means of God's address to his people, accomplished through prophets. It is for this reason that at 63.10, where the MT reads, 'they grieved his holy spirit,' the Targum presents us with, 'they provoked the word of his holy prophets.'[5]

In a recent monograph,[6] Peter Schäfer has provided a comprehensive review of the concept of the holy spirit in rabbinic literature. He agrees with the observation of his predecessors that there is a consistent connection between the holy spirit and prophecy in the sources, including the Pentateuchal Targums.[7] The discussion above may be taken to substantiate Schäfer's findings in respect of the Isaiah Targum, and such passages as Tg Joel 3.1, 2 (where 'holy spirit' renders 'spirit' in the MT; cf. above on Tg Is. 44.3b) show that this substantiation could easily be extended to include the Prophetic Targum generally. In some instances in the Prophetic Targum, however, 'holy spirit' does not appear in a prophetic context when one would have expected it to. For example, Tg Zechariah 7.12 has 'words which the LORD of hosts has sent by his memra (for MT 'spirit') in the hands of the prophets' (cf. Tg Is. 48.16). Moreover, the conventional association between holy spirit and prophecy, which resulted in the meturgeman's rendering of Is. 63.10 observed above, is not always carried through in rabbinic literature—as we can see by considering other documents which cite Is. 63.10. Two passages in Midrash Rabbah (Lamentations 1.22§57 and Ecclesiastes 3.8§2, both in unascribed expositions) speak of God's turning to become the enemy of his people without mentioning their rejection of the prophetic message. In the Mekhilta (Shirata 5.66), it is the failure of Israel to do God's pleasure which occasions this result. 'Spirit,' therefore, is not immediately equated in rabbinic thought (including that aspect represented in the Targum) with the holy spirit active in prophecy.

Rabbinic thought can be said to distinguish between MT uses of 'spirit': sometimes this is taken to refer to prophecy ('holy spirit'), sometimes to a personal aspect of God (cf. the 'memra' usage in Tg Zechariah 7.12, and the 'Memra' section). His acute observation of the way in which the 'holy spirit' is spoken of in rabbinic literature enabled Schäfer to explain why it should not be construed as an ontological hypostasis:

> Der Terminus 'hl. Geist' bezeichnet nicht die Gottheit selbst, also eine bestimmte 'Seinweise' Gottes, sondern allenfalls eine 'Offenbarungsweise' der Gottheit. Diese Unterscheidung zwischen 'Seinweise' und 'Offenbarungsweise' ermöglicht es vielleicht, die mit der Fragestellung 'Identität des hl. Geistes mit Gott' oder 'Hypostasierung des hl. Geistes' zu eng gefasste Problematik zu erweitern.[8]

As an expression of God's revelation, Schäfer writes, 'holy spirit' designates, not the quality of a prophet, 'sondern eine "Gabe," mittels der er bestimmte Offenbarungen empfängt und gegebenenfalls weitergibt.'[9] Seen in the context of rabbinic theology, with which the meturgeman's diction coheres well, 'holy spirit' in the Isaiah Targum is not simply a device to avoid anthropomorphism, but a vehicle to express the relationship of the prophet to God: he is empowered by God through the spirit.

The Isaian meturgeman's usage is also consistent with another aspect of rabbinic teaching noted by Schäfer:

> ... Der hl. Geist wird bei den 'klassischen' Offenbarungen am Sinai, im Dornbusch und im Stiftzelt an keiner Stelle erwähnt. Es handelt sich dort immer um direkte Offenbarungen ...[10]

But building on and extending evidence adduced by A.M. Goldberg, Schäfer goes on to show that there is a strict association in rabbinic thought between the holy spirit and the Shekinah:

> רוח הקודש meint nicht einfach 'heiliger Geist' oder 'Geist Gottes,' sondern konkret Geist des im Heiligtum als Ort der Begegnung zwischen Gott und Mensch sich offenbarenden Gottes.[11]

Schäfer also cites evidence that the eschatological sanctuary, not only the historical sanctuary, was also to be associated with prophetic activity, so that the repentance which leads to Israel's restoration was seen to be prerequisite to the renewed activity of the spirit.[12] He very emphatically points out, however, that there was no universally accepted Jewish teaching about the cessation of the spirit: repeated references to its activity after the time of the prophets, and of the first and second Temples, are available.[13]

Against the background of Schäfer's exposition of the rabbinic understanding of the holy spirit, what stands out—almost anomalously—in the meturgeman's usage is that this theologoumenon is not particularly associated with the sanctuary theologoumenon. That he was possessed of an expectation of Israel's recovery, based on a restoration of the cult, seems clear, but he did not choose to express it by means of his 'holy spirit' diction. The reason for this is not difficult to ascertain (see above): repentance is fundamentally the message of the prophets, and for the meturgeman this is a present, divine demand. It would therefore have been natural for the meturgeman (whether c.70 or Amoraic) to stress more the consistent presence of the spirit in the demand for repentance than the relative cessation of the spirit with the departure of the Shekinah. We cannot claim that 'holy spirit' usage conforms better to either level in the formation of the Isaiah Targum; it fits in very well with the present scholarly understanding of rabbinic thought generally.

I. 'Prophet(s)'

The meturgeman often introduced his renderings with the statement, 'the prophet said,' or a similar locution. This is a rather emphatic historical assertion, so that it is all the more striking that the introduction accompanies innovative readings[1]:

> 5.1
> Tg The prophet said, I will sing for Israel, which is like a
>   vineyard, the seed of Abraham my beloved, a song of my
>   love for his vineyard . . .
> MT I will sing now to my beloved a song of my love for his
>   vineyard . . .
> 5.3
> Tg Say to them, prophet, Behold the house of Israel have
>   rebelled from the law and are not willing to repent . . .
> MT [the Hebrew text begins after this addition]

9.5

Tg The prophet said to the house of David . . .

MT [as above]

22.14

Tg The prophet said, With my ears I was hearing when this
was decreed from before the LORD of hosts, this sin will
not be forgiven you until you die the second death . . .

MT And the LORD of hosts has revealed in my ears, this
iniquity will not be forgiven you until you die . . .

24.16

Tg From the sanctuary house whence joy is about to go forth
to all the inhabitants of the earth, we have heard a song of
praise for the righteous. The prophet says, The mystery
of the reward of the righteous is shown to me, the mystery
of the retribution of the wicked . . .

MT [cf. 'The righteous' section]

Save for the rendering of 22.14, each of these contains theologoumena
which have been dealt with in other sections, so that it is plain that the
early meturgeman availed himself of this introduction. The 'second
death' usage at 22.14 is also at home in this period (cf. Revelation 2.11;
20.6, 14; 21.8), and so is properly included in this list. To some extent,
these passages (and those presented in n.1) evince in their 'prophet'
diction a desire for clarity, since the introductory words serve to
specify the speaker. Full weight, however, should be given to the fact
that the meturgeman included his own concerns as the prophetic
burden: Isaiah is held to speak in the Targum to the people of the
interpreter's own day. One cannot help but be reminded of the
Talmudic statement, 'The Targum of the Prophets was composed by
Jonathan ben Uzziel under the guidance of Haggai, Zechariah and
Malachi' (Megillah 3a).[2] Since Jonathan was a disciple of Hillel, the
statement is historically anomalous, but it accurately conveys the
authoritative impression which the meturgeman's 'prophet' language
makes. The response to the translation ascribed to the בת קול in this
haggadah ('Who is it that has revealed my secrets to mankind?') would
be an appropriate one to any attempt to speak on behalf of a prophet.
Once we place the at first glance paradoxical Talmudic statement
about the Jonathan Targum in the context of exegetical conventions in
the Isaiah Targum, we discover that it is an informative haggadah.

The meturgeman's implicit claim to speak with almost prophetic
authority is more impressive when we observe his refusal to call others

'prophets.' At 9.14 and 28.7 (n.b., in a chapter in which prophetic diction has been introduced), 'scribe' takes the place of 'prophet,' since the prophecy at issue is false. But he did not hesitate to picture Isaiah as representing concerns appropriate to the contemporary situation (8.17):

> Tg The prophet said, For this reason I prayed before the LORD who said to take up his Shekinah from Jacob's house, and I sought from before him.
> MT I will await the LORD, who hides his face from Jacob's house, and I will wait for him.

Once established, the same contemporizing tendency in respect of 'prophet' diction could be manifest at a later period. For reasons already discussed in the 'Repentance' section, this appears to be the case at 21.11b, 12.[3]

Usage of the term in the plural establishes the background of the meturgeman's 'prophet' diction (5.6c):

> Tg and I will command my prophets not to prophesy a prophecy concerning them.
> MT and I will command the clouds not to rain on it.

For him, the consistent rejection of the prophets' call,[4] despite God's faithfulness,[5] despite the prophetic threat of punishment,[6] has brought the age of prophecy to an end (cf. 29.10, substantively following the MT). The hiatus is associated with the departure of the Shekinah (v. 5), not with the close of the canon (as in Megillah 3a),[7] so that the early meturgeman was in a position to claim to have had contact with the now inoperative dispensation. On this basis, he could look forward to a promised restitution when 'the eyes of the house of Israel, which were as if blind to the law, will be opened, and their ears, which were as if deaf to receive the words of the prophets, will attend' (35.5). Then the prophets will be commanded to prophesy consolations (40.1).[8] They are called 'bearers of good tidings to Zion,' and their message is, 'the kingdom of your God is revealed' (40.9). Their message is cognate with their office; as God 'orders the holy spirit in the mouth of all the prophets,' so those messengers announce the vindicating presence of God himself.[9]

In the Isaiah Targum, then, while God's constancy is stressed by emphasizing the consistent appeal of the holy spirit through the prophets, the disastrous consequences of Israel's rebellion are stressed by emphasizing that, with the departure of the Shekinah, prophecy is to cease. To be sure, this cessation is not definitive, in that a renewal of prophecy is anticipated, but it is palpable. In the name of Aquila the proselyte, Is. 5.6 is associated with God's command to the prophets not to prophesy (as in the Targum; Ecclesiastes Rabbah 11.2.1), and an unascribed statement in Genesis Rabbah (42.3.ii) relates Is. 8.16, 17 to the lack of prophets and the departure of the Shekinah. It would therefore appear that, in this respect, the Isaiah Targum coheres with the rabbinic motif of the hiatus of prophecy associated with the taking up of the Shekinah—a motif which Schäfer found expressed in some assertions about the holy spirit.[10] By way of contrast, we would point out that in the Amoraic period, the Shekinah is linked with synagogues and houses of study (Leviticus Rabbah 11.7; Esther Rabbah 11; and see the 'Exile' section, on the rabbinic exegesis of Is. 43.14), whose work continued. The Targum does not appear to represent this idea.

As we have seen, however, the meturgeman does pretend to a quasi-prophetic authority which permits him to speak in the name of the biblical author. Interestingly, the two Amoraim (R. Jacob and R. Aḥa) in whose names the dictum in Genesis Rabbah 42.3.ii is handed down preface the quotation of Is. 8.17 with the introduction, 'Isaiah said,' and they relate the verse to Ahaz' seizure of synagogues and schools.[11] The meturgeman's introductory 'the prophet said' accomplishes a similar purpose in 8.17: Isaiah addresses the concerns of the meturgeman's day, and, as interpreted, is the contemporary voice of prophecy. There is therefore an evident continuity between the quasi-prophetic pretensions of the c.70 meturgeman (whose concern focused on the Temple), and the Amoraim (whose interest, as expressed in the interpretation of the same verse, was in the academies). The Amoraic meturgeman, of course, had no difficulty availing himself of the same convention at 21.11b, 12 (discussed more fully in the 'Repentance' section), and it is notable that 'Isaiah said' prefaces a similarly individualistic reading of the passage (understood in terms of Malachi 3.18) in an unascribed opinion given in Numbers Rabbah 16.23.[12]

As in the case of the 'holy spirit,' one may not claim that this theologoumenon belongs to any one level (much less a single stratum) in the Isaiah Targum; the various interpreters who contributed to it seem simply to have shared in one of the enduring conventions of rabbinic Judaism. In the present case, however, it has been possible to discern that the same theologoumenon has been applied by both the c.70 and the Amoraic meturgeman to underline the preaching of repentance (cf. Tg Hosea 10.12; 11.2; Tg Micah 6.9). The rendering of Is. 22.14 particularly highlights the work of the former. As has already been observed, the parallels in the Revelation to the 'second death' usage already constitute evidence to this effect, and C. Perrot and P.M. Bogaert point out in the second volume of the Liber Antiquitatum Biblicarum that the phrase is also to be found elsewhere in the Targums (citing Deuteronomy 33.6 in Neophyti, Onqelos and the Fragment Targum; Tg Jeremiah 51.39, 57) and also in the Pirqe de R. Eliezer (34).[13] But from the second century, the rabbis regularly refer Is. 22.14 to death in the straightforward sense (Mekhilta Baḥodesh 7.24 [R. Eleazar ha-Kappar on a teaching of Ishmael]; jYoma 8.8; Yoma 86a). More generally, one might also make a distinction between the understanding put forward in Exodus Rabbah 28.6 that Isaiah received his prophecy on Sinai (in R. Isaac's name, citing Is. 48.6), and the Targumic emphasis on the spirit of prophecy seizing the prophet at the time he spoke (Tg Is. 61.1; Tg Ezekiel 3.14; Tg Micah 3.8). But these slight variations seem only to confirm our finding that the present theologoumenon was shared by our interpreters with rabbinic Judaism, and applied according to their particular interests.

f. '*My memra*' (מימרי)

'Word' (מימרא), normally with the pronominal suffix for 'my' (מימרי), is perhaps the best known targumic paraphrase for God, and it predominates over all others in the Isaiah Targum. The locution is not merely used to avoid anthropomorphism; as Stenning observed in the passage from his book cited in the previous section, memra is employed (along with 'glory' and 'presence'), 'when God is described as coming into relation with man.' We can be more specific than that, insofar as our meturgeman used the term in contexts in which the open call of God to his people is at issue. מימרי represents God as he responds to and addresses Israel, and as such it also provides the occasion on which Israel might react. There are so many occurrences of this theologoumenon in the Isaiah Targum that some means of categorization and selection is necessary if its range of meaning is to be appreciated. Accordingly, in what follows eight distinctive, but consistent, motives associated with memra will be isolated. They will be discussed on the basis of the most prominent passages from each category, and in the order of appearance of the first representative from each category. References to other memra renderings of each type will be provided in notes or parentheses.

i. מימרא *as an occasion for rebellion*

The rebellion motif associated with memra usage first occurs at 1.2; the MT reads, 'they rebelled against me,' while the Targum has, 'they rebelled against my memra.' In the same chapter (v. 16), the imperative is voiced, 'put away the evil of your deeds from before my memra' (MT: 'remove the evil of your deeds from before my eyes'). The same verse calls for repentance to the law (see 'Repentance'), so we are encouraged to imagine that there is a relationship between law, as the means of one's access to or apostasy from God, and memra, as God's awareness of which attitude obtains.[1] That is why the meturgeman offerred the following translation of v. 20:

> Tg and if you refuse and do not obey my memra, by the enemy's sword you will be slain; for by the memra of the LORD it is so decreed.
>
> MT and if you refuse and rebel, you will be devoured by sword, for the mouth of the LORD has spoken.

Memra is again that which is insulted by a refusal to repent, and now also appears as that which responds to the insult.[2] We have seen before the pattern of the divine response to repentance or obstinacy, and the motives of holy spirit and prophecy which are seen to make this pattern quite clear, but here we perceive a reference to the noetic centre of the process. 'My memra' was the meturgeman's way of speaking of God as self-consciously taking action along lines which other theologoumena explicate. Human beings may be said to work out their relationship to memra by the attitude they take to the law. The two concepts are so closely related that in 40.13 the meturgeman can speak of the righteous as servants of the LORD's memra, and the appeal for obedience to the law in v. 18 coheres with the call to obey the memra in v. 19.

Of course, this motif might have emerged at any time out of reflection on such theologoumena as we have already discussed. That God responds to Israel necessitates the understanding that there is a responsive divine faculty. But when we read the following, innovative phrase in chapter 28 (v. 21, after 'Gibeon'), which contains so much primitive language, we are led to suspect that 'memra' also was part of such language:

> Tg to be avenged against the wicked who transgressed against his memra...

A particularly close association with the prophet motif is betrayed in 30.1, where the meturgeman added both the plural noun and a reference to memra: 'to make plans and not of my memra, and to take counsel without asking my prophets.'[3] At 63.10, a play on words appears on 'memra' as both word of the LORD and the word of the prophets:

> Tg and they rebelled and provoked the word of his holy prophets, and his memra turned to be their enemy...[4]
>
> MT and they rebelled and grieved his holy spirit and he turned to be their enemy...

This rendering very clearly evidences the meturgeman's understanding of the distinction between 'holy spirit' and 'memra'; the former is the means of address, while the latter is what makes the divine decision as the result of Israel's response to this address.

ii. מימרא *as an agent of punishment*

In the face of consistent rebellion, the divine decision is to punish. At 1.14, 'my memra' (for 'my soul' in the MT) is said to abhor the new moons and appointed feasts, and v. 15 speaks of the removal of the Shekinah, so we may conclude that we are dealing here with an interpretation which post-dates the destruction of the Temple (cf. 'Sanctuary,' on 30.20; 'Jerusalem,' on 54.8). Another indication in this direction is the last clause of 1.14: 'I have increased forgiving,' for 'I have tired of bearing.' The meturgeman has so adjusted to the impossibility of cultic atonement that he has alternative means of forgiveness in mind.[5] God's memra appears as a threat against Israel's refusal to repent at 8.14:

> Tg If you do not obey, his memra will be among you for punishment[6] and a stone...
>
> MT He will become a sanctuary and stone...

In the 'Sanctuary' section, the meturgeman's avoidance of cultic language here has already been discussed. We may venture to add that, in his experience, God's punishing 'word' has replaced the sanctuary as the seal of the divine presence.[7]

If God's memra is a threat to Israel, how much more is it viewed as the agent of final judgment against the nations. This conviction is manifest in a long passage (30.27-33) in which consolation is promised to the 'house of Israel' (v. 32, see the appropriate section), and 'a curse upon the wicked' (v. 27, an innovative rendering). The curse, first of all associated with the name of the LORD, takes the form of God's own memra, pictured as a 'devouring fire' (v. 27), 'a mighty river' (v. 28), a fiery storm (v. 30), and even as the fiery stream which constitutes 'Gehinnam' (v. 33). Historically, God's memra is directed against the Assyrians (v. 31, following the MT), but the meturgeman's belief that the passage has an eschatological dimension is betrayed when he speaks of the 'mighty battle which will be waged for them against the nations' (v. 32), and of the preparation of Gehinnam by 'the eternal king' (v. 33, for 'for the king' in MT).[8] In three rather similar passages, the meturgeman uses the same image to describe the punishment meted out by God's memra:

33.11b
Tg ... my memra, as whirlwind the chaff,[9] will destroy you.
MT your breath is a fire that will consume you.
40.24c
Tg ... and his memra, as the whirlwind the chaff, will scatter them.
MT ... and the gale, as chaff, will take them up.
41.16b
Tg and his memra, as the whirlwind the chaff, will scatter them
MT and the gale will scatter them

The first passage precedes one which speaks of the nations burning (33.12), and itself presents the innovative address, 'you nations'; the second promises retribution to rulers and judges (the antecedent presented in 40.23); the third appears as a promise to Israel (41.14)[10] at the expense of the nations (41.11, innovative). The meturgeman sees his own dissatisfaction with Gentile ascendancy mirrored in divine displeasure, whose natural locus is the memra. Indeed, the feeling of revulsion at Gentile rule is so prominent, and the usages of memra mentioned in this paragraph differ so markedly from the more self-critical theologoumena discussed in the previous paragraph, that one might suspect that we are now dealing with a motif from a time closer to the Simon bar Kokhba movement than to the period of lax Temple practice. The impression that a sudden influx of invaders occasions such usage is strengthened by the rendering at 59.19b:

> Tg　When oppressors will come as the Euphrates River floods, they will be spoiled by the memra of the LORD.
>
> MT　For he will come as a dread[11] stream which the wind of the LORD drives.

Here, however, the diction refers less to final judgment than to God's immediate resistance to invaders. But since an eschatological orientation by no means excludes the hope of divine activity in the present, it would be incautious to posit two strata of anti-Gentile memra motif, and preferable to envisage a consistent usage which reflects various events and circumstances in a considerable period of Jewish history.

iii. מימרא *as a demand for obedience*

> If you are willing and obey my memra, you will eat the good of the land. And if you refuse, and do not obey my memra, by the enemy's sword you will be killed, for by the memra of the LORD it is so decreed.[12]

This rendering, at Targum Isaiah 1.19, 20, is entirely consistent with what we have already seen of memra usage as well as with the repentance and exile theologoumena. Indeed, coming as it does so early in the Targum and including such a repeated usage of memra, we might take it as a normative statement of the meturgeman's understanding of the term. Faced with a threat from aliens (n.b., '*enemy's* sword'), he calls for a rectified relationship with God.[13] With only a slight change of emphasis, the meturgeman can look forward to the time when the remnant of Israel will rely on the LORD's memra (10.20; cf. 17.7; 60.9), because to rely on him is to know him as one's saviour (12.2; 40.13b[14]; 55.2, 3) from whom benefit can be expected (25.9; 26.3, 4; 40.10[15]; 57.13; 61.10). The reward for obedience to the memra is so strongly anticipated that Israel can make claims upon God on the strength of her obedience (26.13, with a reference to the return of exiles in v. 15; cf. 33.2; 36.7, 15).

iv. מימרא *as edict*

The last clause of 1.20 in the Targum (cited above) is the first instance of a slogan ('for by the memra of the LORD it is so decreed') which is repeated at 22.25; 25.8; 40.5; 58.14 (in each case at the end of the verse). Generally speaking, the edict is in the nature of a promise, but the single exception to this generalization (22.25),[16] and the balancing threat of 1.20, should warn us away from thinking that the decree is stereotyped. Legal language[17] is used to stress the authority of God's decision as memra, and emphatically not to suggest a limitation on the flexibility of the divine response.

In two cases, where the MT reads, 'the zeal of the LORD of hosts will do this,' the Targum gives us, 'by the memra of the LORD of hosts this will be done' (9.6; 37.32[18]). In both instances, the locution makes the divine decision seem more considered and therefore more definite, as well as avoiding a certain emotional anthropomorphism. Similarly, it is natural for the meturgeman to say at 34.16b, 17a:

> for by his memra they will be gathered together, and at his pleasure they will be brought near. And he, by his memra, has cast a lot for them . . .

After all, a deliberate decision must be involved, even when God casts a lot. In the same vein, the meturgeman had Rabshakeh say, 'Have I now come up without the memra of the LORD against this land to destroy it?' (36.10a), and he spoke of a covenant with Abraham made by God's memra (48.15; cf. 'Abraham').

v. מימרא *as a voice*

As in the case of Hebrew דבר (which is, however, usually represented by other Aramaic words), Aramaic מימרא refers to a 'word' which may also involve speech and action. We have described God's word in the Targum as the locus of divine decision in an attempt to do justice to the variety of ways in which the term is used, but any description of the meturgeman's usage must also take account of the auditory reference which it sometimes bears. At 6.8, the prophet is pictured as hearing 'the voice of the memra of the LORD' (cf. 30.30, 31; 66.6), and the memra is the subject which speaks at 8.5. More striking is the innovative statement, 'he has spoken by his memra' (in 12.2b); מימרי is the normal means of the divine address in the meturgeman's understanding. This conclusion would suggest that there is a close association between memra and prophecy, and we have already seen that this is the case (see part i, on 63.10).[19] Yet it is important to call attention to 48.16c:

> Tg   The prophet said, and now the LORD God has sent me
>   and his memra.
> MT   And now the LORD God has sent me and his spirit.

It is quite clear that memra belongs to the divine initiative, just as spirit, for the meturgeman, is the source of prophecy. 'Memra' and 'holy spirit' are definitely related, but the former stresses more the God-ward side and the latter the more man-ward side. The present usage also occurs in the context of a reference to Abraham (see the appropriate section).

vi. מימרא *as divine protection*

Despite the infidelity of Israel, which might provoke an appropriate response from God's memra (see parts i, ii, iii above), the consistent support of the memra is an article of faith in the Isaiah Targum. At 17.10a, the meturgeman generally followed the MT, but he added that the God who has been forgotten is he 'whose memra is for your help.' Reference has already been made to 27.3 (in the 'House of Israel' and 'Abraham' sections); it is striking to find after a statement of Israel's past transgressions the assertion, 'night and day my memra protects them.'[20] This divine care appears repeatedly as the ground of an injunction not to fear (41.10, 13, 14; 43.5)[21] and it can be viewed as extending to individuals (42.1; 49.5[22]). On the whole, however, the memra is understood to support the community, both in the past (43.2, 'in the beginning when you crossed over the reed sea, my memra was for your help . . .'; 63.8b,[23] 14a[24]) and in the future (29.19):

> Tg   And they that have received humiliation will increase joy
>   in the memra of the LORD, and the needy sons of men
>   will exult in the memra of the holy one of Israel.[25]

The support of God's memra can amount to a vigorous intervention (45.2a):

> My memra will go before you and I will trample walls.[26]

By his memra diction, the meturgeman expressed his trust in a God who is passionately faithful, even in his severity.

vii. מימרא *as an eternal witness*

God's word is intimately bound up with creation from the beginning, as the rendering at 44.24 makes plain:

> Tg ... I suspended the heavens by my memra ... [27]
> MT ... the one stretching out the heavens alone ...

Each of the passages cited is followed by a promise: it is apparent that the purpose of the reference to the creation is not to make an abstract assertion about which aspect of God was involved in making the heavens and earth, but to assert that the divine pledge for the future is as certain as his activity in the beginning. His word has the eternal validity of the primordial word. The asseverative function of the usage is frequently explicit, as when we read, 'By my memra have I sworn ... ' (45.23[28]). Similarly, God can be said to promise, 'for my memra's sake' (48.11[29]), and at one point the provenience of such a usage in the period after 70 C.E. seems plain (63.17c):

> Tg Restore your Shekinah to your people for the sake of your righteous servants to whom you swore by your memra ...

We may see this language as complementary to the usages which decry the punishment of cultic abuse (see parts i, ii). Further, the general similarity of the memra-as-oath locution to the Johannine prologue, which also links the ideas of creation and witness (cf. vv. 1, 2, 4, 14f.), might also suggest that it was in use early on.[30]

viii. מימרא *as an intermediary?*

While the oath locution does not actually hypostasize memra, it perhaps represents a tendency to see memra as the ground of relationship with God (cf. also vi above). At 48.3, 'the former things' are seen as proceeding 'from my memra' (not 'from my mouth,' as in the MT); this is far from a fully developed doctrine of providence, but the noetic overtones of 'memra' may make the usage a contribution thereto. In one passage, memra is a means of access to God, not merely his own word (65.1):

> Tg I let myself be entreated through my memra ...
> MT I was ready to be sought ...

Later in the verse, the meturgeman uses the verb for 'pray'; his conception of the memra verges on making it an intermediary.[31]

*

Memra diction is sufficiently variable, even within the Isaiah Targum alone, to warn us away from conceiving of its usage as limited to a single period (or even to several periods) in the long process of Targumic formation. Having said that, however, and having acknowledged that some of the motives discussed stem from periods which postdate the formation of the New Testament (see parts ii and viii in particular), we must also remember that some of the usages cohere with primitive theologoumena (see part i—and the themes of repentance, the refusal to repent, sanctuary, prophecy; part ii—and the sanctuary theme; part iii—and the themes of repentance and exile; part v—and the prophecy theme; part vi—and 'House of Israel,' 'Abraham'; part vii—and 'Shekinah'). Even allowing for the possibility that, on occasion, 'memra' may have been added at a later period to earlier renderings, it would at the moment seem arbitrary to deny that the Isaiah Targum attests the use of the theologoumenon in its 66-132 C.E. framework.

The other Prophetic Targumim present a memra usage which is consistent with that of the Isaiah Targum in all of its variety. Israel is pictured as a people that has rebelled against God's memra (cf. Tg Hosea 7.13; 14.1) by transgressing the law (13.14). The last passage cited makes explicit a collateral conception of memra, law and Shekinah:

> ... now my memra will be among them for death and my word for corruption; and because they transgressed my law I took up my Shekinah from them.

'Law,' as in the Isaiah Targum, is the God-given occasion on which Israel accepts or rejects her God; 'Shekinah' is God's presence with his people, especially in the cult (cf. the next section). But memra is the active agent of punishment (cf. Tg Amos 4.11), not the reason for punishment (which is transgression of the law) or the result of punishment (which is the departure of the Shekinah). Naturally, the more positive demand for obedience, understood as obedience to the law, can also be instanced (Tg Malachi 3.7), and the address of the memra can be viewed as a constant appeal or promise in the nature of a decree (cf. Tg Jeremiah 14.19; Tg Ezekiel 17.24; 34.24), voiced through the prophets (cf. Tg Zechariah 7.12). The memra is God's support for his people (cf. Tg Jer. 30.11; Tg Ez. 34.30; Tg Zech. 4.6), his way of acting, sometimes through a human agent (Tg Hos. 13.15). Indeed, memra is the means of the creation itself (cf. Tg Jer. 27.5), and as such is the surety that what God says is established as fact (cf. v. 6). References are also available which present memra as susceptible of entreaty (cf. Tg Ez. 14.7, 13; 20.3). In short, the memra theologoumenon in the Isaiah Targum coheres with that of the Prophetic Targumim in aggregate.

The inference seems inescapable that memra usage is not merely *ad hoc*, but represents a rather more systematic development of theological thought than might have been expected. A difficulty emerges when we observe that the evidence of the rabbinic literature surveyed suggests that the rabbis had no such memra theology; 'memra' itself, of course, does not appear. It is perhaps significant, however, that passages from Isaiah which represent memra in one of its eight varieties are cited in rabbinic opinions which have at least a tenuous relationship to the Targumic interpretation:

i *(occasion for rebellion):* Leviticus Rabbah 13.4 (cf. 35.6 and Pesiqta de Rav Kahana 14.3 [p. 241]) cites Is. 1.20f.; R. Aḥa pointed 'sword' to mean 'carob' and associated Israel's repentance with eating this meagre fare.

ii *(punishment):* Abodah Zarah 44a takes Is. 41.16 to be a reference to scattering, and R. Joseph's translation is noted (but not cited), and a different rendering is proposed.

In Sanhedrin 108a, R. Menaḥem b. R. Jose, speaking of Is. 33.11, refers to the grief in Gehenna of the souls of the generation of the flood. The contrast with the more nationalistic reading of the Targum is obvious.

In Genesis Rabbah 6.6, R. Judah b. R. Illa'i cites Is. 33.11 to show there is 'neither a day nor a Gehenna, but a fire shall come forth from the wicked themselves.' This exegesis is contradictory to the interpretation of the Targum.

On the other hand, Is. 41.6 is cited (in unascribed opinions, unfortunately) in Genesis Rabbah 83.5 and Song of Songs

Rabbah 7.3.3 to speak of Israel's vindication over the nations. This accords with the Targumic rendering, but also with the MT.

iii *(demand for obedience):* In Kiddushin 61b, R. Ḥanina b. Gamaliel cites Is. 1.19f. by way of showing how important it is to be 'willing.' The agreement with the Targum is no greater than the agreement with the MT, although it may be worth noting that the principals in the dialogue (Ḥanina and R. Meir) discuss the fulfilment of statutes in the preceding paragraph (cf. the 'law' reading in Tg Is. 1.18). The thought of R. Simeon b. Yoḥai (Leviticus Rabbah 35.6; cf. 13.4, both of which are mentioned above) is more consistent with that of the Targum, but the mode of expression is quite different: 'If you observe the Torah, behold you shall have a loaf to eat, but if not, behold, a rod to beat you with . . . he meant, you will eat carobs . . . ' (Is. 1.19 is quoted between the two statements). R. Eleazar, on the other hand (Deuteronomy Rabbah 4.2, also citing Is. 1.19), understands the choice to be between the book of law and the sword, while R. Levi speaks of a golden necklace and iron chains as the alternatives *(ibid.)*.

iv *(edict):* lacuna.

v *(voice):* Isaiah is singled out as the recipient of a special revelation in Targumic and Rabbinic interpretation of Is. 8.5. But while the meturgeman spoke of his immediate inspiration by the memra, the rabbis spoke historically of Isaiah's presence on Sinai (see R. Isaac, Exodus Rabbah 28.6, and compare Ecclesiastes Rabbah 10§7).

vi *(divine protection):* R. Levi, speaking of Is. 27.3 (Genesis Rabbah 13.17), refers not to God's protection of Israel, but to the watering of the earth by the cosmic deep.

vii *(eternal witness):* R. Isaac, according to R. Lulian b. Tabri (Genesis Rabbah 1.3) cited Is. 44.24 to show that God created the world without the help of the angels (cf. Pesiqta Rabbati 33.8).

viii *(intermediary):* lacuna.

Aside from the fact that there are important lacuna in the above listing (categories iv, viii), the vagueness of the similarities between the Rabbinic and Targumic interpretations prevents us from concluding that memra was a category in intramural rabbinic discussion. There are many instances of rabbinic דבור or דבר usage, and some of these correspond to the categories of memra usage discussed here,[32] indeed this term also—and frequently—appears in Pseudo-Jonathan,[33] but, so far as the Isaiah Targum is concerned, the coordination of the rabbinic with the Targumic theologoumenon is not apparent. Strack-Billerbeck maintain that הדיבור first appears as a designation for God around the year 250[34]; the composition of the Isaiah Targum's framework before that time would explain the absence of the coordination between memra and dibur which we see attempted in Pseudo-Jonathan, a much later Targum. Moreover, the at first glance anomalous failure of the rabbis to exegete Isaian memra passages in a manner consistent with the Targum is quite explicable, given that they were aware that memra was not the exact equivalent of their dibur usage. This is especially supported by the reference in Abodah Zarah cited above, where the Targumic passage is noted as differing from the rabbinic opinion, but not cited. Further, we have already observed that R. Isaac (the third-century Amora, presumably), in Exodus Rabbah, understands Isaiah to have received his revelation on Sinai, and this is consistent with דבור usage, which was frequently used in the context of the inaugural giving of the law.[35] The failure to use memra, which in the Targum speaks of existential revelation at Is. 8.5, corresponds to a shift to a conception which accords with דבור usage.[36] The relationship between these two words and the conceptions they articulate would require monographic treatment to be explained fully; the evident distinction between the two, and the difference between the Isaiah Targum and Pseudo-Jonathan in דבור usage is, however, enough to serve as another support in the defence of our argument.

In his 1975 Oxford D.Phil. thesis,[37] C.T.R. Hayward attempts to be far more specific, not only in respect of the origin of the term 'memra,'[38] but also in regard to the period in which it was used. He unfortunately does not relate memra usage to דבור usage, but he does cite evidence which tends to support the general contention that memra usage was most fashionable in the period before classical Rabbinica achieved written form. Positive indications of an early memra theology are to be found in Wisdom 16.10-12; 18.14-16; Genesis Apocryphon 22.30-31; Revelation 19.12, 13 according to Hayward.[39] There are also important negative indications, namely, the apparent discrepancy between memra usage and rabbinic locutions. The most interesting of these is that the Targumic memra does not conform to the distinction between יהוה and אלהים (to denote the divine mercy and judgment respectively) which became conventional in rabbinic circles.[40] Such considerations must not be viewed as conclusive, because the relationship between memra and dibur has yet to be fully explained, but they may be held to support Hayward's case, and it is notable that the memra of the Isaiah Targum is similar to that of the Targum with which Hayward is particularly concerned (Neophyti I) in corresponding both to the proper (in the sense of merciful) and strange (in the sense of judgmental) works of God.[41] On the other hand, Hayward appears to press the evidence tendentiously in making the claims that memra usage originated in priestly circles, was associated particularly with the Temple, and fell into desuetude as a result of the destruction of the sanctuary.[42] The argument for such an association at times makes better sense as systematic theology than as exegesis:

> N[eophyti]'s point is therefore clear: the covenant with Jacob at Bethel is God's assurance that He, in His *Memra*, will be with Jacob, and the Jerusalem Temple is the outward and visible proof of the fulfilment of that oath, since it is the point of contact between earth and heaven, the place where God's presence in His *Memra* is most keenly apprehended.[43]

Through the covenant as oath motif, the sanctuary—as the locus of worship according to the divine intent—might well have been seen as the logical place for Israel to attend to the memra, but to speak of the 'presence' of God in the memra is surely to usurp the place of the Shekinah. The clear distinction between the two is shown at Tg Is. 1.14, 15, where the memra's abhorrence of the cult represents the change in God's intention in regard to the place of the Shekinah. Hayward cites Numbers 6.27 in Neophyti to show the special connection of memra with the sanctuary, since there the memra blessing is spoken by the priests and effected by the memra itself.[44] But here again, we have learned from the Isaiah Targum (at 63.10) that men other than priests (namely prophets) might so order their speech that it accords with the memra. Such language more nearly approximates reference to God's intention than to his presence, and it is a matter of regret that Hayward chose not to concern himself with the 'exact relationship of this exegetical term to Shekinah.'[45] As a result, we cannot agree with Hayward that the fall of the Temple spelled the end of memra usage[46]; although this may have been the case—and if it were, our own general thesis would be supported—at the moment the evidence is not so straightforward as to be susceptible of such a schematic solution. One might suspect that memra usage appears complex in relation to rabbinic theologoumena because, as the most characteristic periphrasis in the Targums, 'memra' was directed to non-rabbinic audiences before the rabbis exercised extensive control over synagogue worship.

K. 'My Shekinah' (שכינתי)

Repeated reference has been made to passages in which this theologoumenon occurs, because they reveal the hand of a meturgeman for whom the cessation of Temple sacrifice is a pressing concern. The crucial problem, he felt, was not merely the material destruction which attended the war of 66-70 C.E., but the removal of the divine presence, because this is what made the cult efficacious (1.15a):

> Tg And when the priests spread their hands to pray for you, I remove the face of my Shekinah from you.
>
> MT And when you spread your hands, I will hide my eyes from you.

In addition to its avoidance of anthropomorphism, the passage instances the meturgeman's understanding that there is a divine judgment against the cult. Moreover, the verbs for 'spread' and 'remove' are in the participial form (cf. the infinitive and imperfect in the MT), and this suggests that the judgment is contemporary and durative. For our interpreter, the departure of the Shekinah is explicable in terms of God's just anger (cf. 59.2b, 'and your sins caused the removal of my Shekinah from you . . . '), but it is something which he still feels acutely, as is substantiated by the many passages in which the departure of the Shekinah is lamented.[1]

The acuity of his grief was transmuted by hope into an expectant confidence. The following passage, already cited in the 'Sanctuary' and 'Jerusalem' sections (for the latter term, cf. the following verse), attests both an association with the Temple and a conviction that the Shekinah is a dynamic presence (4.5):

Tg   And the LORD will create upon all the sanctuary mount
     of Zion and upon the place of the Shekinah house a cloud
     of glory . . . for with glory greater than he said he would
     bring upon it the Shekinah will shield it as a shelter.

MT   And the LORD will create upon all the site of Mount Zion
     and upon its assemblies a cloud . . . for over all glory
     there will be a shelter.

This expectation is for what the meturgeman called the 'consolation'
or 'comforting' of Jerusalem (cf. v. 3 and 'Jerusalem,' n.1); it appears to
be a representative of a theology of vindication which is repeatedly
expressed by means of this theologoumenon.[2]

Other renderings in the Targum tend to confirm the observation
that the meturgeman was active in the period around 70 C.E. It was
still natural for him to stress the association of the Shekinah with the
cult in the sanctuary vision of Isaiah chapter six (v. 3):

Tg   And they were crying, each to the other, and saying, holy
     in the high heavens, his Shekinah house, holy on earth,
     the work of his might, holy forever and ever is the LORD
     of hosts, all the earth is filled with the brightness of his
     glory.

MT   And one called to the other and said, holy, holy, holy, is
     the LORD of hosts, all the earth is filled with his glory.

The association, however, is not a complete identification: the
Shekinah house reference occurs with the 'high heavens' phrase, not
the 'on earth' phrase. Considered in isolation, this passage might lead
us to suppose that the meturgeman conceived of the vision as strictly
heavenly, but the fact is that he honoured the word for Temple in the
MT in v. 1 and added 'Temple' and 'Sanctuary' in v. 4. Where, then,
did he understand the Shekinah to be[3]? Our answer appears in v. 6:

Tg   And one of the ministers flew to me and there was a
     speech in his mouth which he received from him whose
     Shekinah is upon the throne of glory in high heavens,[4]
     higher than the altar.

MT   And one of the seraphim flew to me and there was a live
     coal in his hand which he took with tongs from the altar.

By his careful exposition, the meturgeman managed to present the
divine presence as the epicentre of the sanctuary and yet as in no way

limited by the Temple building. The association between Shekinah and cult is loose enough to militate against the notion that God was successfully dethroned in 70 (cf. Revelation 4.5; Hebrews 10 and n.4), and close enough to suggest that the renewal of his influence on the Temple is as near as his proximity to the altar site.

Given the interpreter's care in qualifying the link between Shekinah and cult, it is curious to find renderings which locate the Shekinah in Zion quite specifically.[5] The first of these occurs at 8.18, and is cited in the 'Exile' section; since the threat here is that Israel might be exiled from the Shekinah which, it is assumed, remains in Zion, the pre-70 provenience of this passage is suggested.[6] A very free rendering of 17.11, which has already been cited in the 'Repentance' section, includes the objection, 'and even when you entered the land of my Shekinah house, where it was proper for you to serve, you forsook my service and served idols.'[7] The implied antithesis between idolatry and service in the land of the Shekinah house assumes a closer identification between the Temple and the divine presence than would have been appropriate after 70 (indeed, the point of view is retrospective), and reminds us of the attacks on improper cultic practice (discussed in the 'Sanctuary' section). Coherence with the early 'Sanctuary' theologoumenon is confirmed when we come to 28.10 (end):

> my Shekinah there (i.e., in the sanctuary) was a small thing in their eyes.

'Shekinah,' then, seems already to have been a traditional term by the time the events around 70 were explicated by its use. Indeed, in a very early usage, the LORD is pictured as revealed to judge the wicked 'from the place of his Shekinah house' (26.21a, for 'from his place' in the MT), so that the Temple is still viewed as the locus of vindication.[8] This sort of language had to be revised by the more qualified theology of the post-70 period; the meturgeman of 6.6 shows how he understood the assertions of his own predecessors,[9] whose renderings are taken up into his own theologoumenon. This locutional shift, which concerns the relation of the Shekinah to the physical Temple, is explicable on the hypothesis suggested above (cf. 'Sanctuary,' 'Exile,' 'Jerusalem'), viz. that distinct interpretative strata from the c.70 period have been woven into the framework of this Targum.

The recent study of 'Shekinah' in Talmud and Midrash by Arnold M. Goldberg provides us with an opportunity to collate our findings with those of a scholar working in a related area.[10] Goldberg argues convincingly, on the basis of a thorough catalogue of relevant texts, that 'Shekinah' is not merely a substitute for a reference to God, 'sondern erklärt, wie Gott, der doch erhaben im Himmel thront, in der Mitte Israels gegenwärtig sein kann, nämlich als Schekhinah' (p. 450).[11] As he points out, the Targumic usage of the term (which he treats from a small selection of readings) is scarcely explicable on the grounds of a programmatic avoidance of anthropomorphism, since the Targums do not always avoid anthropomorphic imagery. Given that 'Shekinah' is an explanatory term, which functions to assert how God is present, what manner of presence was envisaged? Under the heading 'Gegenwartsschekhinah,' Goldberg sees in the Shekinah's presence in the sanctuary the most original referent of the term (p. 455). With this is contrasted the 'Erscheinungsschekhinah,' which speaks in a derivative way of God's presence 'bis der Terminus Schekhinah schliesslich jede Form der Offenbarung und Gegenwart Gottes in der Welt bezeichnen konnte' (p. 455). Goldberg recognizes that the contemporary experience of the rabbis led them to look again at the strict connection of the term with the Temple (pp. 455, 457), so that by the time of the exile this aspect was attenuated (p. 486). Indeed, later passages in Babli so equate Shekinah with the holy spirit that the former can be pictured as merely conferring prophetic ability (p. 466).[12] From the point of view of this inquiry, it is immediately striking that all Shekinah usages in the Isaiah Targum belong to Goldberg's primary type of idiom. Further, both aspects of the 'Gegenwartsschekhinah' as analyzed by Goldberg are in evidence: 'Die sakrale Gegenwart, d.i. der reale Vollzug der Gemeinschaft zwischen Gott und Israel verbunden mit dem Kultus ... und die daraus resultierende schützende Gegenwart, die zur Erfüllung der Verheissungen führt' (p. 472). Even though two strata in our Targum become evident, one in which Shekinah and Temple are virtually identified, and another in which a more critical relationship between them is supposed,[13] in no case did we see the dissociation of the two which Goldberg documents from later Rabbinic sources.

Confronted with the dissolution of the cult, the rabbis to some extent rationalized their predicament by insisting that the Shekinah had departed with the destruction of the first Temple[14]; in principle, Israel had already come to terms with what confronted her in 70 C.E. The Shekinah was held to remain in the heavens,[15] and yet later rabbis taught that the Shekinah went with Israel into exile.[16] That is, the conception of the Shekinah seems to have grown progressively attentuated in rabbinic thought, and we can substantiate Goldberg's insight in respect of the Targums by observing how passages characteristic of the meturgeman's Shekinah theology are treated in the Rabbinic literature selected for comparison. Consistently—and usually without the use of the term 'Shekinah'—the rabbis interpret the passages in question to refer to the circumstances of the individual. From the early Amoraic period (third century), R. Johanan b. Nappaha and R. Eleazar refer Is. 1.15 to the transgressions of individual priests (cf. Berakhoth 32b and Niddah 13b). Later, the often-cited Rabbah insisted that Is. 4.5 proves that 'the holy one, blessed be he, will make for everyone a canopy corresponding to his rank' (Baba Bathra 75a).[17] As we have remarked above (in 'The Prophet(s)' section), the rabbis also associated the Shekinah with their academic centres, and even disputed its precise location (cf. Megillah 29a). The attenuated use of Shekinah, in order to assert divine immanence, and its usage in the context of individual ethics, is well illustrated in Kiddushin 31a:

> R. Isaac said: He who transgresses in secret is as though he pressed the feet of the Shekinah . . . R. Joshua b. Levi said: One may not walk four cubits in a proud manner, for it is said, the whole earth is full of his glory. R. Huna son of R. Joshua would not walk four cubits bareheaded, saying: The Shekinah is above my head.

The opinions of these third and fourth century teachers are obviously a far cry from the interpretation of the Isaian meturgeman.[18] The relevant texts in Jerushalmi can be divided into texts which are concerned with priestly conduct (Berakhoth 4.1 and Taanith 4.1, both of which are less individualistic, referring to normal practice and the efficacy of prayer respectively), and the names of the seraphim.[19] The absence of an individual, ethical interest in Jerushalmi should not be deduced from this survey, since comments on only Is. 1.15 and 6.6 were available, while the opinions expressed in Babli in respect of Is. 1.15; 4.5; 6.3, 6; 66.1 have been considered. In Exodus Rabbah 22.3, the early Amora Hama b. Hanina cites Is. 1.15 to assert that anyone, not only a priest, who commits violence defiles his prayer[20]; in Pesiqta Rabbati (31.6), R. Hama is also credited (by R. Levi) with the view that the holy one will prepare canopies for the righteous according to rank (cf. above on Baba Bathra 75a). Generally speaking, therefore, the tendency in Rabbinica to individualize an attenuated understanding of the Shekinah seems established when we collate our findings with Goldberg's. This is to be contrasted with the more literal and communal understanding apparent in the Isaiah Targum, and with other Prophetic Targum, in which the Shekinah is said to be present with Israel (Tg Ezekiel 38.35), removed in view of her wickedness (Tg Jeremiah 33.5; Tg Hosea 13.14), yet ready to return (Tg Ez. 37.27; Tg Habakkuk 3.4, 9; Tg Zechariah 9.8).

Without using the word 'Shekinah' (in discussing the feast of Succoth), R. Aqiba is cited in the Mekhilta de R. Ishmael (Beshallah 1.174) as adducing Is. 4.5, 6; 35.10 to substantiate the communal redemption of Israel. The suspicion is raised that the Bar Kochba episode is a watershed in rabbinic theology, that before this time the Shekinah was thought of as soon to return to be the common focus of Israel and that after this time it was seen more as a numinous presence which each individual had to take account of. Quite apart from the sort of considerations which have been offered in this monograph, Goldberg suggests both that the notion of individual offence against the Shekinah developed after the revolt, and that in this period the connection of the Shekinah and the sanctuary was still viewed as normal:

> Sollte meine Annahme zutreffen und die Ausbildung der Vorstellung von der Entfernung der Schekhinah durch Blutvergiessen, Unzucht, Götzendienst und Verleumdung ihren Höhepunkt unmittelbar nach dem Bar-Kokhba Aufstand erfahren haben, dann ist dies ein Zeichen dafür, wie lebhaft und real damals, etwa siebzig Jahre nach der Zerstörung des Heiligtums, die Vorstellung von der Schekhinah noch war, denn bei fast allen in Frage kommenden Texten ist die Entfernung real gedacht. Der Vergleich der Werte war also noch voll wirksam. (Dies wäre kaum möglich gewesen, wenn man sich das zweite Heiligtum ohne Schekhinah gedacht hätte.) [21]

Goldberg's argument is not that there was a univocal usage of Shekinah before 135, and an equally unvarying idiom thereafter: he categorizes the extant Shekinah texts into sixty-eight groups.[22] Indeed, his major thesis, expressed in the last paragraph of the book, is that the term 'Shekinah' came to include more and more 'Einzelvorstellungen' as time went on.[23] Neither is it any part of the present thesis to suggest that the Shekinah of the Isaian meturgeman is a static, unireferential term. Rather, as we have seen, the meturgeman uses the word (a) to refer to Israel's action against the cult as an act against God, (b) to speak of the divine removal from the cult, (c) to hope for the renewed presence of God in a fully consoled Jerusalem, and (d) to evoke the imagery of the heavenly dwelling. Goldberg has shown that each of these usages, along with many others, had a place in rabbinic Shekinah language.[24] The present point is certainly not that the rabbis chose to forget the Shekinah's connection with the Temple after the Bar Kokhba episode, or that they invented a new meaning for the theologoumenon; but the evidence of the Targum matches well against the theory proposed by Goldberg in respect of Talmud and Midrash, suggesting again that the Isaiah Targum's earliest framework was developed in the difficult period from shortly before 70 until the revolt of Bar Kokhba. Within this level of material, two distinct, but theologically consistent, strata emerge, one of which assumes that the cult continues to function and that the Shekinah is present in the Temple, while the other presupposes the temporary removal of the divine presence.

L. *'Glory'* (יקרא)

The term 'glory' frequently appears with 'Shekinah' in the passages discussed in the previous section. The awesome visual aspect of the divine presence is evoked by some of these usages,[1] but in other instances they serve within almost theoretical expressions of God's majesty.[2] Such distinctions in usage are obviously not contradictory, and on the whole we can say 'glory' is used of God to emphasize his incomprehensible splendour. Sometimes this is seen as a terrifying reality, as at 2.10, 19, 21, where men are said to flee 'from the brightness of his glory' (for 'from the splendour of his majesty' in the MT), and in the latter two verses, an eschatological dimension is added to this terror: 'when he reveals himself to destroy the wicked of the earth' (for MT: 'when he arises to terrify the earth').[3] In his own time, however, the meturgeman acknowledged that the LORD's glory is not manifest to all; the wicked can be said to ignore 'the praise of your glory' (26.10[4]). When the exiles return, the story will be different: 'a cloud of glory will cover your heads' (35.10[5]).

'Glory' is not the sole possession of God; men also can have glory or pretend to do so, although it is repeatedly asserted in the Targum that this is nothing compared to what God now possesses or will possess (3.17):

> Tg And the LORD will enslave the glorious ones of the daughters of Zion, and the LORD will take away their glory.
>
> MT And the LORD will make scabby the head of the daughters of Zion, and the LORD will uncover their secret parts.

Alongside the motif of the divine glory, which culminates in open manifestation, there is, then, a conviction that purely human glory is destined to perish. 'Their [sc. my people's] glorious ones' are seen as headed for destruction in 5.13, 14,[6] even though it was God that 'glorified' Israel in the first place (5.2).[7] Nor is transitory glory an affliction of Israel alone: the taunt is raised against Babylon (which is addressed through its king in v. 4), 'Your glory is brought down to Sheol' (14.11, for 'your pride' in the MT).[8] A similar motif, with reference to all peoples, comes to expression at 25.6, where the LORD's feast is described:

> ... they think that it is of glory, but it will be a disgrace to them ... [9]

Repeatedly, the glory which once belonged to the Gentiles is promised to Israel,[10] and again the glory is promised in association with early theologoumena, namely 'exile' and 'Jerusalem.'[11] The antiquity of the usage may also be supported by McNamara's observation that John 12.41 agrees with Targum Isaiah 6.1, 5 in the understanding that Isaiah saw God's glory.[12]

Although 'glory' is a theologoumenon which seems consistent with the perspective of the early framework, it is clear that the term cannot be construed to be limited to the rabbinic period in Judaism, much less to any particular time within that period. Even in the Old Testament, as von Rad has shown, כבוד is the means of God's manifestation which attests his sovereignty (Psalm 19), dazzles men (Exodus 33.17-34.35) and which is in the end 'the final actualisation of His claim to rule the world.'[13] Both as כבוד and יקרא, 'glory' was a conventional theologoumenon in the Judaism of the rabbinic period,[14] and a usage such as we have seen in the Targum to Isaiah is evident in Jewish works which enjoyed currency in the first century. For example, IV Ezra 7.42 associates judgment with the 'radiance of the glory of the most high,'[15] and Psalms of Solomon 17.30 particularly links δόξα with the vindication of Jerusalem.[16] We cannot pretend that this proves or even suggests that 'glory' is a characteristic motif of the c. 70 meturgeman; neither would we be advised to argue that it falsifies that assertion.

M. 'Kingdom of God' (מלכותא דאלהא)

In the Targum to Isaiah, the phrase 'kingdom of God' or 'kingdom of the LORD' is a distinctive, though comparatively rare, periphrasis for God himself, employed in respect of divine and saving revelation, particularly on Mount Zion. The first two usages make this apparent:

> 24.23b
> Tg because the kingdom of the LORD of hosts will be revealed on Mount Zion...
> MT because the LORD of hosts will reign on Mount Zion...
> 31.4c
> Tg so the kingdom of the LORD of hosts will be revealed to dwell on Mount Zion
> MT so the LORD of hosts will descend to fight upon Mount Zion.

The former usage may be held to be a reasonably straightforward representation of the Hebrew, in that 'kingdom' with 'to be revealed' simply renders 'reign' (מלך). The latter instance, however, betrays a more deliberate association between God's kingdom and Mount Zion; moreover, the Targumic revelation of the kingdom corresponds to the Masoretic Text's image of God's purposeful and violent descent, in face of considerable opposition (cf. v. 4a, b), on behalf of Jerusalem (cf. v. 5 MT and Tg). The referent of kingdom seems to be God's saving (24.23b) and vindicating (31.4c) presence, his activity in reasserting his rule.[1] Later in the Targum, the very mention of God's mighty intervention on behalf of Jerusalem (cf. 40.10, 11 and 40.9a, b) brings the kingdom catchword to the meturgeman's lips:

40.9d
Tg   the kingdom of your God is revealed
MT   behold your God.

The less vindictive, more positive face of the kingdom appears again at 52.7 end ('the kingdom of your God is revealed') and corresponds to the presence of מלך in the MT ('your God reigns').

Such a dynamic understanding of the kingdom is also apparent in Tg Zechariah 14.9a:

Tg   and the kingdom of the LORD will be revealed upon all
     the dwellers of the earth
MT   and the LORD will reign upon all the earth.

The addition of 'dwellers of' savours of a more universalistic (but no less vindicatory; cf. v. 12) understanding of the kingdom's revelation, and such a conception becomes obvious (albeit still nationalistic; cf. the previous half verse) at Tg Obadiah 21b:

        and the kingdom of the LORD will be revealed upon all
        the dwellers of the earth.

This rendering accords with all the passages so far adduced in construing the kingdom as God positively acting upon others, but the insertion of the 'all the dwellers' phrase is a startling departure from the practice of the Isaian meturgeman, for whom the actual mention of Mount Zion in v. 21a would have provided another occasion to posit the Temple site as the kingdom's locus of revelation. What is the reason for the discrepancy between an exclusively Zion-associated and a more universalistic construction of the kingdom? The Zion association is fully consistent with the work of the c.70 Isaian meturgeman (whose characteristic concern was with the restoration of the Jerusalem sanctuary), and passages in which this association is exploited to the point that it becomes exclusive are found only in the Isaiah Targum. We may, therefore, reasonably infer that the kingdom-Zion connection, when it is so emphasized as to be nearly an identification, betrays the theology of this interpreter. Logically, the more universalistic rendering may be taken to be the antecedent or the reaction to the Zion-association; a reading from the Mekhilta inclines us toward the former possibility. There,[2] in the name of R. Eliezer b. Hyrkanos (a noted first century traditionalist),[3] the clause 'and the Place will be alone in eternity and his kingdom will be forever' prefaces a citation of Zechariah 14.9. Evidently, 'kingdom' was felt by R. Eliezer to be naturally related to the universal promise articulated in Zechariah. The relative antiquity of the Targumic rendering of Zech. 14.9 is supported by its verbatim reproduction (without MT warrant for the addition of 'upon all the dwellers of the earth') at Obadiah 21b. The conservative understanding of 'kingdom' represented by Eliezer and spelled out at Tg Zech. 14.9; Tg Obad. 21[4] was apparently superseded by the Zion association, which arose in response to the situation after 70, when the restoration of the sanctuary seemed the most desirable vindication one could expect from God's saving presence.

Aside from these two strata within first century kingdom usage (which may, indeed, have been contemporaneous to some extent), one can discern other distinctive idioms in the Prophetic Targums which include the use of the term. In the Targum to Ezekiel, 'kingdom' unqualified can stand for 'kingdom of God' or 'of the LORD' (7.7, 10); this is a natural abbreviation and could have arisen in any period (cf. Matthew 4.23; 9.35). But the last usage in the Prophetic Targumim represents a particularistic theology in a way which is much more systematic than that in which the Isaian meturgeman presented the kingdom-Zion association (Tg Micah 4.7b, 8):

> Tg and the kingdom of the LORD will be revealed upon them in Mount Zion from now and forever, and you, Messiah of Israel that is hidden from before the sins of the congregation of Zion, to you the kingdom is about to come, even the former kingdom will come to the kingdom of the congregation of Jerusalem.
>
> MT and the LORD will reign upon them in Mount Zion from now and forever, and you, tower of the flock, hill of the daughter of Zion, to you it will come, even the former dominion will come, the kingdom of the daughter of Zion.

The Mount Zion-kingdom connection (exclusively understood) is the point of departure for the present meturgeman's interpretation, but his distinctive contribution lies in a progressive narrowing of the kingdom concept. The first use of 'kingdom' simply replaces the verbal root: the interpreter does not seem concerned substantively to alter the meaning of this clause, whose Hebrew version already provides him with the association of מלך with Mount Zion. What does consume his interest is the scope of the revelation of the kingdom. The Targum announces that the kingdom is about to come to the messiah addressed, and this kingdom is subsequently identified with the 'former dominion.' This practical equation between God's kingdom and Jerusalem's autonomy is underlined in the last clause, in which the 'congregation' (not presently a national unit)[5] becomes the recipient of the blessing. Such a limited kingdom conception is not that of Tg Zechariah 14.9; Tg Obadiah 21, nor does it cohere very well with Tg Is. 24.23; 31.4; 40.9; 52.7.[6] Relatively speaking, this passage appears to be a late-comer to the Targumic traditions which corrects earlier notions. Several other indications direct us towards the same conclusion. Aside from the 'congregation' reading (cf. n. 5), the rendering coheres with the fourth century dictum that one day of Israelite repentance would bring the messiah (so that her sins delay his appearance).[7] Of more particular interest from the point of view of the kingdom conception in Tg Micah 4.7b, 8 is the exegesis of Obadiah 21 offered by R. Aibu (fourth century), in which Israel's repentance causes God to return the kingdom to her.[8] This supports the picture of the development of the kingdom theologoumenon which we have suggested.

To explain the heightened particularism of the Amoraic kingdom theology, one might suppose that the rabbinic tendency even before that period was to associate the kingdom with Israel (not merely Mount Zion, as the Isaian meturgeman did) exclusively. According to H.L. Strack and P. Billerbeck, the rabbis achieved precisely this connection:

> Auf Grund vorstehender Gedankenreihe wird man den rabbin. Begriff מלכות שמים zu definieren haben als die Herrschergewalt, die Gott durch die Offenbarung seines Names u. seines Willens über seine Bekenner ausübt.[9]

Of course, 'seine Bekenner' are identical with Israel, those who know God as 'our father, our king.'[10] Keeping laws of cleanness is equated with taking on the yoke of the kingdom from the end of the first century (in the name of R. Eleazar b. Azariah),[11] and recitation of the Shema' is even more strongly associated with this image in the same period (in the name of R. Gamaliel).[12] One might easily imagine how this more nomistic kingdom theology, developed in rabbinic circles,[13] came to supplant the understanding implicit in Tg Zech. 14.9; Tg

Obad. 21 and Tg Is. 24.23; 31.4; 40.9; 52.7, and to influence such passages as Tg Mic. 4.7b, 8.

At the same time, one can still see traces of the older, more dynamic kingdom understanding in rabbinic literature, especially in the ancient prayers. In the תפלת מוסף הרגלים , the cry goes up: אבינו מלכנו גלה כבוד מלכותך עלינו , and is associated with the expectation of return to ירושלים בית מקדשך.[14] The general coincidence with the theology of the Isaiah Targum is evident, and it is interesting that in an opinion dated in the Aqiban period divine judgment is said to occur with the elders of Israel (cf. Tg Is. 24.23).[15] Such evidence certainly does not show that the Isaiah Targum was extant at the time the prayers were composed and Aqiba taught, but it does demonstrate that the dynamic understanding of the kingdom is not merely a Targumic innovation, and that it may very well be early. Indeed, in one sense it is as early as Psalm 103.19, which is reflected in the prayer אמת ויציב (וכסאו נכון ומלכותו ואמונתו לעד קימת).[16] The rabbinic exegesis of those passages of Isaiah which are interpreted in terms of the kingdom in the Targum makes it evident, however, that the rabbis did not adhere to the kingdom usage of the early meturgeman. In Pesaḥim 68a, for instance, R. Ḥisda (third century) applies Is. 24.23 to the world to come, and this confirms the shift in usage postulated by Gustav Dalman.[17] In his apprehension of the kingdom as God's strong action on behalf of his people, the Isaian meturgeman distinguishes himself from those who use the term 'kingdom' merely to refer to the force exerted by someone in authority (cf. Daniel)[18] and from those in a later period who understood the kingdom as the nomistic recognition that God is king. To this extent, the meturgeman's theology is comparable with that of Jesus,[19] but the meturgeman's characteristic association of the kingdom with Zion differentiates his usage from that of Jesus and from other early Jewish teachers (R. Eliezer and the interpreters of Zechariah and Obadiah).

N. 'The Righteous' (צדיקיא)

These are the recipients of God's promised vindication in the Isaiah Targum. This is clearly established in chapter five. The people of God are gone into exile 'because they did not know the law' (v. 13), and the glorious ones have descended into Sheol (v. 14), but an innovative rendering of v. 17 provides assurance:

Tg The righteous will be cared for as was said concerning
them, and the righteous will take possession of the riches
of the wicked.

MT And the lambs will graze as in their pasture, and
strangers will eat the waste places of the fat ones.

Faced with a very difficult Hebrew text,[1] the meturgeman took the
flock imagery to apply (as it often does in biblical language) to God's
care of his chosen, rather than to the complete wastage to which the
MT appears to refer. One is reminded of the place of the 'poor' in
biblical theology. The theme of the debasement of men's pride is
prominent in this chapter (cf. v. 15), and v. 20a evokes a vision of
retribution in which the righteous poor gain at the expense of those
who prosper:

Tg Woe to the ones saying to the wicked who prosper in this
age, You are good, and to the poor saying, You are
wicked. When light comes to the righteous, will it not be
dark to the wicked?

MT Woe to the ones saying to evil good and to good evil,
placing darkness for light and light for darkness.

The eschatological dimension of the reward and punishment is
evident in the phrase, 'in this age,' which implies that the reversal of
fortunes is to take place in the next age.[2]

A specific association between the righteous and the messiah is
betrayed in chapter eleven (in which משיחא is used in vv. 1, 6)[3]:

v. 5a

Tg And the righteous will be round about him

MT And righteousness will be the girdle of his loins.

Again, an eschatological and clearly collective hope attaches to the use
of this term. In describing the hope as 'eschatological,' the adjective is
meant to refer to a definitive divine action; nothing other-worldly is
intended by this description. Indeed, the meturgeman conceived of the
reward of the righteous in a realistic way. At 17.6b, after referring to
the departure of Gentile and Israelite 'glory' (vv. 3, 4, with a usage of
the verb for 'exile' in the latter), the meturgeman provided us with his
understanding of the gleanings image[4]:

so the righteous will be left solitary in the midst of the
world among the kingdoms . . .

Occurrences of memra (vv. 7, 10), Shekinah (v. 11) and the refusal to
repent motif (v. 11) follow, and 'among the kingdoms' is somewhat
reminiscent of the exile theme, so that we may reasonably conclude
that the meturgeman who was responsible for the early framework
addressed his hope to the righteous, and this is quite coherent with
other theologoumena (sanctuary, Jerusalem, exile, house of Israel).

The lively and early expectation concerning the sanctuary (cf. that
section) is specifically associated with the righteous at 24.16:

> Tg From the sanctuary house whence joy is about to go forth
> to all the inhabitants of the earth, we have heard a song of
> praise for the righteous. The prophet says, The mystery
> (רז) of the reward of the righteous is shown to me, the
> mystery of the retribution of the wicked is revealed to me.
> Woe to the oppressors that are oppressed, and to the
> spoiling of the spoilers, behold, they are spoiled.
>
> MT From the end(s) of the earth we have heard songs, beauty
> for the righteous (one).[5] And I say, Leanness to me (רזי ־
> לי),[6] leanness to me. Woe to me, defrauders defraud,
> defrauders defraud with fraud.[7]

At a time, then, when there was still hope for a vindication of which the
Temple would be the matrix, eschatological reward and punishment[8]
could be announced using the theologoumenon under discussion.
There is a very positive aspect of this promise (cf. 32.16b, 'and those
who do righteousness will dwell in the fruitful field'),[9] but, as in the
case of Jerusalem usage, the consolation of the righteous may partially
consist of a vindictive triumph over the oppressors. This is manifest in
the last verse of the Targum (66.24c):

> Tg and the wicked will be judged in Gehinnam until the
> righteous say of them, we have seen enough.
>
> MT and they will be an object of aversion to all flesh.

Again, a final hope is expressed, but one which is tangible enough to
satisfy a desire for vengeance (cf. the passages cited in n. 8). Moreover,
this early hope is so imminent an expectation that the righteous can be
said already to be blessed (30.18 [end]—except for the terms 'righteous'
and 'salvation,' this rendering follows the MT), and this in a context in
which Jerusalem (v. 19, as in the MT) and Shekinah (v. 20, innovative)
also appear.[10]

The meturgeman was not in the least doubtful about who, precisely, the righteous were (32.2):

Tg   And they will be righteous who hide themselves from the
     wicked as those who hide themselves from a storm, they
     will return and be appointed, and their teaching will be
     accepted . . . [11]

MT   And a man will be as a hiding place from the wind and a
     shelter from a shower of rain . . .

What characterizes the righteous in the meturgeman's mind, then, is their teaching. Their vindication comes with the acceptance of their teaching, and it is a reasonable inference that their teaching is understood to have occasioned the oppression by the wicked. These wicked are not Gentiles, but those who are styled righteous themselves,[12] and their deeds result in the destruction of the sanctuary (v. 14). Nonetheless, a restoration of the Shekinah is still expected (v. 15), and the meturgeman spoke later of the righteous dwelling in the sanctuary (33.16, cited in the 'Sanctuary' section). This picture of confusion, dispersion, internecine conflict and, nonetheless, confidence reminds us of the circumstances surrounding and following the 66-70 war, and coheres with the previous finding that the early sanctuary theologoumenon promised joy to the righteous. But this is not to deny that 'the righteous' would appeal as a self-designation to any rabbinic group that stood by its teaching in times of difficulty.[13]

These righteous teachers already enjoy a favoured relationship with God by virtue of their obedience (40.13b):

Tg   And to the righteous doing his memra he makes the
     words of his good pleasure known.

MT   And (who) as a man of his counsel has instructed him?

The opening half of this verse in the Targum refers to 'the holy spirit in the mouth of all the prophets,' and the meturgeman at 62.10 had the prophets proclaim 'consolations to the righteous, who have removed the wicked thoughts of the yetzer.'[14] The promise to the righteous comes from God, and its certainty is especially emphasized at 65.8 in the Targum:

Tg   . . . As Noah was found worthy in the generation of the
     flood, and I said not to destroy him . . . so I will act for the
     sake of my servants, the righteous . . .

MT   ... As wine[15] is found in a cluster and he says, Do not
      destroy it ... so I will act for the sake of my servants ...

The righteous, then, may be said to stand in relation to the patriarchs
(cf. n. 15) in respect of their blessing as well as in respect of their
obedience.

The basic hope for the vindication of the righteous, to some extent at
the expense of the wicked, is ascribed by Volz to Judaism from the time
of the Psalms of Solomon:

> Ausserdem wissen die Psalmen, dass die Frommen das Leben
> erben, die Sünder die Verdamnis ... näher bezeichnet ist er
> (sc. der Tag) als: gnadenreiche Heimsuchung der Gerechten
> 3.11, als Tag der Gnade über die Gerechten 14.9, als Gericht,
> an dem die Frommen von dem Druck der Gottlosen Befreiung
> finden 2.33ff., als allgemeines Weltgericht, an dem die Sünder
> verdammt, die Gerechten begnadigt werden 15.12f.[16]

Volz illustrates the prominence of the motif by citing the expectations
of the rule of the righteous (Wisdom 3.7f.; 4.16),[17] and of their vision of
God in Jerusalem,[18] and by demonstrating that the glory of the
righteous is already thought of as 'creata et praeparata' (II Baruch
66.7).[19] Moreover, the relationship between the righteous and law is
emphatically stressed in the literature treated by Volz, as it is in the
Isaiah Targum:

> Die Gerechtigkeit hat ihre Quelle im Gesetz (justitia ex lege)
> Bar 67.6; 51.3, das Leben des Gerechten ist eine Unterwerfung
> unter das Gesetz Bar 54.5; ein Wandeln auf dem Wege (den
> Wegen) Gottes oder des Gesetzes Esr 7.88; Hen 99.10; Bar
> 44.3; Ps Sal 14.2.

Volz was also struck by the conception of judgment as vindication,
'besonders da, wo die Frommen unter dem Druck ihrer gottlosen
Volksgenossen seufzen'[20]; his observation might apply as well to the
Isaiah Targum, as we have seen. Of especial interest is Volz's reminder
that R. Aqiba applied Is. 66.23 to the duration of the punishment of the
godless in Gehenna.[21]

Of course, the righteous are the natural recipients of God's blessing,
and they are so designated in the Shemoneh Esreh in both the
Palestinian (benedictions twelve and thirteen) and Babylonian (benediction thirteen) recensions. The usage in the Habînenû prayer, where

the righteous are said to rejoice in 'your city,' 'your Temple' and 'your messiah' is even more similar to the Targumic theologoumenon.[22] Such a motif of messianic vindication in respect of the righteous is common to the Prophetic Targums (cf. Tg 1 Samuel 2.8-10; Tg 2 Samuel 23.4; Tg Jeremiah 23.5; Tg Ezekiel 17.23), and the nomistic definition of righteousness which we have seen in the Isaiah Targum can also be instanced elsewhere in the Prophetic Targum corpus (e.g., Tg Jer. 31.6). The wide attestation of this motif makes it impossible reasonably to argue that its currency was restricted to the period we hold likely to be the era of the early Isaian framework meturgeman. But it is noticeable that later opinion construes righteousness in a more individualistic way. In Babli, R. Eleazar[23] applies Is. 5.20 to flatterers, and the legal emphasis of the Targum is not echoed explicitly (although a nomistic context is surely implied). This is of some note, because the Targum understands the righteous to advance a 'new teaching' of law, and it has been argued that this has influenced the wording of Mark 1.27.[24] Further, R. Judah's[25] exposition of Is. 24.16 in Sanhedrin 37b (cf. 94a) does not speak of the public song of praise for the righteous, but takes 'edge of the earth' as distinct from 'mouth of the earth' to imply an element of secrecy.[26] In the Pesiqta de Rav Kahana (16.1, p. 264), this verse is used as proof that the earth has wings. A definite tendency away from the Isaian meturgeman's confident expectation of the tangible vindication of communal, law-oriented righteousness would seem apparent in later rabbinic exegesis.[27]

O. 'Messiah'

Broadly speaking, one may conclude from the theologoumena so far considered that an early meturgeman provided an interpretative framework, manifest in the repeated usage of key terms and phrases, on which later interpreters built. Whether his work was transmitted in oral or written form, or, putting the question in another way, when the transition was made fom one medium to another, is beside the point for our purpose; it is enough for us to say that transmission of his work was conservative enough to make it identifiable in the extant Targum text. This meturgeman's interpretation was deeply influenced by the events around 70 C.E., and his confidence in concrete restoration and vindication in communal terms seems unqualified by the bitter experience of the Bar Kokhba period. To be sure, the faith of the rabbis after that time entailed messianic hope, but this tended to be expressed in a more circumspect, often more individualistic, manner.

Usage of the term 'messiah' in the Isaiah Targum manifests a teaching which is consistent with the early meturgeman's theology. The messiah is a figure intimately associated with the restoration (4.2):

> Tg In that time the messiah of the LORD will be for joy and for glory, and the servants of the law for increase and for praise for the spared of Israel.
>
> MT In that day the branch of the LORD will be for beauty and for glory, and the fruit of the land for the pride and for the honour of the spared of Israel.

The messiah here is a figure distinct from the servants of the law, even as their fortunes are congruent with the messiah's, while 'the branch' in the MT is a collective in parallelism with fruit. (For the Davidic connection of 'branch,' cf. Jeremiah 23.5.) The integration of the messianic teaching of the meturgeman with his view of the law is confirmed by the promise in v. 3, 'he who has done the law will be established in Jerusalem.' Moreover, the phrase 'consolation of Jerusalem' occurs at the end of the same verse, and a promise of the Shekinah appears in v. 5, so that this 'messiah' usage fits in neatly with what have appeared to be primitive motives.

The next usage of 'messiah' in the Targum clearly emphasizes the importance of keeping the law, both for the (explicitly) Davidic figure and his followers (9.5, 6):

> Tg The prophet said to the house of David that a child has been born to us, a son has been given us, and he has taken the law to himself to keep it, and his name has been called from of old, wonderful, counsellor, mighty God, living forever, messiah, in whose days peace will increase on us. The repute of those doing the law will increase . . . by the memra of the LORD of hosts this is done.
>
> MT Because a child has been born to us, a son has been given to us, and the dominion will be on his shoulder, and his name will be called, wonderful, counsellor, mighty God, everlasting father, prince of peace. Of the increase of the dominion . . . The zeal of the LORD of hosts will do this.

Both of the Hebrew uses of the term 'dominion' (מָשְׂרָה) occasioned a reference to the law by the meturgeman, as the only ruling agency sanctioned by God. What qualifies this ben David as messiah is that he adheres to the law; the same qualification attaches to those who enjoy the benefits of his rule. The congruence with 4.2 is obvious; the congruence with the Davidic expectation expressed in the Psalms of Solomon does nothing to hurt our case for the early provenience of this theologoumenon.[1]

Not unexpectedly, chapter eleven of the Targum is most explicit in its conviction that the messiah is of Davidic descent (v. 1):

> Tg   And the king will come forth from the sons of Jesse, and
>   the messiah from his sons' sons will grow up.
> MT   And a shoot will come forth from the stump of Jesse, and
>   a branch will grow from his roots.

Again, 'branch' terminology has occasioned the messianic associations manifest in 'king' as well as 'messiah.' In the Psalms of Solomon, 'king' is also associated with 'son of David' (17.23) and 'messiah' (17.36) as well as standing on its own (17.35, 'righteous king'; 'messiah' stands alone at 18.8; further, 'king' appears unqualified in the Targum in evidently messianic contexts: 41.25 ['I will bring quickly a king who is strong as the north wind . . .']; 66.7 end ['her king will be revealed']). The phrase 'from his sons' sons,' as already suggested, stresses Davidic descent, but it does so in such a way that, using Moore's description of Tannaitic sources, 'there is no trace . . . of any idea that the Messiah himself was an antemundane creature.'[2] Another general indication that we are dealing with an early interpretation comes at 11.6, where the idyllic description (following the MT) is prefaced with the clause, 'In the days of the messiah of Israel peace will increase in the earth.' That is, the meturgeman seems not to have embraced the idea which came into vogue at the end of the first century (cf. IV Ezra 12.34; II Baruch 40.4) that the messiah's reign is merely preparatory to divine intervention.[3] When, in v. 10, we hear that 'the kingdoms will be obedient to him [viz. to 'the son of the son of Jesse'],' it appears to be an echo of sentiments which are also expressed in the Psalms of Solomon.[4] The uses of 'the righteous' in v. 5 and of 'exile' in v. 12 are further pointers to the antiquity of this interpretation.

The meturgeman also understood the messiah to be an agent of vindication in respect of Israel's enemies, e.g. Philistia (14.29b):

Tg For from the sons of the sons of Jesse the messiah will come forth and his deeds among you will be as a harmful serpent.

MT For from the root of the snake a viper will come forth, his fruit a flying seraph.

The term 'root' (cf. 11.1) brought the Davidic messiah to his mind, and, once introduced, this figure so dominates the rendering that the vivid imagery of the MT is given only cursory attention.[5] The rendering of 16.1, 5 is less striking in this regard, but the theme of community vindication in Jerusalem again comes to expression:

Tg They will bring up tribute to the messiah of Israel, who prevailed over him who was as a wilderness, to the mount of the congregation of Zion.

MT Send a lamb to the ruler of the earth, from Sela to the wilderness, to the mount of the daughter of Zion.

Tg Then the throne of the messiah of Israel will be established in goodness, and he will sit on it in truth in the city of David . . .

MT And a throne will be established in mercy and he will sit on it in truth in the tent of David . . .

The use of the precise title 'messiah of Israel' in these passages (as at 11.6) would seem to be occasioned by the meturgeman's conviction that Israel as such joins in the benefits of the messiah's reign. In general terms, we could say that such a conviction is characteristic of Judaism in most periods, but it is interesting that this title plays an important part in the documents found at Qumran.[6]

In chapter twenty-eight, to whose apparent antiquity we have repeatedly called attention, it is the 'messiah of the LORD,' not the LORD himself (as in the MT), who is to be the crown of the remnant (v. 5). As such, he is the antithesis of the crown of the 'proud, foolish prince (רבא) of Israel,' and of the 'one who gives the turban to the wicked one of the sanctuary house' (vv. 3, 4). Here, then, the messiah's rule is portrayed as an alternative to the present corruption of Israel, and in this sense the expectation of the meturgeman should be characterized as realistic rather than as idealistic: the messiah embodies the hope for the community in its prevailing circumstances, which included philo-Roman simony. There is nothing fanciful about this eschatological messianic hope.

Targumic usages of 'messiah' in association with the occurrence of 'servant' in the MT are of particular interest, since such texts played a part in the development of Christology. In making this statement, full cognizance must be taken of Morna D. Hooker's convincing thesis that, so far as the New Testament is concerned, 'The use which is made of these quotations from Deutero-Isaiah does not support the suggestion that they imply an identification of Jesus with the "Servant".'[7] But this denial that a suffering servant Christology was *appropriated* by Jesus or the Church leaves us to explain why servant passages were *associated* with Jesus.[8] Of course, the term παῖς/עבד may be considered one condition of the association, insofar as it is applied in the Old Testament to such worthies as Abraham (Genesis 26.24, LXX: διὰ Αβρααμ τὸν πατέρα σου), Isaac (Genesis 24.14), Jacob (Ezekiel 28.25, LXX: δούλῳ), Moses (Exodus 14.31, LXX: τῷ θεράποντι αὐτοῦ), Joshua (Judges 2.8, LXX: δοῦλος), David (2 Samuel 3.18, LXX: δούλου), Elijah (II Kings 9.36, LXX: δούλου) and Isaiah (20.3).[9] Such applications, however, are not a sufficient condition for the use of servant passages from Isaiah in particular. If, however, Isaian servant diction was referred to the messiah in the pre-Christian period, that, along with the simple fact that Jesus did die, would account for the New Testament association between Jesus and this servant. It is to be stressed that we are positing a pre-Christian messianic servant, *not* a pre-Christian 'suffering' servant, as a sufficient condition for the development of this stream of New Testament diction.

The meturgeman first identified the Isaiah servant as the messiah at 43.10:

> Tg   You are witnesses before me, says the LORD, and my
>   servant the messiah in whom I am well pleased . . .
> MT   You are witnesses, says the LORD, and my servant whom
>   I have chosen . . .

The MT 'servant' may be taken in a collective sense, and the meturgeman took it to refer to the figure who for him is the hope of communal vindication. At Zechariah 3.8, 'servant' and 'branch' (צמח) were already brought together, so that the present interpretation could have occurred at almost any time in the development of the Targum. For two reasons, however, this rendering should probably not be assigned to the early exegetical framework. First, the messiah here is a present witness, as if he existed before he was active; we have already taken the hint from Moore that such an implication of the messiah's pre-existence is not altogether consonant with Tannaitic messianology. Second, at v. 14, as has already been indicated in the 'Exile' section, the rendering is apparently from the Amoraic period. It is quite conceivable that the servant-messiah identification is primitive, and even that the 'in whom I am well pleased' rendering is a precedent for New Testament usage,[10] but the present context of Targum Isaiah 43.10 warns us away from citing it as evidence from a pre-Christian period.

The case is quite the reverse when we come to Targum Isaiah 52.13; 53.10:

    Tg Behold, my servant the messiah will prosper...
    MT Behold, my servant will prosper...
    Tg And it was a pleasure before the LORD to refine and purify (רכא) the remnant of his people / to cleanse their soul from sin. / They will gaze upon the kingdom of the messiah; they will increase sons and daughters; they will prolong days, and the servants of the law of the LORD will prosper in his pleasure.
    MT And the LORD took pleasure to crush (רכא) him; he has made him ill. / If his soul will place a sin-offering, he will see his seed, he will prolong his days, and the pleasure of the LORD will prosper in his hand.[11]

The first of these renderings requires no special comment, except to say that its position assures us that this servant song is to be read as a messianic passage, as the use of 'messiah' in the second rendering confirms. But the latter is obviously the more striking of the two readings, and it exhibits a feature which is characteristic of 52.13-53.12 in the Targum: 'the exaltation of the Servant is applied to the messiah, but his sufferings fall in part upon Israel, in part upon the Gentiles.'[12]

Is this interpretation an instance of anti-Christian polemic? If one believes that the meturgeman deliberately placed the sufferings of the messiah on others to avoid congruence with the Gospel's account of the messiah, one will answer this question in the affirmative.[13] On the other hand, one may think that no tendency is evident but the primitive motif of a victorious messiah in whom suffering would be anomalous. The latter view has the advantage that we have seen evidence for such a primitive messianology; the former suffers the corresponding disadvantage that the primitive suffering servant Christology of which, on this view, the Targum represents a correction, is merely hypothetical. The reading of the Targum at 53.12 seems to clinch the case for a negative answer to the question: where the MT has 'he poured out his soul to death,' the meturgeman rendered, 'he delivered his soul to death.'[14] In v. 7, he had no trouble converting 'as a lamb led to the slaughter' to 'he will deliver the mighty ones of the peoples as a lamb to the slaughter,' and in the course of his reference to Israel or Gentiles he had to construe singular constructions as plural; and yet at this point, where self-imposed death is at issue, he translated more literally. As anti-Christian polemic, this is incompetent, especially since the messianic identity of the servant had already been stressed. It is far more plausible to suppose that the meturgeman, who was unperturbed by Christian claims, was influenced by primitive messianology as he rendered the MT.

The position here defended was well argued, more than fifty years ago, by Robert A. Aytoun. His starting point was *Contra Celsum* I.iv, where Origen mentioned the collective interpretation of the Isaian servant espoused by Jews of his time:

> When we turn to the Targum we find that it hardly accords with this Jewish interpretation, except to this extent, that it does represent the Jewish people as being in a state of dispersion and suffering . . . But on the other hand, and this is the most important point, nowhere in this passage is the Servant identified with the chosen race. Instead, the distinction between the two is more clearly drawn in the Targum than in the original Hebrew. That is to say, even if the Jews of Origen's time were rightly understood by him to have held the 'collective' interpretation of the 'Servant' in this particular prophecy, it is ruled out in this Targum.[15]

Aytoun wrote at a time when a 'Suffering Servant' Christology was in vogue, and, correctly observing that it was 'inconceivable that this specific identification can have been made officially accepted by the Jews after Isa. liii came into the forefront of the Christian apologia,' he concluded that 'the Messianic interpretation of Isa. lii 13—liii 12 . . . was officially recognized and popularly held at least as early as the time of our Lord.' Taking cognizance of references to contemporary Gentile domination, he dated the 'present form somewhere between about 50 B.C. and A.D. 30.'[16]

There are general and specific considerations in the light of which Aytoun's dating seems to be about a century too early. Generally speaking, one has no warrant to presume that the gospel was instantly presented in connection with Isaiah 53.12, that 'the Jews' instantly recognized it in connection with the passage as an exegetical challenge, or that the Targum would instantly be reformed to deal with the challenge. After all, the initial efforts of evangelization were short of totally effective, and the Targum endured much transmission, long after the decisive split of Church and synagogue, before it was committed to the extant manuscripts. More specifically, our passage refers to the removal of the Shekinah (v. 3), and announces that the messiah will build the sanctuary (v. 5). Again, we seem to have before us the work of the c. 70+ interpreter. If so, then the consistent refusal to countenance messianic suffering may instance anti-Christian exegesis, although the basic conception, which at least involved the messiah in risking his life, clearly was not a part of such a (secondary) tendency. Moreover—and on Aytoun's own admission—the stress on the oppression of the Jews could well be Amoraic, so that our acceptance of his basic position must remain qualified.

In addition to these usages of 'Shekinah' and 'sanctuary,' we find references in this messianic passage to 'house of Israel' (52.14), 'the righteous' (53.2), 'glory' (53.3), 'exile' (53.8) and 'law' (53.11, 12), all of which instance congruence with the work of the early meturgeman. The last term mentioned is especially important: in v. 11 it is the messiah's purpose 'to subject many to the law' and the statement in v. 12 that he delivered his soul to death is followed by the assertion that he 'subjected the rebellious to the law.' Each of these clauses is the preface to a statement about the forgiveness which is available through the messiah[17]:

> 53.11 (end) and he will pray concerning their sins
> 53.12 (end) and he will pray concerning many sins and for
> him it will be forgiven the rebellious.

The messiah does not forgive sin, he prays concerning it, and there is no question of his ministering to individual transgression.[18] His programme is of restoration and law, which leads to communal forgiveness:

> 53.5 And he will build the sanctuary house which was
> profaned by our sins and delivered by our iniquities and

> by his teaching his peace will be increased upon us, and
> by our devotion to his words our sins will be forgiven us.

As in the Psalms of Solomon,[19] the promise of vindication to Israel in respect of sin necessitates a corresponding threat to the nations (53.8b, 9):

> Because he will take away the rule of the peoples from the
> land of Israel, the sins which my people sinned he will
> bring on them. And he will deliver the wicked to
> Gehinnam . . .

In a word, the hopes of the primitive meturgeman centered on a messiah as he looked forward to recovery from the disaster of 70. The gospel of Jesus was not yet of sufficient concern to make him alter his interpretation for apologetic reasons, and it is permissible to infer that, in his messianic understanding of the Isaian servant, the meturgeman attests a primitive exegesis common to Judaism and Christianity.

In his article, entitled 'Le Messie dans le Targum des Prophètes,'[20] Paul Humbert came to conclusions very similar to those recommended in the present study. He also observed, 'Dans tout le Targum des Prophètes il n'est jamais parlé de la mort (expiatoire, salutaire) du Messie; ce silence absolu interdit de trop presser les termes d'Es. 53.12.'[21] Accordingly, Humbert accepted Jastrow's assurance that מסר למותא נפשיה in the Targum means simply that the messiah risks his life. We would agree that such an attenuated meaning (in comparison with the MT) was probably accorded the passage by the Amoraic tradents of the Isaiah Targum (who, in addition to 43.10, may also have inserted their own renderings into the wording of Isaiah 53) and perhaps also by their Tannaitic predecessors, for whom the ultimate victory of the messiah was of first importance. Our point is not that the Aramaic phrase unequivocally means the messiah did die, but merely that it is susceptible of the interpretation that he did so, and that therefore the Targumic rendering of Isaiah 53 should not be characterized as univocally anti-Christian (and post-Christian). But after a review of messianic passages in the Prophetic Targumim,[22] Humbert offered a synthesis of messianic doctrine in the Targums which is of particular relevance to our dating of the Isaian framework meturgeman. Humbert realized that 'le Targum distingue franchement les temps du Messie du présent siècle,'[23] and proceeded on that basis to discuss the relationship between the messianic era and the age to come in Targumic theology. He concluded that Klausner's characterization of the Tannaim in this regard suited 'le Targumiste' as well: "'La distinction de ces deux notions n'a pu être effectuée avec une conséquence parfaite".'[24] In this sense, he concluded that the Targumic theology derived from the 'primitive piety of Israel,' not from apocalyptic circles (cf. n. 24). The messiah functions as an intercessor (p. 37: 'non pas qu'il soit sans péché, mais il est un grand saint!'),[25] a military victor (p. 38), a man led by the Torah (p. 39), and even (p. 46) 'un saint rabbi' whose reconstruction of the Temple is the seal of his success and his piety (pp. 40, 41). Time and again in his conclusion, Humbert was driven— as we have been— to describe the messianism of the Targum as nationalistic and primitive:

> L'intérêt de l'auteur se confond avec ceux de sa nation: son messianisme est national au premier chef et rappelle à s'y méprendre celui des Psaumes de Salomon.[26]

In his recent monograph on the messiah in the Prophetic Targums, Samsom H. Levey agrees with the judgement of Pinkhos Churgin on Isaiah 53, namely, 'that this Targumic passage stems from the time when Bar Kokhba stood at the head of warring armies, and therefore the Targumist would not have taken literally the picture in Is. 52-53, but rather makes a glorious presentation of the Messiah, who is for him present in the flesh at that time.'[27] One has difficulty imagining that Bar Kokhba is actually portrayed by the meturgeman; given the outcome of his military campaign, he would be an odd person to base the ideal of the messiah on. But one could easily imagine that such a portrait of the messiah may have driven Bar Kokhba, and inspired rabbis to take his lead; he was even willing, as the Targumic messiah, to risk his life, subjecting the rebellious to the law (cf. Tg Is. 53.12).

Such general considerations as have been presented above cannot be said to suggest positively that only the c. 70-135 period could have seen the development of the exegetical framework of the Isaiah Targum. David is associated with Jerusalem's restoration in classical prayers,[28] and a specific benediction (numbered fifteen) for the prosperity of David appears in the Babylonian recension of the Shemoneh Esreh.[29] Surely, the repeated use of such texts kept the messianic hope and the motives associated with it alive, as the very preservation of such documents as the Isaiah Targum attests. But two remarks made by Paul Volz encourage us to suggest that the 70-135 period was the likely temporal origin of the messianic portrait of the (Tannaitic) Isaian framework meturgeman. Both remarks highlight the specific association of the messiah and the restoration of the Temple cult at this time. Bar Kokhba, he reminds us (who had Numbers 24.17 applied to him by Aqiba), caused coins to be minted 'auf denen ein Stern über einem Tempel abgebildet ist.'[30] Secondly, Volz twice calls our attention to Pesaḥim 5a, where the three rewards promised the sons of Israel according to the school of Ishmael are the extirpation of Esau (Rome), the building of the Temple and the name of the messiah.[31] Moreover, the Davidic identity of a concretely victorious messiah such as we see portrayed in the Isaiah Targum is authorized as an obligatory element of the Shemoneh Esreh by none other (if Volz's inference is accepted) than R. Eliezer: 'Whoever does not mention the kingdom of the house of David in the benediction "builder of Jerusalem" (i.e., the fourteenth) has not discharged his duty.'[32] Such evidence suggests that the provenience of the messianic portrait in the Isaiah Targum is Tannaitic. As it happens, in this case we can see in classical rabbinic literature more positive coherence with our findings in respect of the Targum than is usually available. Babli (Sanhedrin 94a) associates Is. 9.5, 6 and 24.16, so that the connection between the messiah and the righteous such as is typical in the Targum is also presented. A more specific dependence on exegesis also attested in the Targum is manifest when 'It is my secret, it is my secret' (MT: רזי־לי רזי־לי) is said to be spoken by a heavenly voice, and the association is contexted in a discussion of the time of the reward of the righteous.[33] A secrecy motif was also present in R. Judah's exposition of Is. 24.16 (in Sanhedrin 37b, cf. the previous section), and the present passage's ascription takes us back to the second century (Bar Kappara, in whose name R. Tanḥuma speaks). The messianic portrait of the Prophetic Targumic corpus as a whole seems reasonably coherent with the messiah envisaged by the Isaian meturgeman: he is a figure associated with the vindication of the righteous and the punishment of the wicked in Gehenna (Tg 1 Samuel 2.8-10), his ministry is conducted with a priestly colleague (Tg 1 Sam. 2.35; Tg Zechariah 6.12, cf. Tg Jeremiah 33.21, 22), and so has implications for the worship of Israel (Tg Jer. 30.21; Tg Hosea 3.5). In short, he stands for the law (Tg Jer. 23.5; 33.15).

CONCLUSION

Our attempt to isolate and describe the exegetical framework of the Isaiah Targum has proved to be complicated by a factor which we already called attention to in the introduction: the long process of Targumic formation involved contributions from many interpreters. There is no such thing as a single exegetical framework which served as a skeleton for later additions. Rather, we have seen that the work of a c. 70-135 meturgeman, either an individual or a group (but in any case supposing now the existence, now the destruction of the Temple), provided a principal framework, some of whose characteristic terms were taken up by an Amoraic framework meturgeman with a theology of his own. Moreover, some characteristic theologoumena in the Isaiah Targum cannot be fixed securely as having their most likely currency in the period of either meturgeman, although the available evidence and the present state of scholarly discussion would seem to suggest that we can claim general support for our thesis from the presence of such terms in the Targum. The initial purpose of this conclusion is to describe selectively the sort of evidence which has led to these findings, without the detailed analysis we have already provided (and to which the reader may refer for more specific exegetical treatment).

1. The exegetical framework(s) of the Isaiah Targum

Before proceeding to distinguish between one framework and the other, one must have some grasp of the overall framework to which the framework interpreters contributed, because the contribution of the individual meturgemanin becomes more distinctive when viewed within the context of the total edifice they built with their colleagues. The coherent usages of various terms in the overall framework centre on the restoration of the house of Israel. This restoration involves a return from the dispersion to the land appointed by God, and therefore victory over the Gentile dominion. The entire earth will have to recognize that true glory which is uniquely God's. The Temple and Jerusalem, the designated geographical associates of the Shekinah itself, are very much at the heart of the restoration, and the sanctuary features particularly both as the locus of divine power and the focus of Israel's obedience. For obedience to law is the *sine qua non* of divine favour, just as rebellion occasions God's wrath. But in the wrath or favour of his memra, God remains constant in his choice of Israel, to whom he issues the call to repent through the prophets, the agents of his holy spirit. Israel may accept or reject the divine work, but God's choice of Abraham is unchanging. Still, it is righteousness akin to Abraham's which the interpreters demand from their people in the prophet's name; a return to the law and correct Temple service were to them the content of repentance. Only such repentance could put Israel in a position to receive the vindication willed him by God. That is why the messiah's programme—of restoring law so as to occasion forgiveness—is so crucial in the Targum.

The principal and most striking feature of this overall Targumic framework is its perennial relevance to Israel. This is what permitted the Amoraic framework meturgeman to incorporate the contribution of his Tannaitic predecessors into his own work, what enabled the rabbis of Babylonia to authorize the transmission of the Targum itself, and what encouraged medieval scholars to make enough copies to ensure (substantively) the textual integrity of the Stenning and Sperber editions. Here is a message, in the name of the greatest literary prophet, which speaks to a dispersed and disoriented Israel living on the sufferance of Gentile officials, without a cult and yet expectant of a messiah who will restore the Temple and the autonomy of Israel. The Targum acknowledges these circumstances—indeed it speaks (at one level) from an immediate experience of them—and it also articulates these hopes. But the Targum is no broadsheet whose purpose is to foment the uncritical expectation for vengeance among those who lived under various forms of oppression[1]; hope is appropriate only for those who repent to the law; the promises of Abraham belong to those who behave as Abraham; the memra is always with Israel, but it might support or punish. The Targum has addressed all dispersed Israel in the time since the desolation of Mount Zion seemed final, and it has done so—not as generality—but as comfort and challenge. To those to whom rabbinic literature is nothing more than academic legal discussion and speculative haggadah, the Isaiah Targum is a most eloquent answer, and the dearth of accessible modern language editions is unfortunate.

Yet the very success of the Targum in its extant form as a contribution to the spiritual life of dispersed Israel (that is, Israel as disoriented by the desolation of the cult, not only as geographically scattered) means that it is problematic to assign the overall framework to a single given period. Indeed, the usage by different framework meturgemanin of the same characteristic terms often makes it impossible with any certainty to decide when the work of one leaves off and that of another takes up, and the echoes between the Targum and the Shemoneh Esreh (for example) demonstrate that rabbis might responsibly have encouraged the use of such a paraphrase in almost any period between the dissolution of cultic practice and the medieval attestation of the document.

By itself, the Targum's understanding of the law as the central means of Israel's approach to God and the secret of her communal identity serves only to highlight the coherence of the interpreters' faith with the spiritual movement which found its voice in the Seleucid challenge and culminated with the rabbis.[2] But the specific and emphatic association between the law and the cult in the Targum, and the expectation that a messianically restored Israel would attend to teaching which comes from the Temple, seemed especially (although not exclusively) similar to the fervent, literally expressed hope expressed in Intertestamental literature. Such similarity was far more apparent in respect of 'sanctuary' usage, because—while the concrete restoration of the Temple is a prominent expectation shared by the Targum, Intertestamental literature and early rabbis—the Amoraim appeared less eager to emphasize the building of the Temple as an immediate and central hope. At this point also, the internal evidence of the Targum suggested that two strata within the earlier framework should be distinguished, the first of which takes restoration to be a matter of regulating the cult properly, and the second of which assumes that physical rebuilding is necessary. The early framework meturgemanin hoped as passionately for Jerusalem's consolation as did one of their contemporaries, the author of the fifth Sibylline book, and their attitude was contrasted in our study with the tendency of rabbinic exegesis to see Jerusalem's vindication in ethical terms. Moreover, the Targumic descriptions of Jerusalem's oppression made it clear that the hope of the interpreters was articulated in critical circumstances: the Roman campaign against the city (stratum one) and its eventual success (stratum two) seem to have influenced the choice of language. A cognate differentiation between the attitude manifest in Intertestamental literature, the early Targumic framework and the Shemoneh Esreh on one hand, and rabbinic opinion from the second century onward on the other was made in respect of 'exile' usage: a development from a literal hope for immediate, militarily triumphal return to the land to a more positive approach to exile as a condition endured by God with his people seemed apparent. At the same time, 'exile' within the early framework is both a threat (at stratum one) and a reality (at stratum two). All usages of the term 'Shekinah' in the Targum cohere with the primary type of idiom isolated by A.M. Goldberg ('Gegenwartsschekhinah')[3] and suppose an identification with the Temple such that the Shekinah is either sinned against by cultic abuse (stratum one) or removed because of such sin, but soon to return (stratum two). A more attenuated use of the term characterizes the Amoraic period. 'Kingdom' in the Targum is associated with Zion, as is consistent with the viewpoint of the early meturgemanin. Their usage represents a development in the meaning of the term (which is evident in comparison with the usage of other Prophetic Targumim and the Mekhilta), in that the earlier understanding saw the kingdom in less restricted terms. But the connection of the kingdom with the sanctuary is also attested in the musaf prayer for pilgrimages, and is only a step in the direction of a nomistic understanding of the kingdom which was achieved at or near the end of the first century. The early framework interpreters' view of righteousness is, as in Intertestamental literature, communal and motivated by the hope of vindication; the Amoraim were no less emphatic in their call to be righteous, but they understand righteousness as a more individual duty and associate it more with obedience to the law (an association which is presupposed in their demand for right behaviour) and less with the teaching of the law (which was a crucial necessity in the days of the early meturgemanin).

For the Amoraic framework meturgeman(in), sin in general, rather than specifically cultic abuse, is the cause of the exile to Babylon, and his hope for the eventual end of the Babylonian tyranny is linked more to individual than to ethnic repentance. In the sense that exile is the situation in which the individual is to cultivate righteous behaviour, the Amoraic acceptance of exile as the *status quo* seems presupposed, and we found a near parallel to an 'exile' reading from the later framework (Tg Is. 43.14) in the Pesiqta Rabbati (30.2), and many Amoraic parallels to a later and individualistic 'repentance' reading (at Tg Is. 57.19). Moreover, Israel for this interpreter is more a 'congregation' than a 'house' (again, cf. Pesiqta Rabbati 37.3); a post-nationalistic perspective seems evident. On the other hand, it must be acknowledged and stressed that the Amoraic interpreter was an ardent traditionalist. He was willing, for example (at Tg Is. 48.15, 16), to let the work of his predecessors stand and transmit to his readers an imperative to follow Abraham in a vocation of cultic service rather than voice the call, fashionable in his day, for scholars to be heard with the respect due to Moses. Likewise, the Amoraic Isaian framework meturgeman (unlike his, or another's, practice in Tg Micah) effaced his own kingdom theology in favour of the viewpoint of a Tannaitic framework meturgeman. Interpreters at both the Tannaitic and Amoraic levels availed themselves of the introductory phrase, 'The prophet said.' The former typically employed it to articulate the demand for communal repentance and the hope for the renovation of prophecy thereafter; the latter used it to insist on right conduct in view of eschatological judgement (cf. Tg Is. 21.12 with Numbers Rabbah 16.23). The Amoraic meturgeman also developed the earlier picture of the messiah ben David who, with a priestly counterpart, gives the law from the Temple he restores into a figure who is proleptically active (Tg Is. 43.10, and not in name only) as a witness to God's sole efficacy as God.

What we have postulated to explain the growth of the Isaiah Targum is not a series of mechanical redactions, but the unfolding of an interpretative continuum. There is no way of determining the number of meturgemanin who were responsible for each of the individual readings contained in the extant manuscripts, and yet the evidence has substantiated our hypothesis, developed in the introduction, that the repetition of characteristic terms manifests an organizing framework. We have collated that evidence against selected data from Intertestamental literature, the Qumran finds, ancient Jewish prayers, Rabbinica and the New Testament, and we were have been led by our exegeses to differentiate between the applications of these characteristic terms within the Targum itself. We have come to the conclusion— gradually, as the inquiry progressed, and term after term appeared to bear now one meaning, now a distinct (albeit related) meaning—that we must think of the framework itself as a developing organizing principle which permitted more ancient readings to be transmitted even as their theological significance was adapted to the points of view of the meturgemanin and their readers. As rings on a tree, the two strata of the Tannaitic level and the single, although less substantial, Amoraic level stand out as witnesses to stages of growth. The shape of the tree was at each stage distinctive, but related to its shape at the next stage, and at every point it was recognizably the same tree that was growing. The last observation proceeds directly from the remarks offered above; if it were not so, one could not speak of the overall framework, nor could one describe each constituent framework with reference to the same characteristic exegetical terms. But we can substantiate our observation further by recollecting that certain key terms ('holy spirit,' 'memra,' 'glory') are simply impatient of categorization into strata or levels in that they seem to be the common property of the various framework interpreters.

This brings us around full circle within this section of conclusions: our analysis of individual terms within constituent frameworks has sharpened our appreciation of the overall framework. One achieves greater insight into the vitality of this durable document by observing how it developed through various exigencies and in different theological climates. The Isaiah Targum endures as a testament to the faith of early and rabbinic Judaism. Fed by many hands, dominated by no single person and yet carefully shaped and pruned at crucial stages, its survival, as a tree's, depended on its ability to grow during the changing conditions of the years. But our simile of organic growth invites us to ask how successful our method has been at apprehending the development of the Isaiah Targum. The business of the next section is to answer that question.

2. Methodological

For reasons explained in the introduction to this monograph, linguistic and atomistically exegetical approaches to the Targums have not thus far produced coherent results in respect of their theology and provenience. Nonetheless, the present inquiry has attempted to take account of linguistic questions, and has profited greatly from the individual exegetical insights of previous investigators. Discussion of the language of the Targumim has served to delimit (if broadly) the period in which Targumic formation most probably occurred, and it has provided an advance warning against the easy assumption that linguistic criteria alone can fix an Aramaic document securely in a single time and place. And the at first sight confusing array of early and late Targumic readings (whether dated from a historical or a theological point of view) is an indispensible substantiation of Churgin's foundational insight that the investigator of the Prophetic Targums must be prepared to take account of a very long process of development.[4] Our attempt has been to move beyond these results in

(1) describing the theology of the Isaiah Targum by analysing the characteristic terms in its (hypothetical, at first) exegetical framework and (2) determining the provenience of the framework by comparing the use of these terms with readings in Intertestamental literature, Rabbinica, the Septuagint and the New Testament.

At each stage in the work, a process of selection has been necessary, and—having come to the end of the inquiry—we must ask whether the method and its application have proved viable. In the first place, we would assert that the hypothesis of an exegetical framework has been substantiated by consideration of the characteristic terms here exegeted. Admittedly, some of the terms are the common property of post-biblical Judaism, but the particular fields of meaning to which the theologoumena belong, their repetition in a consistent fashion, and the coherence between the various usages to articulate an identifiable theology, demonstrate that there is an exegetical framework within this Targum which is its ordering principle. As such, it is what makes the Isaiah Targum identifiable as a thorough-going paraphrase which is evidenced in extant manuscripts, with or without the more primitive and more recent material which was no doubt included in the course of transmission.

We must, however, set some cautionary considerations alongside our suggestion. Our selection of terms on the basis of which the theology of the Targum was described was heuristic, and it is virtually certain that another investigator would have selected a somewhat different collection of terms for analysis.[5] Nonetheless, the prevalence of the terms selected and their coherence with one another suggests that they cannot be ignored as evidence for the theology of the meturgemanin. Further work could, and probably will, offer refinements in the description of the theology they express, but that some account should be taken of them in future inquiries of this sort does seem appropriate. Secondly—and substantively perhaps more important— our analysis has not isolated a single framework, but the work of framework interpreters at two levels (Tannaitic and Amoraic), with the earlier level distinguished into two strata (before and after the destruction of the Temple). Our initial hypothesis has therefore been refined as we took account of Targumic readings and developed a theory of the evolution of the document as we know it. It is conceivable that the scheme here proposed will have to be developed further as more Targumic terms are studied and evaluated.

Selection has also been required in choosing the documents, and the interpretations of or allusions to Isaian passages therein, with which to compare the Targum. The choice of Isaian passages was justified by the extent to which the characteristic exegetical theology of the Targum was manifest in them; a different choice may have led to somewhat different results, depending on the prominence of the passages chosen in the work of the rabbis, those responsible for the Septuagint and Intertestamental material, and the contributors to the New Testament. Further, while the selection of rabbinic literature for the purpose of comparison was defended in the introduction, no guarantee is available that a different selection of documents would not have led us to formulate different conclusions. These potential defects in the work must be acknowledged openly, since such a recognition might be taken as a spur to further research.

Having admitted the limited and limiting nature of our selection, it would be invidious to suppose that we can generalize authoritatively about the relationship of interpretations in the Isaiah Targum to those in other rabbinic works. It may nonetheless aid the course of further research to list the passages in the Targum which we have considered characteristic for the purpose of comparison and the rabbinic documents which seemed to us to present relevantly analogous or variant[6] interpretations:

Law
>Tg 2.3: Midrash Rabbah (Leviticus 24.4); Babli (Pesaḥim 88a); Jerushalmi (Nedarim 6.9); Pesiqta Rabbati (39.2; 41.1).
>Tg 26.19: Midrash Rabbah (Ecclesiastes 1.7.7); Babli (Kethuboth 111a, b; Sanhedrin 90b); Jerushalmi (Berakhoth 5.2); Pirqe de R. Eliezer (34: p. 260).

Sanctuary
>Tg 22.22: LXX.
>Tg 24.16 (cf. 38.11): Babli (Kethuboth 112b); Pesiqta de R. Kahana (16.1: p. 264); Pirqe de R. Eliezer (37: p. 282); cf. 'The righteous.'
>Tg 28.13: none.
>Tg 53.5: none.

Jerusalem
>Tg 25.2: none.
>Tg 54.1b: Midrash Rabbah (Song of Songs 1.5.3 and 4.4.9); Babli (Berakhoth 10a); Pesiqta Rabbati (32.2).

Tg 54.15b: Babli (Yebamoth 24b).

Tg 56.9: none.

Exile

Tg 43.14: Mekhilta (Pisḥa 14.103); Midrash Rabbah (Exodus 15.16; cf. 33.5; Leviticus 32.8; Numbers 7.10; Lamentations 1.19-20§54; Song of Songs 4.8.1); Babli (Megillah 29a); Jerushalmi (Taanith 1.1); Pesiqta Rabbati 8.4; 29/30.1; 30.2).

Tg 53.8: none.

Tg 54.1: none.

House of Israel

Tg 27.2: Midrash Rabbah (Numbers 10.2; cf. Song of Songs 8.14.1).

Tg 27.4: Mekhilta (Shirata 5.62); Babli (Abodah Zarah 4a).

Tg 51.11: Pesiqta Rabbati (37.3).

Repentance

Tg 21.12: Midrash Rabbah (Exodus 18.12; Numbers 16.23); Jerushalmi (Taanith 1.1); Pesiqta Rabbati (33.4); LXX.

Tg 28.10: none.

Tg 57.18, 19: Midrash Rabbah (Leviticus 16.9; Numbers 8.4; 11.7); Babli (Berakhoth 34b; cf. Sanhedrin 99a); Pesiqta Rabbati (44.8).

Tg 65.12: none.

Tg 66.12: none.

Abraham

Tg 48.15, 16: Midrash Rabbah (Exodus 28.6; Leviticus 1.9-10; Ecclesiastes 10§1); Babli (Mo'ed Ḳaṭan 16b; cf. Shabbath 86b).

Holy Spirit

Tg 40.13a: none.

Tg 63.10: Mekhilta (Shirata 5.66); Midrash Rabbah (Lamentations 1.22§57; Ecclesiastes 3.8§2.

Prophet(s)

Tg 5.6c: Midrash Rabbah (Ecclesiastes 9.2.1).

Tg 8.17: Midrash Rabbah (Genesis 42.3.2; Leviticus 11.7; Esther 11; Ruth 7); Jerushalmi (Sanhedrin 10.2); LXX.

Tg 21.11b, 12: Midrash Rabbah (Exodus 18.12; Numbers 16.23); cf. 'Repentance.'

Tg 22.14: Mekhilta (Baḥodesh 7.24); Babli (Yoma 86a);
Jerushalmi (Yoma 8.8).

Tg 40.9: none.

Memra

i   Tg 1.20: Midrash Rabbah (Leviticus 13.4).

Tg 63.10: none.

ii Tg 8.14: Babli (Sanhedrin 38a).

Tg 33.11b; 40.24c; 41.16b: Midrash Rabbah (Genesis 6.6; cf.
35.6; 83.5; cf. Song of Songs 7.3.3); Babli (Abodah Zarah
44a and Sanhedrin 108a).

Tg 59.19b: Babli (Sanhedrin 98a).

iii Tg 1.19, 20: Midrash Rabbah (Leviticus 35.6; Deuteronomy
4.2); Babli (Kiddushin 61b); Pesiqta de R. Kahana (14.3:
p. 241).

iv Tg 36.10a: none.

v   Tg 8.5: none.

Tg 48.16c: Midrash Rabbah (Exodus 28.6; cf. 'Abraham').

vi Tg 17.10a: none.

Tg 27.3: Midrash Rabbah (Genesis 13.17).

Tg 45.2: none.

vii Tg 44.24: Midrash Rabbah (Genesis 1.3; cf. 3.8); Pesiqta
Rabbati (33.8).

Tg 63.17c: none.

viii Tg 65.1: none.

Shekinah

Tg 1.15a: Midrash Rabbah (Exodus 22.3); Babli (Berakhoth
32b; Niddah 13b); Jerushalmi (Berakhoth 4.1; Taanith
4.1).

Tg 4.5: Mekhilta (Beshallah 1.174); Midrash Rabbah (Genesis
44.22; Exodus 50.5); Babli (Baba Bathra 75a); Pesiqta
Rabbati (31.6).

Tg 6.3, 6: Mekhilta (Beshallah 1.174); Midrash Rabbah (Exodus 33.4); Babli (Berakhoth 4b; Ḥagigah 13b; Kiddushin
31a; Baba Bathra 75b); Jerushalmi (Rosh Hashanah 1.1-
2); Pesiqta Rabbati (33.3); Pirqe de R. Eliezer (10: p. 66).

Tg 28.10: none.

Glory

Tg 2.19, 21 (cf. v. 10): LXX.

Tg 14.11: LXX.

Kingdom
> Tg 24.23: Midrash Rabbah (Exodus 45.5; Leviticus 11.8; Ecclesiastes 1.2); Babli (Pesaḥim 68a; cf. Sanhedrin 91b; Baba Bathra 10b); Jerushalmi (Sanhedrin 11.3).
>
> Tg 31.4: none.
>
> Tg 40.9: none.
>
> Tg 52.7: Midrash Rabbah (Deuteronomy 5.15); Pesiqta Rabbati (15.14/15; 35.4).

The righteous
> Tg 5.20a: Babli (Soṭah 41b).
>
> Tg 24.16: Midrash Rabbah (Song of Songs 2.1.2; Ecclesiastes 1.7.7); Babli (Sanhedrin 37b; 94a); LXX; cf. 'Sanctuary.'
>
> Tg 32.2: none.

Messiah
> Tg 9.5, 6: Midrash Rabbah (Genesis 97 [N.V.]; Numbers 11.7; Ruth 7.2); Babli (Sanhedrin 94a; Shabbath 55a); Jerushalmi (Sanhedrin 10.1).
>
> Tg 16.1: none.
>
> Tg 43.10: none.
>
> Tg 53.5: none.

We are now in a position to remark on the general distribution of these parallels and, stressing again the limited scope of the sample comparisons, to suggest in a provisional way some implications for further research. The distinctive purpose of the Targum within rabbinic discussion is immediately indicated by the absence of rabbinic analogues to Targumic readings. This serves only to illustrate what we have seen repeatedly during the course of the study, that Rabbinica frequently present interpretations of Isaian passages which develop very different motives from those manifest in the Targum (cf., for example, the varying treatments of Is. 24.16 and 27.3). In some cases the documents compared with the Targum did not present relevant readings (*Bellum Judaicum, Liber Antiquitatum Biblicarum*, Mishnah, Yalkut Shimoni). In the instance of Mishnah, the lacuna would appear to support the contention that the purpose of the Targum is to be distinguished qualitatively from that of intramural rabbinic discussion and, *mutatis mutandis*, the special purposes of *Bellum Judaicum* (apologetic) and the *Liber Antiquitatum Biblicarum* (as haggadic midrash[7]) would seem to account for the situation. The

relatively late date of the Yalkut Shimoni as compared to that of both
levels of the Isaiah Targum's framework helps to explain its apparent
silence for our purposes.[8] Relevant readings in the Septuagiut are not
numerous, but their very existence at least suggests that the postulation
of an early date for a framework is not implausible.[9] Given their sheer
bulk, and the range of material they present, the comparative
dominance of readings from Midrash Rabbah, Babli and Jerushalmi
among the documents listed is far from surprising. The expositional
nature of Midrash Rabbah may also account for the relative frequency
of its citations here, and for the at first sight striking number of
pertinent readings from the Mekhilta de R. Ishmael. The early date of
the Mekhilta, and of the Pesiqta de R. Kahana, may also be important,
and serves to confirm the postulation of a Tannaitic framework.
On the other hand, the Amoraic framework hypothesis finds support
in the Targumic coherence with Pesiqta Rabbati and (to a lesser
extent) with Pirqe de R. Eliezer. Of particular note is the degree to
which certain passages are given full treatment in documents compiled
for different purposes at different times. Thorough discussion of this
material, although it is beyond the scope of the present study, might
yield insights into developing techniques and tendencies in rabbinic
discussion.

The systematic search discussed above, however, did not provide all
of the references to Rabbinica in the present study. Simple perusal of
the sources uncovered much relevant material, most notably in the
prayer texts collected by D.W. Staerk.[10] The Targumic law, sanctuary,
Jerusalem, exile, Israel, repentance, Abraham, Shekinah, kingdom,
righteousness and messiah motives—that is, the very substance of the
early framework meturgeman's theology—all find important echoes
here. The heuristic supplementation of systematic checking was
crucial in the case of Intertestamental sources, in which explicit
citation of biblical works is not a regular feature, and in this field, as for
Rabbinica, the contribution of Paul Volz[11] has proved indispensible.
The foundational descriptive work of George Foot Moore[12] has
consistently served as a means of orienting oneself to the rabbinic
sources, and the complementary analyses of specific terms undertaken
by P. Schäfer,[13] A.M. Goldberg[14] and C.T.R. Hayward[15] have also
greatly enhanced our capacity to set Targumic interpretations in the
context of rabbinic exegesis. For New Testament parallels, Martin
McNamara's two books are, of course, the basic contributions.[16] Only
a handful of the most important teachers to have instructed us have
been mentioned in order to emphasize that our method has not been

pursued dogmatically to the exclusion of considering the work of others. It may be claimed this has helped us to refine our approach and counterbalance a weakness inherent in any procedure which is based on a selection of data.

3. Collationary

In this conclusion, we have argued that our results are coherent and consistent with the evidence (1) and that our method has proved viable (2). It is left for us to suggest that our findings are plausible within the context of such consensus as has emerged within the secondary literature. Paul Volz already cited the 'second death' reading of Tg Is. 22.14 as Tannaitic,[17] and we have been able (in the 'Prophet(s)' section) to substantiate this claim with reference to the Revelation, the Mekhilta and both Talmuds. Our contention that dominical 'kingdom' diction is to be related to Targumic usage can be viewed as lineally descendant from Volz's understanding that Tannaitic theology can be isolated by comparing Rabbinica with early Jewish literature (including the New Testament).[18]

Linguistically, recent discussion would tend to support the view that the earliest Isaian meturgeman could have been Tannaitic,[19] but the case can be put no more forcefully than that. Not only does consensus on how Aramaic developed seem impossible of attainment at the moment, but the Isaiah Targum itself—which, whether our thesis be accepted or not, does appear to be the product of centuries of development—manifests internal differences in respect of theological idiom (cf. especially 'Jerusalem,' n. 4, 'Exile,' nn. 4, 14, 28, 'House of Israel,' nn. 4, 10 and 'Kingdom,' n. 5), but not (evidently) in respect of grammar or syntax. But at the level of theology, our findings do cohere with those of Goldberg (cf. n. 3) on 'Shekinah,' and those of Paul Humbert,[20] Robert A. Aytoun,[21] Samson H. Levey[22] and Klaus Koch[23] on 'messiah.' In the case of 'memra,' however, we were unable to accept the support C.T.R. Hayward's thesis would have offered had we found his position convincing.[24]

Our recollection of those contributions which have most prominently presented results similar to or cognate with our own only strengthens our conviction of the importance of Pinkhos Churgin's monograph (cf. n. 4), which we discussed in the introduction. The present study can be seen as an attempt to resolve his general picture of the continuous development of the Targum into a more detailed account of its literary evolution.[25] Our thesis takes account of the range of historical allusions he identified, although our catalogue of Amoraic parallels to Targumic readings shows that his attempt to identify the Amoraic meturgeman personally was probably not successful, in that framework meturgemanin at both levels reflect the views of more than one of their contemporaries (cf. particularly nn. 9-11 in the introduction, and the references to R. Eleazar and R. Aqiba in the 'Law' section). Of more basic significance, Churgin showed that the way forward in Targum studies was to undertake the patient description of a given Targum's perspective, rather than to seize on a few selected readings as if they characterized the whole. If this monograph has shown that his method remains viable, given that it is supplemented by the application of a modified form of redaction criticism and a due cognizance of rabbinic exegeses, its purpose has been achieved.

Jacob Neusner's recent history of the Babylonian Rabbinate would tend to support Churgin's contention that readings from the Sassanian period are manifest in the Targum, a contention which our specification of Amoraic parallels might be taken to support. Neusner contrasts the Tannaitic expectation of the messiah with that of the Babylonian Amoraim by claiming that the former was characterized by a desire 'to avenge the sanctuary and make possible its restoration,'[26] while the latter 'constituted an irenic and spiritualized, mostly passive expectation.'[27] We have considered evidence which tends to support the view that an ethical and individualistic expectation (reflected in the Amoraic framework) gained dominance, to some extent at the expense of a more communal and nationalistic hope, in the process of Targumic formation, but the one never seems to have excluded the other. Moreover, the genuine persecution of the late Sassanian period[28] would seem to have infused the messianic vindication theology of the Tannaitic framework with fresh relevance for its Amoraic tradents. Recent discussion has tended to confirm the suspicion that Aqiba's acclamation of Bar Kokhba was no idiosyncratic outburst, but the culmination of a fervent Tannaitic belief in concrete messianic vindication.[29] The earlier framework of the Isaiah Targum would seem to represent that movement (particularly in its second, but also in its first, reform-oriented, stratum).

Translation in the synagogue provided the raw material for our framework meturgemanin, and from these renderings—as well as from the teaching of their rabbinic contemporaries and their own philologically acute understanding of Isaiah—they produced an exegetical framework. They did so in stages and under various conditions, but what stands out in their enterprise is their realistic faith under harrowing circumstances in Israel's concrete vindication. This observation is pertinent both to the robust nationalism of the Tannaitic framework and to the more circumspect ethical teaching of the Amoraic framework. The edifice as a whole manifests the conviction that God will act on behalf of Israel; precisely when Israel was most threatened, the earlier and foundational level of the framework was produced, and an enduring interpretation of Isaiah as a whole was born. The Targum to Isaiah stands as a monument to the urgent need to express and develop the faith attested by this biblical book, no matter how dreadful the challenges to it may be, by means of patient and acute reflection on the biblical text.

Appendix

'Messiah' in Prophetic Targumim other than Isaiah

Professor Hengel, in a letter dated 18 June 1980, quite rightly points out that the foregoing study raises 'die Frage, wieweit der Jesajatargum mit dem übrigen Prophetentargum zusammenhängt, ob sich dort ähnliche Tendenzen finden wie bei Jesaja, oder starke Abweichungen.' We have repeatedly drawn attention to particular similarities and dissimilarities between the Isaiah Targum and other Latter Prophets Targumim, but, before a detailed comparison of the Targumic frameworks could proceed, the characteristics of each Targum would have to be discovered individually, as in the present monograph. As a preliminary investigation, however, it does seem appropriate to take up Professor Hengel's suggestion, and to compare the usage of Targum Isaiah in respect of 'messiah' (which is both a central theologoumenon in the Isaiah Targum and evidenced generally in the Prophetic Targumim) with that of the other Latter Prophets Targums.

In his monograph, *The Messiah: An Aramaic Interpretation* (cited in 'Repentance,' n. 16), Samson H. Levey was able to discern distinctive tendencies in these Targums (p. 102), even though he cautioned against generalizing too much in the face of their variety (p. 103). By considering the evidence he very usefully draws together against the background of the interpretative framework of the Isaiah Targum, one can offer tentative conclusions in regard to similarities and differences among the Latter Prophets Targums in their teaching about the messiah.

Levey has the Jeremiah Targum twice refer to the Davidic messiah enacting 'a righteous and meritorious law in the land' (23.5, p. 69; 33.15, p. 74), where the Masoretic text has only 'judgment and righteousness.' This would be a significant and interesting departure, but Levey's translation here seems to make the Targum appear more paraphrastic than it is. He renders דין as 'law,' and takes וזכו with דקשוט rather than as an apposition to דין; taking the text more straightforwardly (especially given the Masoretic text),[1] we would translate, 'true judgement and righteousness.' On this understanding, only the rendering of 'branch' as 'messiah' (as at Tg Is. 4.2) stands out as an innovation in the Targum. The exact phrase 'messiah, son of David their king' appears at 30.9 (where there is a misprint in the Sperber edition), while the Isaiah Targum speaks of the 'house of David' (at 9.5, and cf. 11.1, 10; 14.29). This possibly reflects a change in preferred usage: Berakhoth 48b (ascribed by Volz, *op. cit.* ['Law,' n. 16], 176 to Eliezer, who also used 'messiah' unqualified [cf. Sanhedrin 99a], as in the Isaiah Targum) assumes that the phrase found in the Isaiah Targum is in the Shemoneh Esreh, and Sanhedrin 97, 98 shows that more fully developed speculations attached to 'son of David.' But no such speculation is characteristic of Targum Jeremiah, and it should be borne in mind that the meturgeman here renders 'David' in the MT (which is preserved in Tg Is. 29.1; 37.35; 38.5; 55.3 without the use of 'son'); the present usage is contexted in a reference to a return from exile (30.10), which is consistent with the messianic teaching of the Isaiah Targum. Finally, when Tg Jer. 30.21 mentions the messiah in asociation with Israel's return to God's 'service,' it may be understood that cultic praxis is at issue, as at Tg Is. 48.15, 16.[2] If so, the reading presupposes that the meaning of 'service' has already been clearly agreed. In the main, then, the Jeremiah Targum is restrained and curiously allusive in its statements about the Davidic messiah. Apart, perhaps, from 30.9 it seems more a pale reflection of such teaching as we find in the Isaiah Targum than a further development of it.

Levey considers it a 'major problem' (p. 85) that the Ezekiel Targum does not use the term 'messiah.' A member of David's house, however, is here to be made king, to subdue the nations and delight the righteous in his powerful rule (17.22-24; cf. 34.24, and the reference to the sanctuary, which is so closely connected with the messiah in the Isaiah Targum, in v. 26). Levey counts this as evidence of 'an eschatological, non-Messianic outlook' and of the distinctive authorship and provenience of this Targum (p. 87).[3] But if the terminology of Tg Ez. 17.22-24 is not messianic, its substance is, and, taken together with 34.26, the coherence with the messianic teaching of the Isaiah Targum is evident, although far from comprehensive. Moreover, the designation of David as king has been picked up by the meturgeman from the Hebrew text of Ezekiel (37.24), and repeated by him (v. 25 end, for MT 'prince' cf. 34.24), so that there can be no question of the word 'king' being neutral in his understanding. The use of 'kingdom' in 17.22, 24 and 'king' itself in 17.23 is to be taken as similarly evocative, especially when the reference to Davidic kingship in vv. 22-24 is seen to be reminiscent of the description of the messiah's role in the Isaiah Targum.

The Hosean meturgeman was much more forthcoming in his messianic expectation than the interpreters of Jeremiah and Ezekiel. When speaking of the 'head' at 2.2, it was natural for him to specify the figure as 'from the house of David' and to refer expressly to a return from exile. 'King' bears the same qualification at 3.4, and in the following verse the full phrase 'messiah, son of David, their king' appears in the context of Israel's return to God's 'service' (cf. above, on Tg Jer. 30.21). Finally, 'messiah' innovatively occurs at 14.8 in association with the return from exile, the resurrection of the dead, and a metaphorical reference to sanctuary ritual (cf. v. 7). As Levey observes (p. 91), the eschatological aspect of this interpretation is 'a rarity for the Messianism of official Targumim.' This, along with the non-realistic usage of cultic imagery and the possibly late provenience of the 'exile' phrase,[4] suggests that this interpretation is more recent than that which characterizes the Isaiah Targum.

The reading at Tg Micah 4.8, as reflecting Amoraic teaching, has already been discussed (in the 'Kingdom' section). Levey characterizes the interpretation as 'a reflection of apocalyptic rabbinic teaching, as well as Christian' insofar as it refers to a hidden messiah.[5] But as he himself observes (p. 93), Tg Mic. 5.1b implies that the messiah, not merely his name, is pre-existent:

> from you the messiah will come forth before me, to be a wielder of power over Israel, even he whose name was spoken from the beginning, from the days of the world.

The meturgeman seems to have moved a step beyond the dictum that the name alone of the messiah was one of the seven things created before the world was made (Pesaḥim 54a), and Levey cites the later view in Pesiqta Rabbati 33.6 by way of comparison. This would tend to support our reading of 4.8, and suggests the later provenience of the messianic teaching of the Micah Targum as compared to the framework of the Isaiah Targum.

The Habakkuk Targum contains a single reference to the messiah in a highly paraphrastic rendering of 3.18:

> Then, because of the sign and deliverance you will do for your messiah and for the remnant of your people that are left, they will give thanks . . .

The expectation is for the salvation of the remnant, not for the return of the exiles, and this departure from the usual convention in the Prophetic Targums is not required by the Hebrew text. The meturgeman of Habakkuk seems to be operating in a context different from that of his colleagues. The previous verse also voices the most explicit disapproval of a specific Roman policy to be found in this Targum. The last sentence of the rendering predicts, 'The Romans will be destroyed, and will not levy the tax from Jerusalem.' Generally, vehement sentiments of an anti-Roman nature can be instanced in the Isaiah Targum (e.g., at 54.1), but the present paraphrase (cf. the Hebrew text) is striking for its rebellious response to a named aspect of Roman rule. Levey thinks the meturgeman writes in support of 'Judas the Galilean, a zealot who had the backing of the school of Shammai' (p. 95).[6] He undoubtedly presses the evidence here for a more exact historical allusion than it can reasonably be held to involve, since the Roman taxation of Jerusalem was perennially vexatious to the Jews. Nonetheless, a prediction of this kind would hardly have been seen as appropriate by the mainstream of rabbis after Hadrian coopted the Temple tax for the cult of Aelia Capitolina, so that Levey's suggestion is chronologically plausible. Further, the express nationalism of this Targum, which extends to a remnant theory of vindication in place of the more usual (and inclusive) expectation of the return of the exiles, presumably proceeds from a confidence in local political, social and financial structures not yet ravaged by war with Rome. The Habakkuk Targum appears to represent even more starkly than the Isaiah Targum the sort of propaganda which led Israel as a whole on two occasions within a century to seek her autonomy from Rome.

The initial messianic reading in the Zechariah Targum (3.8) is straightforward (cf. צמח in Is. 4.2; Jer. 23.5; 33.15, in all of which 'messiah' appears as the rendering in the Targums), rendering 'branch' in the Hebrew text, but the context of the interpretation makes it characteristic of this Targum as a whole: Joshua the high priest is addressed with the promise of the coming messiah. In 4.7, 'messiah' appears for 'head stone' (האבן הראשא). Levey observes (p. 98) that this understanding of 'stone' imagery, although quite in line with Mt. 21.42 // Mk. 12.20 // Lk. 20.17, is unique; but this is not quite accurate. The 'cornerstone' of Zech. 10.4 becomes 'king' in the Targum, and 'nail' becomes 'messiah.' The military aspect of the messianic exegesis is evident, not only in the exact rendering of 'mighty men' (גיברין for גברים) in v. 5, but especially in the qualification 'of the house of Israel' (cf. the Isaiah Targum), which is an addition. Also, in Tg Is. 28.16, stone imagery occasions Targumic reference to the divinely appointed king, although he is not explicitly called the messiah here. Understood as a metaphor for the Temple, 'stone' (and similar words) is probably rendered by reference to the messiah because the messiah is understood to build the Temple (so Tg Is. 53.5; Tg Zech. 6.12) and to be associated with a priest (Tg Is. 22.22; Tg Zech. 6.13; cf. 'Sanctuary').

On the whole, the other Latter Prophets Targums appear to reflect messianic teaching consistent with that represented in the Isaiah Targum, but not so fully. The restrained usage of the Jeremiah and Ezekiel Targums is expressive enough to enable us to see in the former an expectation of the messiah son of David who would bring Israel back to geographical and, perhaps, cultic integrity, and in the latter an expectation of the Davidic king who is to be the leader appointed in God's vindication of his people, a vindication in which they are to enjoy the blessing of the sanctuary. The central emphasis of the Isaiah Targum on the messiah as a teacher of the law who effects repentance is notably absent from these Targums, and indeed from all Prophetic Targums except that to Isaiah. It is arguable whether this phenomenon is to be explained on the basis of the earlier or later provenience of the messianic material in the other Latter Prophets Targums, but the precise usage 'son of David' (cf. above, on Tg Jer. 30.9) suggests that they allude to more than they explicitly say. Moreover, the reference to the association between the messiah or king and the cult in the Jeremiah and Ezekiel Targums suggests that this association was well established, and required only allusive mention, at the time their meturgeman(in) provided their interpretations. The Hosea Targum appears equally evocative in its use of 'service' (3.5), and this with the full phrase 'messiah, son of David, their king.' (The use of 'king' with 'messiah' warns us away from the supposition, as in Levey's analysis of the Ezekiel Targum, that this term reflects the programmatic avoidance of 'messiah.') Although this Targum refers to a return from exile, it does so with what may be a slogan from the Amoraic period, and its metaphorical reference to sanctuary ritual (14.7, 8) and express teaching of the resurrection in the closest connection to the messiah (14.8) suggest its messianic material comes from a day later than that of the Isaian framework meturgeman. Similarly, the messianic teaching of the Micah Targum appears to be substantively Amoraic, in that the messiah is a definite figure whose name is from of old (5.1b), and he is hidden as a result of Israel's sin (4.8). Theologically, then, the Jeremiah and Ezekiel Targums appear more proximate to the Isaiah Targum than the others so far considered, while the Hosea and Micah Targums seem more elaborate developments in respect of their view of the messiah. But that they are developments is manifest: the Hosean meturgeman continues to speak of a return from exile, and associates the Davidic messiah—albeit in an attenuated way—with cultic integrity; the Mican meturgeman understands the messiah, however exalted his status, primarily as the one who restores Israel.

The programmatic assumption that the Isaiah Targum provides the basis for the other Latter Prophets Targumim would, however, be facile. Although Isaiah was long understood to be pre-eminent among the literary prophets (cf. 'Prophet(s)'), and the preponderance of haftarot from Isaiah supports the general contention that this was one of the first Prophetic books to be interpreted as a whole, that is no reason to assume that the Isaiah Targum as we know it fully represents interpretative activity at the earliest period. Further, we must bear in mind that, in this appendix, we have focused on uses of 'messiah'; since Isaiah is most susceptible of an understanding along messianic lines, it is perhaps only inevitable that the Isaiah Targum should provide the fullest messianic exposition. More specifically, the Habakkuk Targum is more fiercely nationalistic, and the Zechariah Targum more emphatically cultic, than the Isaiah Targum, and they may represent the interpretation of a period earlier than that of the Isaian framework meturgeman.

This monograph offers a method for establishing, within limits of certainty imposed by the availability and specificity of evidence relevant to our purpose, the theology, provenience and date of a given Targum. Whether it succeeds in respect of its target document, the Isaiah Targum, is for readers to judge. This appendix is presented only as a codicil, in order to suggest that the method can be applied to other Targums, especially Prophetic Targums in their relationship to the Isaiah Targum, and that, once applied, we might begin to comprehend the development of documents which are crucial to the understanding of our Jewish and Christian heritage.

NOTES TO INTRODUCTION

Throughout this study, references to works already cited will include in parentheses the notes where they are first mentioned.

1. A lucid account of the impact of this 'discovery' on Targum studies is provided by Martin McNamara (who himself began work on his thesis one year after the identification of Neophyti) in chapter I of *The New Testament and the Palestinian Targum to the Pentateuch*, Analecta Biblica 27 (Rome: Pontifical Biblical Institute, 1966). See also Alejandro Diez Macho, 'Le Targum palestinien' in: J.E. Ménard (ed.), *Exégèse Biblique et Judaïsme* (Strasbourg: Faculté de Théologie catholique, 1973), 17-77 and in: *Recherches de science religieuse* 47 (1973), 169-231; R. Le Déaut, *Introduction à la littérature targumique*. Première partie (Rome: Institut Biblique Pontifical, 1966) and 'The Current State of Targum Studies' in: *Biblical Theology Bulletin* 4 (1974) 3-32. Secondary literature on the Targums has reached such a proportion that exhaustive references would be neither practicable nor desirable. In this study, only a selection of my background reading is represented, it is hoped in the interests of clarity. Readers in any case have ready access to the two volume work of Bernard Grossfeld, *A Bibliography of Targum Literature*, Bibliographica Judaica 3, 8 (New York: Ktav, 1972, 1977).

2. Mention might be made of the following (some from before the period in which Kahle's influence was felt): J.R. Harris, 'Traces of Targumism in the New Testament' in: *Expository Times* 32 (1920-21), 373-376; A. Wikgren, 'The Targums and the New Testament' in: *Journal of Religion* 24 (1944), 89-95; R. Le Déaut, 'Traditions targumiques dans le Corpus Paulinien?' in: *Biblica* 42 (1961), 28-48; S. Schulz, 'Die Bedeutung der neueren Targumforschung für die synoptischen Tradition' in: O. Betz, M. Hengel, P. Schmidt (eds.), *Abraham unser Vater* (Festschrift O. Michel) (Leiden: Brill, 1963), 425-436; J.R. Diaz, 'Palestinian Targum and New Testament' in: *Novum Testamentum* 6 (1963), 75-80; M. Black, *An Aramaic Approach to the Gospels and Acts* (Oxford: Clarendon, 1967[3]); McNamara, *op. cit.* (n.1) and *Targum and Testament. Aramaic Paraphrases of the Hebrew Bible: A Light on the New Testament* (Shannon: Irish University Press, 1972); R. Le Déaut, 'Targumic Literature and New Testament Interpretation' in: *Biblical Theology Bulletin* 4 (1974), 243-289; C. Perrot, 'Le Targum' in: *Etudes théologiques et religieuses* 52 (1977) 219-230.

3. He has frequently made this point in reviews, for which see Grossfeld, *op. cit.* (n.1). In particular, see *The Genesis Apocryphon of Qumran Cave 1*, Biblia et Orientalia 18 (Rome: Pontifical Biblical Institute, 1971[2]), 30-39 and 'Methodology in the Study of the Aramaic Substratum of Jesus' Sayings in the

New Testament' in: J. Dupont (ed.), *Jésus aux Origines de la Christologie*, BETL 40 (Gembloux: Leuven University Press, 1975), 73-102. An attempt to reconstruct the haggadah common to the Palestinian Targums is made by Avigdor Shinan in: *The Form and Content of the Aggadah in the 'Palestinian' Targumim on the Pentateuch and its Place within Rabbinic Literature* (Hebrew University: Ph.D., 1977). Now cf. Fitzmyer, 'The Aramaic Language and the New Testament' in: *JBL* 99 (1980), 5-21.

4. For challenges to the antiquity of these targums in linguistic terms, cf. G.J. Cowling, 'New Light on the New Testament? The significance of the Palestinian Targum' in: *Theological Students' Fellowship Bulletin* 51 (1968), 6-15; J.A. Fitzmyer, 'The Languages of Palestine in the First Century A.D.' in: *CBQ* 32 (1970), 500-531; M. Delcor, 'Le Targum de Job et l'araméen du temps de Jésus' in: *Rec.S.R.* 47 (1973), 232-261 (also in: Ménard, *op. cit.* [n.1], 78-107); Fitzmyer, 'The Contribution of Qumran Aramaic to the Study of the New Testament' in: *NTS* 20 (1973-74), 382-407. For such challenges in substantial (i.e., halakhic and/or haggadic) terms, cf. M. Delcor, 'La Portée chronologique de quelques interprétations du Targoum Néophyti contenues dans le cycle d'Abraham' in: *JSJ* 1 (1970), 105-119; A.D. York, 'The Dating of Targumic Literature' in: *JSJ* 5 (1974), 49-62; J. Heinemann, 'Early Halakhah in the Palestinian Targumim' in: *JJS* 25 (1974), 114-122; M. Ohana, 'La polémique judéo-islamique et l'image d'Ismaël dans Targum Pseudo-Jonathan et dans Pirke de Rabbi Eliezer' in: *Augustinianum* 15 (1975), 367-387; (cf. J. Faur, 'The Targumim and Halakha' in: *JQR* 66 (1975-76), 19-26); A.O.H. Okamoto, 'A Geonic Phrase in MS. Targum Yerushalmi, Codex Neofiti I' in: *JQR* 66 (1975-76), 160-167; P.R. Davies and B.D. Chilton, 'The Aqedah: A Revised Tradition History' in: *CBQ* 40 (1978), 514-546.

5. The passage continues: 'He further sought to reveal a targum of the Hagiographa, but a bath qol went forth and said, Enough. What was the reason?—Because the date of the Messiah is told in it.' Prima facie, then, the date of composition of the Prophets Targum is distinguished from that of the Hagiographa Targum. (Unless otherwise stated, the renderings are based on those of the Soncino edition.) Cf. the statement of Díez Macho: 'Etant donné que le Targ P des Prophètes est practiquement disparu et que les Targums des Megillot sont des compositions tardives, nous nous bornerons dans cette conférence au Targ P du Pentateuch' (*art. cit.* [n.1], 17).

6. Geiger's theory was dismissed by Pinkhos Churgin, *Targum Jonathan to the Prophets*, Yale Oriental Series—Researches XIV (New Haven: Yale University, 1907, 1927) 15, 16, but resuscitated (without reference to Geiger or Churgin) by Bowker, *op. cit.* (n.2), 27; cf. McNamara, *Targum and Testament* (cited in n.2), 174, 206, and P. Schäfer, 'Bibelübersetzungen II. Targumim' in: G. Krause and G. Müller (eds.), *Theologische Realenzyclopädie* VI (Berlin: de Gruyter, 1980), 216-228, 222.

7. I allude to the famous 'akhnai stove incident, in which Eliezer was supported by a bath qol (among other things), but the majority overruled him. Note that Gamaliel also claims to act for God's honour, lest strife increase in Israel. For both references, see Baba Metzia 59a, b.

120 *The Glory of Israel*

8.   G.F. Moore, *Judaism in the First Centuries of the Christian Era* I (Cambridge: Harvard University Press, 1946), 46, 80f., 86.

9.   *Zu dem Targum der Propheten*, Jahresbericht des jüdisch-theologischen Seminars (Breslau: Schletter, 1872), 10, 11. In passing, Frankel attacks the view that 'Jonathan' derives from 'Theodotion': 'es ist keine Spur, dass man die Uebersetzung des Theodotion in Palästina gekannt hat . . . .' He insists that 'das uns vorliegende Targum ist reich an R. Joseph nicht ungehörenden Uebersetzungen und hagadischen Zusätzen.' Frankel's fourth century dating of R. Joseph is supported by the analysis of Jacob Neusner in *A History of the Jews in Babylonia* IV: SPB (Leiden: Brill, 1969) 93, 288. Cf. J.J. Slotki's index in the Soncino edition of the Babylonian Talmud, where Joseph is placed in the third century. But Joseph b. Ḥiyya need scarcely be assumed to be the rabbi in question whenever Talmud refers to the translational activity of a rabbi named 'Joseph' (without further qualification).

10.   Berakoth 28a: 'It [viz. Zeph. 3.18] is rendered by R. Joseph: Destruction comes upon the enemies of Israel because they put off till late the times of the appointed seasons in Jerusalem.' Cf. Targum Jonathan on this verse: 'The ones hindering in you the times of your feasts I will remove from your midst . . . .' Pesaḥim 68a: 'As R. Joseph translated [viz. Is. 5.17]: and the estates of the wicked shall the righteous inherit.' The even more striking similarity of the Jonathan Targum in this case shows that Joseph was involved with a targum tradition which was at least associated with the presently known text. But the discrepancy between Joseph's renderings and Targum Jonathan's makes us stop short of the assertion that one used the other or even that they proceeded on the basis of an identical tradition. Churgin, *op. cit.* (n.6), 15 n.12 also cites Kethuboth 6b, cf. (Churgin, p. 14 n.7) Kelim 29, 30 and Oholoth 18.

11.   As Churgin also observed, *op. cit.* (n.6), 14, citing Megillah 3a. Sanhedrin 94b (in a discussion of Is. 8.6): 'R. Joseph said: But for the Targum of this verse, I would not know its meaning . . . .' The rendering which follows accords with that found in Targum Jonathan. Mo'ed Ḳaṭan 28b: 'R. Joseph said, Had we not the rendering of that text [viz. Zech. 12.11], I would not have known what it said there . . . .' Again, the congruence with Targum Jonathan is striking (but cf. the previous note). Churgin, p. 15, gives instances of the citation of Targumic passages in the names of other rabbis; cf. also pp. 146f.

12.   We refer to his two volume work, *Eliezer ben Hyrcanus: The tradition and the man*, Studies in Judaism in Late Antiquity III, IV (Leiden: Brill, 1973). For the traditions about Jonathan, cf. *The Rabbinic Traditions about the Pharisees before 70* I (Leiden: Brill, 1971) 206-208, 252, 264, 279, 296, 299, 393f.

13.   Moore, *op. cit.* (n.8), chapter v; Le Déaut, *op. cit.* (n.1); Bowker, *op. cit.* (n.6); McNamara, *op. cit.* (n.2), chapter 3; D.E. Gowan, *Bridge between the Testaments. A Reappraisal of Judaism from the Exile to the Birth of Christianity*, Pittsburgh Theological Monograph Series 14 (Philadelphia: Pickwick, 1976), 384.

14.   Cf. in particular Fitzmyer, 'The Languages' (cited in n.4).

15. On this point, John F. Stenning's introductory matter is very illuminating in: *The Targum of Isaiah* (Oxford: Clarendon, 1949).

16. Gustav Dalman, *Grammatik des jüdisch-palästinischen Aramäisch* (Leipzig: Hinrichs, 1905), 12 (citing Genesis Rabbah 79).

17. See Moses Aberbach and Bernard Grossfeld, *Targum Onkelos on Genesis 49: Translation and Analytic Commentary*, SBL Aramaic Studies 1 (Missoula: Scholars Press, 1976). Cf. N. Wieder, 'The Habakkuk Scroll and the Targum' in: *JJS* 4 (1953), 14-18, 18; Y. Komlosh, 'Etymological Elucidations in the Aramaic Targum of Isaiah' (Hebrew, English abstract) in: *Tarbiz* 37 (1967), 15-23 (II), 18, 19, 21, 22, 23; P.S. Alexander, 'The Rabbinic Lists of Forbidden Targumim' in: *JJS* 27 (1976), 177-191 (*pace* Alexander, I do not see that the attempt of the rabbis to exert control implies they succeeded in revising all those targumic readings which struck them as unsatisfactory); Shinan, *op. cit.* (n.3); A.D. York, 'The Targum in the Synagogue and the School' in: *JSJ* 10 (1979), 74-86; Schäfer, *art. cit.* (n.6), 217.

18. This is argued very persuasively by York, *art. cit.* (n.4); J. Heinemann, *art. cit.* (n.4); M.P. Miller, 'Targum, Midrash, and the use of the Old Testament in the New Testament' in: *JSJ* 12 (1971), 29-82. Cf. J. Faur, *art. cit.* (n.4). Quite correctly, the last writer attacks the view that targumic renderings were ad hoc and personal, and demonstrates the rabbinic concern with Targumic versions. It nonetheless seems to me that he does not sufficiently distinguish the nature and process of Targum formation from those of the formation of intramural rabbinic literature. Cf. Shinan, *op. cit.* (n.3); Schäfer, *art. cit.* (n.6), 218.

19. As we have been reminded by John A.T. Robinson, *Redating the New Testament* (London: SCM, 1976). *Pace* Robinson, it is not appropriate to disregard the theology of documents when dating them, especially when they are more theological than historical in intent.

20. 'Woe to him who gives the crown to the proud foolish one, the prince of Israel, and gives the turban to the wicked one of the sanctuary house . . .'; cf. Stenning, *op. cit.* (n.15) and Alexander Sperber, *The Bible in Aramaic. III: The Latter Prophets according to Targum Jonathan* (Leiden: Brill, 1962).

21. 'Who dwell in houses that they build from the dust of graves and with corpses of the sons of men . . . .'

22. ' . . . for the sons of desolate Jerusalem will be more than the sons of inhabited Rome . . .'; this is evidently an allusion to the post-70 situation.

23. ' . . . Babylon has fallen, and is also about to fall . . .'; cf. Moses Aberbach, 'Patriotic Tendencies in Targum Jonathan on the Prophets' in: *Hebrew Abstracts* 15 (1974), 90, where the verse is seen as 'an unmistakable allusion to Rome.' Aberbach's position is discussed in the 'Repentance' section in Part II.

24. See also the following possible allusions of note (in all cases, cf. the Masoretic Text):

> *References to a dissolute cult, the Temple and its destruction,*
> 17. 11: ' . . . even when you came up to the land of my Shekinah . . . you forsook my service . . .' 29.1: 'Woe to the altar, the altar which they built in the city where David dwelt; because of the congregation of armies which will

gather upon it in the year the feasts in you will cease.'
And cf. the following verses:

32.14: 'For the sanctuary house is laid waste . . .'
61.10: ' . . . as the high priest adorned with his garments . . .'
References to Babylon,
13.22: ' . . . the time of Babylon's destruction is near to come . . .'
21.2: ' . . . I have sighed for all that were sighing for the king of Babylon.'
References to lax practices,
5.10: 'For because of sin that they did not give tithe . . .'
28.12: 'to whom the prophets were saying, This is the sanctuary house,
serve in it, and this is the inheritance of the house of rest, and they did not
wish to receive teaching.'
References to Rome,
27.1: 'At that time the LORD will punish with his great and strong and
powerful sword the king who exalts himself as Pharaoh the first king,
even the king who acts proudly as Sennacherib the second king, and he
will kill the king who is strong as the dragon in the sea.'
34.9: 'And the streams of Rome will be turned to pitch . . .'
References to Arabs,
21.16: ' . . . all the glory of the Arabs will come to an end.'
42.11: ' . . . the villages that dwell in the wilderness of the Arabs . . .'
60.6, 7: 'Caravans of the Arabs . . . All the sheep of the Arabs . . . .'
For evidence of a pre-Islamic Arab incursion into Babylonia, cf. J.
Neusner, *A History of the Jews in Babylonia* (cf. n.9) IV (1969), 44f. and V
(1970) 69, 114.

25.   For Jewish and Christian usage of 'Babylon' for Rome, cf. E.G. Selwyn,
The First Epistle of St. Peter (London: Macmillan, 1961²), 243.

26.   'A man must speak in the words of his master,' quoted (with references)
in Bowker, *op. cit.* (n.6), 49.

27.   Cf. Dalman, *op. cit.* (n.16), 15, on Targum Jonathan, 'Da dies Targum
nicht wie das zum Pentateuch im vollständig vorgetragen wurde, ist indes
anzunehmen, dass hier die Tradition weniger feststand als bei dem Thoratargum.' But precisely the same consideration encourages us to think that the
production of a continuous Prophetic Targum evidences the scholarly
contribution of the rabbis.

28.   So Perrot, *art. cit.* (n.2), 224.

29.   For one view of the position of the Aramaic of Onqelos (which is to be
associated with that of Jonathan) within the dialectical variations of the
language, cf. Franz Rosenthal, 'Das Jungaramäische' in: *Die aramaistische
Forschung seit Th. Nöldeke's Veröffentlichungen* (Leiden: Brill, 1939), 104–
172. Dalman had already observed (*op. cit.*, 40), 'dass die Sprache der
Targume ein Produkt gelehrter Tätigkeit war, welcher Nachbildung des
hebräisches Originals wichtiger ist als die Übersetzung in gemeines Ara-
mäisches.' Schäfer, *art. cit.* (n.6), 217 observes, ' . . . Sif Dev 161, S.212

erwähnt ganz allgemein das Targum gleichberechtigt mit der Schrift und der Mischna als Gegenstand des Studium.'

30.   Wieder, *art. cit.* (n.17); W.H. Brownlee, 'The Habakkuk Midrash and the Targum of Jonathan' in: *JJS* 7 (1956), 169-186; R. Marcus, *Josephus' Jewish Antiquities Books V-VIII*, Loeb Classical Library (Cambridge: Harvard University Press, 1958), x. Brownlee seems to go well beyond the evidence adduced when he concludes: 'The frequent dependence of 1QpHab upon the Targum indicates that the Targumic text had taken definite shape by the middle of the First Century B.C. The evidence drawn from Josephus, the Talmud, and the Greek Version of Job serves to suggest that the Targumic text employed by the author of our *pesher* may have been in writing' (p. 184). Wieder is much more circumspect, in that he acknowledges that ancient traditions can be transmitted and used at a later period in new circumstances (p. 18). It is nonetheless interesting that the term כתים is used in the Isaiah Targum (23.1, 12). Cf. also Komlosh, *art. cit.* (n.17).

31.   'The Date of Targum Jonathan to the Prophets' in: *VT* 21 (1971), 186-196, 192, 194f.

32.   There are many similar phrases in the Isaiah Targum alone which do not appear to be dependent on the Islamic slogan:

לית בר מנך, 37.16, 20; 64.3 (cf. 26.13)

לית בר מני, 43.11; 45.6; 47.8, 10 (of Babylon!) (cf. 46.9)

בר מני לית אלה, 41.4; 43.10; 44.6; 45.5; 48.12 (cf. 44.8)

לית עוד אלה בר מנה, 45.14

לית עוד אלה בר מני, 45.21.

Cf. the prayer of Rav, cited in J. Neusner, *A History of the Jews in Babylonia* (cf. n.9) II (1966), 163.

33.   Cf. the Sperber edition. The reading in question is ארמילוס (= Romulus). For an instance of an obviously appended later reading in Pseudo-Jonathan, cf. V. Hamp, *Der Begriff 'Wort' in den aramäischen Bibelübersetzungen. Ein exegetischer Beitrag zur Hypostasen-Frage und zur Geschichte der Logos-Spekulation* (München: Filser, 1938), 1, 2.

34.   *Art. cit.* (n.2), 226.

35.   Frankel, *op. cit.* (n.9), 13-16. For place names, cf. 25-28.

36.   Dalman, *op. cit.* (n.16), 32, 33.

37.   This insight is convincingly substantiated by A. Sperber, 'Zur Sprache des Prophetentargums' in: *ZAW* 45 (1927), 267-287.

38.   So M. Black, 'Aramaic Studies and the Language of Jesus' in: M. Black and G. Fohrer (eds.), *In Memoriam Paul Kahle*, BZAW 103 (Berlin: Töpelmann, 1968), 17-28, 18. The famous argument between Kahle and Kutscher about ραββουνί is summarized on pp. 22, 23. This might be cited as an example of the way in which slight variations of spelling—often of dubious textual origin— have been taken as evidence to support rather sweeping theories of the evolution of Aramaic language. Within the Kahle school, the major works are Kahle's own *The Cairo Geniza* (Oxford: Blackwell, 1959[2]) and Black's *Aramaic Approach* (cf. n.2).

39.   'Fragmento de una nueva recensión del Targum Jonatán ben 'Uzziel a los Profetas (T.-S.B. 12)' in: *Sefarad* 16 (1956), 405-406; 'Un nuevo Targum a los Profetas' in: *Punta Europas* (1956), 141-159; 'Un nuevo Targum a los Profetas' in: *Estudios Biblicos* 15 (1956), 287-295; 'Un segundo fragmento del Targum palestinense a los Profetas' in: *Biblica* 39 (1958), 198-205. Cf. Churgin, *op. cit.* (n.6), 132-134, 139-140, 142, 151; Schäfer, *art. cit.* (n.6), 223. Wilhelm Bacher showed long ago, however, that the variant readings indicated marginally in the Codex Reuchlinianus are most often paralleled in 'Babylonian' sources, although he recognized this did not militate against the 'Palestinian' provenience of the readings ('Kritische Untersuchungen zum Prophetentargum. Nebst einem Anhange über das gegenseitige Verhältniss der pentateuchischen Targumim' in: *Zeitschrift der deutschen morgenländischen Gesellschaft* 28 (1874), 1-72, 56-57.

40   For more recent treatments, cf. Etan Levine, 'Some Characteristics of Pseudo-Jonathan to Genesis' in: *Augustinianum* 11 (1971), 89-103; M.C. Doubles, *The Fragment Targum: A Critical Reexamination of the Editio Princeps* (St. Andrews: PhD, 1962); cf. 'Indications of Antiquity in the Orthography and Morphology of the Fragment Targum' in: Black and Fohrer, *op. cit.* (n.38), 79-89; McNamara, *Targum and Testament* (cf. n.2), 183 (on the movement since Kahle to date the manuscripts even later).

41.   *Art. cit.* (n.1), 46.

42.   'The Apocryphal Halakhah in the Palestinian Targums and in the Aggadah' (Hebrew) in: J.L. Fishman (ed.), *Jubilee Volume to Dr. Benjamin Menashe Lewin* (Jerusalem, 1940), 93-104.

43.   *The New Testament* (cited in n.1), 62-63, but cf. *Targum and Testament* (cited in n.2), 12, 186.

44.   Cf., e.g., G.J. Cowling, 'New Light on the New Testament?' and J.A. Fitzmyer, 'The Languages' (both cited in n.4); McNamara's rejoinder in *Targum and Testament* (p. 61) does not amount to a refutation.

45.   Klaus Koch, 'Messias und Sündenvergebung in Jesaja 53-Targum. Ein Beitrag zu der Praxis der aramäischen Bibelübersetzung' in: *JSS* 3 (1972), 117-148, 118, 119 (n.5, citing Le Déaut). Koch also makes the important observation, 'Angesichts der breiten Streuung von aramäischen Dialekten um die Zeitenwende im Dreieck zwischen Iran, Kleinasien und Unterägypten und der Verbreitung vorchristlicher Synagogen in eben diesem Raum, scheint es eine unerlaubte Vereinfachung, für die Entstehung der Targume nur die Antithese Palästina-Babylonien bereitzustellen' (also in n.5). In addition, it might be remarked that linguistic criteria of provenience are still being developed, while the literary assignment of Targums to 'Palestine' is largely a matter of *faute de mieux*.

46.   As a matter of fact, Kahle himself used this argument against Kutscher's assessment of the Genesis Apocryphon; cf. 'Das palästinische Pentateuchtargum und das zur Jesus gesprochene Aramäisch' in: *ZNW* 49 (1958), 100-116, 108.

47.   'The Job Targum from Qumran' in: *Journal of the American Oriental Society* 93 (1973), 317-327; and see McNamara, *Targum and Testament* (p. 64 n.4) on חיא in 4QtgJob. Kaufman does not deal with the argumentation from

place names in *Targum and Testament* (chapter 18), which seems to tell against his position. See also A. Tal, *The Language of the Targum to the Former Prophets and Its Position within the Aramaic Dialects* (Hebrew): Texts and Studies in the Hebrew Language and Related Subjects 1 (Tel-Aviv: Tel-Aviv University, 1975).

48. This 1976 Cambridge Ph.D. thesis is now available in published form: *God in Strength: Jesus' announcement of the kingdom*, Studien zum Neuen Testament und seiner Umwelt (Monographien) 1 (Freistadt: Plöchl, 1979).

49. My method is to be distinguished from that of Aberbach and Grossfeld, *op. cit.* (n.17), in that their attempt is 'to analyze every deviation from the Masoretic text with reference to provenance, historical background, relevant rabbinic, Patristic and Septuagintal material, as well as evaluating the contributions made by modern commentators' (p. xiv). Cf. Etan Levine, *The Aramaic Version of Jonah* (Jerusalem: Jerusalem Academic Press, 1975), and M.J. Mulder, *De targum op het Hooglied: Inleiding, vertaling en korte verklaring* (Amsterdam: Bolland, 1975). A preliminary but important step in the direction I propose pursuing was taken by L.H. Brockington, 'Septuagint and Targum' *ZAW* 66 (1964), 80-86 (see p. 82 in particular). I fully agree with his findings in respect of the term פורקנא, and believe that the present contribution accords with them and provides them with a theoretical basis as well as supporting evidence. That my method is a development of redaction critical approaches to the New Testament will be obvious to many; cf. *God in Strength*.

50. Cf. J. Ziegler, *Isaias*, Septuaginta. Vetus Testamentum Graecum Auctoritate Academiae Litterarum Gottingensis editum 14 (Göttingen: Vandenhoeck und Ruprecht, 1967²). We will also have occasion to mention the work of Y. Komlosh in this connection (cf. 'Messiah,' n.13).

51. In addition to the edition supervised by Charles, *The Apocrypha and Pseudepigrapha* (Oxford: Clarendon, 1913), we have consistently referred to the work of Paul Volz (cited in 'Law,' n.16), since he collated the literature with early rabbinic dicta.

52. Again, cf. the contributions of McNamara in particular (nn.1, 2).

53. In order to appreciate the theological tendencies of the Isaiah Targum, one must compare its renderings with the understanding of the same passages in rabbinic literature. Obviously, it would be an impracticably immense task to collate every verse in the Targum with every rabbinic utterance connected with that verse; some method of selection must be employed. From the point of view of the Targum, a principle on the basis of which such a method may be developed will become immediately apparent. As we discuss the characteristic targumic theologoumena, certain passages will stand out as being particularly representative of the meturgeman's theology and as suggesting the provenience of the theologoumena concerned. So in each section we will compare the most representative renderings with passages from our selection of rabbinic literature. From the point of view of rabbinic literature, we must seek a principle for choosing which documents' readings we should compare our Targumic renderings with. To some extent, our principle here is purely ad

hoc, in that we are limited from the outset to those documents for which there are good, accessible editions and reasonably accurate biblical indices. But even such a selection would involve us in an unacceptably protracted survey. We therefore propose to choose documents (where possible, both early and late) from typical genres of rabbinic literature. Midrash is obviously of especial interest in this context, and we may compare Targumic renderings with references or allusions to Isaiah in the Mekhilta de R. Ishmael[a] (a Tannaitic midrash) and with such passages in the essentially Amoraic Midrash Rabbah[b]. Under the category of mishnah, we may treat of the Mishnah proper[c], and of the two great Talmudim, Babli[d] and Jerushalmi[e]. Among the homiletic midrashim, we may compare our Targum to the Pesiqta de Rab Kahana[f] and (from a later period) to Pesiqta Rabbati[g]. Among later but useful works we may also include the midrashic anthology, Yalkut Shimoni[h], and the haggadic midrash, Pirqe de R. Eliezer[i]. Though very far from exhaustive, this selection should insure that we sample some of the most important wines from the rabbinic cellar as we attempt to appreciate the particular bouquet of the Isaiah Targum. As the argument develops, it will become clear that the relationship of our Targum to the understanding of Isaian passages in Josephus and Pseudo-Philo is relevant, since our contention is that the earlier framework was in existence near the time of the destruction of the Temple. Along with the *Liber Antiquitatum Biblicarum*[j], we choose *De Bello Judaico*[k] for comparison, since this book represents the attempt of Josephus in that period to defend his people in a Hellenistic milieu. We refer the reader to the following editions:

a. J.Z. Lauterbach, *Mekilta de-Rabbi Ishmael* I-III (Philadelphia: Jewish Publication Society of America, 1933, 1961, 1976).

b. H. Freedman, M. Simon, *Midrash Rabbah* (London: Soncino, 1939); cf. M.A. Mirqin, *Midrash Rabbah* (Genesis-Deuteronomy) (Tel Aviv: Jabne, 1956-1967).

c. P. Blackman, *Mishnayot* I-VII (London: Schoenfeld, 1951-1956 and New York: Judaica Press, 1964).

d. I. Epstein, *The Babylonian Talmud* 1-35 (London: Soncino, 1938-1952); cf. J. Hunter, *The Babylonian Talmud* (Jerusalem: Insititute for the Complete Israeli Talmud, 1977-).

e. M. Schwab, *Le Talmud de Jérusalem* I-III (Paris: Maisonneuve, 1871-1890); cf. אור תורה—עם עולם (publishers), תלמוד ירושלמי (Jerusalem, 1960).

f. B. Mandelbaum, *Pesikta de Rav Kahana* 1, 2 (New York: Jewish Theological Seminary, 1962); A. Wünsche, *Pesikta des Rab Kahana* (Leipzig: Schulze, 1885).

g. W.G. Braude, *Pesikta Rabbati* 1, 2: Yale Judaica Series 18 (London: Yale University Press, 1968); M. Friedmann, פסיקתא רבתא (Wien: Kaiser, 1879/80).

h. B. Lorje, *Jalkut Schimoni* (חלק שני נביאים) (Zolkiew: Madfis, 1858); cf. M. Krupp, 'New Editions of Yalkut Shim'oni' in: *Immanuel* 9 (1979), 63-71; A.B. Hyman, *The Sources of the Book of Isaiah* (Jerusalem: Mossad Harav Kook, 1965).

i. G. Friedlander, *Pirkè de Rabbi Eliezer* (London: Kegan Paul, Trench,

Trubner, 1916 and New York: Benjamin Blom, 1971).

    j. D.J. Harrington, C. Perrot, P.M. Bogaert, *Les antiquités bibliques* I, II: Sources Chrétiennes 229, 230 (Paris: Les Editions du Cerf, 1976).

    k. O. Michel and O. Bauernfeind, *Flavius Josephus. De Bello Judaico/Der jüdische Krieg* I-III (I—Bad Homburg vor der Höhe: Gentner, 1960; II, 1—München: Kosel, 1963; II, 2—München: Kosel, 1969; III—München: Kosel, 1969).

In addition, we would call special attention to the monumental index of A.M. Hyman, . . . ספר תורה (Tel Aviv: Debir, 1938).

NOTES TO CHAPTER II

NOTES TO SECTION A.

1.   Cf. the command, 'take away your evil deeds from my memra' in the same verse; 5.3, '. . . the house of Israel have rebelled against the law . . .' (and v. 5 refers to the removal of the Shekinah), v. 12, ' . . . they have not attended to the law of the LORD . . . ,' v. 13, ' . . . they did not know the law . . . '; 26.10, ' . . . if they repent to the law . . . '; 27.4, ' . . . if the house of Israel set their face to do the law . . . '; 27.5, 'Or if they took hold of the words of my law . . . '; 30.9b, nearly following the MT, 'sons who do not wish to receive the teaching of the law of the LORD'; 30.10, ' . . . and to the teachers, teach us not the law . . . '; 30.15, ' . . . and I said that you would return to my law . . . '; 31.6, 'Return to the law . . . '; 35.5, ' . . . the eyes of the house of Israel, which were as blind to the law . . . ' (the same rendering appears at 42.7); 42.14, ' . . . if they would return to the law . . . '; 43.22, ' . . . you wearied in the teaching of my law . . . '; 48.8a, ' . . . you did not receive the teaching of the law'; 57.9, 'When you did the law for yourself . . . '; 57.11, ' . . . if you would return to my law . . . '; 63.17, ' . . . as the peoples who have no portion in the teaching of your law . . . '; 65.1, ' . . . I sought the teaching of my law from those who did not seek my fear . . . .'

2.   This interpretation is inspired by the next clause in the MT, 'for the law will go forth from Zion' (so the Targum). Cf. v. 5, 'Those of Jacob's house will say, come and we will go in the teaching of the law of the LORD.'

3.   Cf. 9.5, 6 (discussed in the section on 'Messiah').

4.   On the other hand, in 13.12 God is said to cherish 'the servants of the law more than the refined gold of Ophir.' For statements of punishment, cf. 24.1, ' . . . because they transgressed the law . . . '; 31.9b, 'whose splendour is in Zion for servants of his law, and his burning furnace of fire in Jerusalem for those who transgress his memra'; 33.8b, 'because they have changed the covenant they are distanced from their cities.'

5.   Cf. 26.16 (end), 'they were secretly teaching the teaching of your law'; 32.6, ' . . . and the words of the law, which they (the righteous) as one who is thirsty for water . . . '; 33.13, 'Hear, righteous, who have kept my law from the beginning . . . '; 35.4, 'Say to the eager in their heart to do the law . . . '; 38.17, 'Behold, for servants of the law peace increases before you . . . '; 40.29, 'He

gives wisdom to the righteous who faint for the words of his law...'
(similarly, 50.4); 50.10, 'Who is there among you... who does the law in
affliction...'; 58.12b, 'and they will call you the establisher of the way, who
turns the wicked to the law' (cf. the function of the messiah, in that section).
6.   Likewise, in a promise to Jerusalem, 'And all your children will be
learning in the law of the LORD, and the peace of your children will be great'
(54.13). Cf. 37.32, 'For from Jerusalem the remnant of the righteous will go
forth, and the escaped upholders of the law from mount Zion...'; 42.21,
'... he will make great the servants of his law...'; 57.2 (end), 'servants of his
law'; 57.19, '... peace will be made for the righteous who kept my law from
the beginning...' (and see n.5).
7.   In addition to 1.2, cf. 33.22b, 'the LORD is our teacher, who gave us the
teaching of his law from Sinai'; 43.12, '... I caused you to hear the teaching of
my law from Sinai....'
8.   Cf. 63.19, '... you did not give your law to the peoples....'
9.   40.14, 'To those who seek from before him he revealed wisdom and taught
them the way of judgment, and gave the law to their sons...'; cf. 59.20,
'... and to turn the rebellious of Jacob's house to the law....'
10.   29.21b, 'and seek words of the law as a snare for him who reproves them
in the judgment house.'
11.   8.20, 'So you will say to them, to the law we listen, which was given to us
as testimony. But you will go into exile... from now on he has no one who
inquires and seeks him'; 8.16, '... seal and hide the law...'; 29.10b, 'he has
hidden the scribes and teachers who were teaching you the law.'
12.   Cf. J.J. Petuchowski, 'Jewish Prayer Texts of the Rabbinic Period' in:
Petuchowski and M. Brocke, *The Lord's Prayer and Jewish Liturgy* (New
York: Seabury, 1978), 21-24, 26. All of the texts cited by Petuchowski have
been checked against, and supplemented by, the Hebrew edition of D.W.
Staerk, *Altjüdische liturgische Gebete ausgewählt und mit Einleitungen*,
Kleine Texte für theologische und philologische Vorlesungen und Ubungen
(Bonn: Marcus and Weber, 1910). In the present case, the vocabulary of the
Targum and that of the Shemoneh Esreh are consistent.
13.   Petuchowski, 31.
14.   In Soṭah 5a, Eleazar links resurrection with one's humility during his
lifetime.
15.   Both are dated in the third century in the *Index Volume to the Soncino
Talmud*, compiled by J.J. Slotki. Cf. the lists compiled by H.L. Strack, *An
Introduction to Talmud and Midrash* (New York: Atheneum, 1972), 107-134,
and J.W. Bowker, *An Introduction to the Targums and Rabbinic Literature*
(Cambridge: Cambridge University Press, 1969), 368-370. For our purposes
we cannot assume that rabbinic attributions (or modern chronologies) are
accurate, but they may at least furnish us with approximate indications of the
circles and periods in which certain views and dicta were current. In the
present instance, note that there is no positive correlation between 'Babylonian'
or 'Palestinian' Amoraim and 'Babylonian' or 'Palestinian' recensions of the
Shemoneh Esreh.

16. Volz, *Die Eschatologie der jüdische Gemeinde im neutestamentlicher Zeitalter* (Hildesheim: Olm, 1966), p. 41. Cf. especially 84.8, 'And remember the law and Zion . . . and the covenant of your fathers, and do not forget the festivals and sabbaths.' For the proposed understanding of פולחנא, cf. C.T.R. Hayward, *The Use and Religious Significance of the Term Memra in Targum Neofiti I in the Light of the Other Targumim* (Oxford: D.Phil. thesis, 1975), p. 114 n.4.

17. *Op. cit.*, 55, 'v. 710-723 [sc. of III]: allgemeines Heilsbild: infolge des Glüches der Juden bekehren sich die Menschen zu Gott, zu dem Tempel und dem Gesetz.'

18. *Op. cit.*, 43. In the literature cited by Volz, as in the Isaiah Targum, it is evident that the law in question is none other than that derived from Sinai, cf. P. Schäfer, 'Die Torah der messianischen Zeit' in: *Studien zur Geschichte und Theologie des rabbinischen Judentums*, AGAJU 15 (Leiden: Brill, 1978), 198-213.

NOTES TO SECTION B

1. The Targum also reads, 'the place where my Shekinah dwells,' while the MT has, 'the place of my feet.' For the use of היכל, cf. D. Juel, *Messiah and Temple. The Trial of Jesus in the Gospel of Mark*, SBLDS 31 (Missoula: Scholars, 1977), 188 n.47.

2. Cf. G.B. Gray, *A Critical and Exegetical Commentary on the Book of Isaiah I-XXXIX*, ICC (Edinburgh: Clark, 1912, 1962), 153. In a private conversation, P.R. Davies has suggested to me that the original sense of the oracle was that God, more than the Temple, is the proper object of worship (cf. Ezekiel 11.16). E.J. Young, *The Book of Isaiah I*, New International Commentary (Grand Rapids: Eerdmans, 1965), 312, argues that the passage means that God is 'to some a sanctuary, but to others, a stone of stumbling'; for him, then, the use of the term here is rather more literal, but it is still metaphorical. Cf. the various emendations and interpretations in H. Wildberger, *Jesaja*, Biblischer Kommentar (Neukirchen-Vluyn: Neukirchener, 1972f.), 335. While the sense of the term here is problematic, it does seem clear that the Jerusalem Temple is not the primary reference. That is the only point at issue for the present purpose.

3. This comment should not be construed to suggest that the meturgeman arbitrarily introduces מקדשא. At 4.5, 'Zion' appears, and מגדל in 5.2 can plausibly be related to Temple architecture.

4. Here, however, 'mount of the *daughter* of Zion' appears as 'the mount of the sanctuary *house*, which is in Zion' in the Targum. 'Daughter' is a *qere*; the *ketib* is 'house.' The meturgeman took the latter alternative, and, as usual, מקדשא was appended.

5. Here also, בית may have encouraged the innovation, but the immediate implication of the meturgeman is that the sanctuary is the natural place for wealth.

130   *The Glory of Israel*

6. The first two passages have already been explained. For 38.2, cf. 37.14, 15 in both Tg and MT; for 52.11, it is a reasonable inference that the 'vessels of the LORD' (MT) were located in the sanctuary.

7. Even though the slogan speaks of joy 'upon all the inhabitants of the earth,' in the same passage the meturgeman refers to 'the reward of the righteous' and to 'the punishment of the wicked.' For the 'all the inhabitants of the earth' phrase, see my 'Regnum Dei Deus Est' in: *Scottish Journal of Theology* 31 (1978), 261-270.

8. בנף, which also means 'wing' or 'garment.' The meturgeman may have thought of the seraphic wings of 6.2.

9. The author of Jubilees could already assert, 'Mount Zion will be sanctified in the new creation for a sanctification of the earth; through it the earth will be sanctified from all guilt and its uncleanness throughout the generations of the world' (4.26).

10. Before the destruction of the Temple there was considerable friction between factions over cultic matters. Tg Is. 28 reflects the vociferous complaint about laxity and uncleanness which a 'Pharisee' would have made. Cf. J. Jeremias, *Jerusalem in the Time of Jesus* (London: SCM, 1969), 264-267.

11. Such confidence was grist for the Bar Kokhba mill, whose revolt this passage apparently antedates. Cf. R.P. Gordon, 'The Targumists as Eschatologists' in: *SVT* 29 (1978), 113-130, for a more general discussion of messianism which tends toward the same conclusion (see pp. 121, 122 and 125 in particular). On p. 125, Gordon adds significantly to Churgin's discussion of Tg Is. 65.4 (cf. Introduction).

12. Cf. McNamara, *op. cit.* (Introduction, n.1), 41, and Churgin, *op. cit.* (Introduction, n.6), 47-49.

13. See F.F. Bruce, *New Testament History* (Garden City: Doubleday, 1972), 389. The evidence in view of which I am inclined to look particularly to the period of Roman dominance is discussed below.

14. Volz, *op. cit.* (cf. 'Law' n.16), 26. On p. 32, he also mentions the Testament of Benjamin in this connection, but recent discussion of the Testaments suggests that they cannot be assumed to evidence first century Judaism, although they may be cited as supporting the currency of a motif in that sphere if it is already attested in an early source. Cf. H.D. Slingerland, *The Testaments of the Twelve Patriarchs. A Critical History of Research*, SBLMS 21 (Missoula: Scholars Press, 1977).

15. Cf. Volz, 15, 104 (and 172); Petuchowski, *op. cit.* ('Law,' n.12), 29 (the fourteenth benediction in the Palestinian recension).

16. Volz, 137; cf. 10.

17. Volz, 176; cf. 310.

18. I exclude from consideration rabbinic usages of 24.16 which take up the verse for altogether different reasons, and generally I have followed that practice in the present study. In the 'Conclusion,' comments of a comparative nature (with some supporting examples) will be offered in respect of the Targums and Rabbinica.

19. Cf. M. Hengel, *Judaism and Hellenism: Studies in their Encounter in*

Palestine during the Early Hellenistic Period I (London: SCM, 1974), 277f.
20. Cf. *Bellum Judaicum* V and VI.
21. Cf. J.C. O'Neill, 'The Lamb of God in the Testaments of the Twelve Patriarchs' in: *JSNT* 2 (1979), 2-30, and the English revision by G. Vermes and F. Millar of Emil Schürer, *The History of the Jewish People in the Time of Jesus Christ* I (Edinburgh: Clark, 1973), 544. The LXX rendering of the verse may be held marginally to cohere with the Targum, in that τὴν δόξαν Δαυιδ renders מפתח בית דוד. This view is also taken by Arie van der Kooij, *Die alten Textzeugen des Jesajabuches. Ein Beitrag zur Textgeschichte des Alten Testaments*, Orbis Biblicus et Orientalis 35 (Göttingen: Vandenhoeck und Ruprecht, 1981), 161 n.3. On the following pages, however, the author attempts to relate the verse to Aristobulus II, Hyrcanus II and the occupation of the Temple by Pompey. This interpretation is problematic, in that van der Kooij repeatedly finds that Tg Isaiah 22.15-28 does not accord with the history of the period it is held to reflect.

NOTES TO SECTION C

1. The usage of the name at 4.3 corresponds to the usage of the MT, but here again the meturgeman speaks of the 'consolation' of Jerusalem (and cf. 66.10). To continue the thought, a reference to the city is added to v. 6. In the same way, the addition at 51.19 follows the uninnovative usage in v. 17.
2. עליך; the meturgeman took the preposition as 'upon.' The only startling innovation here is 'the kings of the peoples.'
3. Even at his most inventive, the meturgeman has his text somehow in mind. In the present case, כל in the Hebrew text is the occasion for adding the statement about Gentile kings.
4. 49.18 and 60.4: 'Jerusalem, lift up your eyes round about, and see all the children of the people of your exiles . . . .' Though possibly written at a later period (n.b.: 'children of . . .'; although בני here could be taken as a simple collective), the slogan may represent the situation envisaged in the Targum's earlier exegesis. The fact that 60.4 is congruent with the tangible consolation announced to Jerusalem in chapter 60 (see below) tells against the view that this slogan is late, however, since settlement in Jerusalem was forbidden by the Romans after 135 (Bruce, *op. cit.* ['Sanctuary,' n.13], 389). Comparison with the MT suggests that 60.4 occasioned the initial use of the clause, which then was inserted as the rendering of 49.18, which influenced v. 20. Cf. 'Exile,' n.4.
5. At the opening of this verse, another reference to the city is added.
6. *The Sibylline Oracles of Egyptian Judaism*, SBLDS 13 (Missoula: Scholars Press, 1972), 89f.
7. Of course, the geographical provenience of the fifth Sibylline book is different from that of the Targum, but this makes its hope for Jerusalem all the more striking.
8. Cf. Volz, *op. cit.* ('Law' n.16), 17, citing from chapters 24 and following, and p. 211, citing chapter 90. Cf. David Flusser, 'Jerusalem in the Literature

of the Second Temple Period,' in: *Immanuel* 6 (1976), 43-45.

9. Volz, 26 (cited in the 'Sanctuary' section), 139, 372.

10. Volz, 225, 372 (citing chapter 17).

11. Volz, 31 (cf. the Testament of Zebulon 9, 'Der Herr geht auf als Licht der Gerechten, sie schauen Gott in Jerusalem . . . ,' and the Testament of Dan 5f., 'Jerusalem wird nicht mehr verwüstet, Israel nicht mehr gefangen . . . '). Cf. p. 49 on the Apocalypse of Abraham.

12. Volz, 41, 43 (cf. p. 48), 138, 310. As Volz mentions, this document is of particular interest because the hopes for the heavenly Jerusalem and for the physically rebuilt Jerusalem are both articulated.

13. Cf. Petuchowski, *art. cit.* ('Law' n.12).

14. Volz, 176. Volz (p. 146) also understands the statement of Jose b. Kisma in Sanhedrin 98a to refer to the destruction and rebuilding of Jerusalem, but the Soncino editor (J. Shachter) takes it to apply to Caesarea Philippi. Cf. also P. Schäfer, 'Die messianische Hoffnungen des rabbinischen Judentums zwischen Naherwartung und religiösem Pragmatismus' in: *op. cit.* ('Law,' n.18), 214-243, esp. 219f.

15. Berakhoth 10a (Beruria). M. Simon, on p. 52, n.2 of the Soncino edition, observes, 'Probably Beruria was thinking of Rome as "the married wife" and Jerusalem as "the desolate."' This would make the Talmudic passage an ethicization of an interpretation such as we see preserved in the Targum, but Simon's observation is speculative. A similar view of Is. 54.1 is expressed (in the names of R. Bibi and R. Reuben) in Song of Songs Rabbah 1.5.3.

16. Song of Songs Rabbah 4.4.9 (R. Abba and R. Johanan). In the interpretation of Is. 54.15 found in Ecclesiastes Rabbah (1.7.6, R. Johanan) and Yebamoth (24b, cf. W. Slotki's note in the Soncino edition, p. 149), proselytes are at issue.

NOTES TO SECTION D

1. See n.4 of that section.

2. So Young, *op. cit.* ('Sanctuary' n.2), 264, 265, and Wildberger, *op. cit.* ('Sanctuary' n.2), 258.

3. The usage at 11.12 for נפשות in the MT is so natural that nothing should be deduced from it. Cf. also 49.6, for נצירי, which again may represent the transition from a remnant motif to an exilic motif, although it has been argued (Young III, 275) that a return from exile is already implied in the MT.

4. And the verb גלא is introduced in v. 13. As mentioned in the discussion of 'Jerusalem' in the Targum (n.4), it is just possible that 'sons' diction was in vogue at a later period. It was apparently first used in connection with 60.4, where the Hebrew text already speaks of sons. But its usage where 'exiles' alone would have done may be taken to suggest that a later situation is presupposed in which only the offspring of exiles (or those who have decided not to settle outside their own land) could reasonably be expected to return (49.18, 20). It is notable in this regard that Tg Is. 27.6 openly speaks of

offspring: 'there (viz. in their land) those of Jacob's house will beget children, those of the house of Israel will increase and multiply, and will fill the face of the world with children's children' (cf. the MT).

5. See Stenning, *op. cit.* (Introduction, n.15), xii-xiv.

6. For this phrase, see n.4.

7. On the basis of this interpretation, it is also understandable that 'my chosen people' (43.20) becomes 'exiles of my people in whom I am well pleased.' Other occurrences of the term which are quite natural in context are found in 52.12; 56.8.

8. V. 10, with its reference to the crossing of the ים סוף, explains why the meturgeman was inclined to this interpretation.

9. There is also an 'exile' usage at 54.15a which manifests the motif of consoling vengeance, and this has been discussed in the 'Jerusalema section. The use of the term here is occasioned by גור יגור in the MT, and the Hebrew verb is taken to mean 'sojourn.'

10. At 60.8, the imagery of cloud and doves is specifically applied to 'the exiles of Israel.'

11. And see the use of the verb in v. 20; cf. 17.4; 23.6. For the argument that a similar motif is represented in the DSS, see Paul Garnet, *Salvation and Atonement in the Qumran Scrolls*, WUNT 3 (Tübingen: Mohr, 1977). Cf. Berakhoth 3a (in Rav's name).

12. Less explicable is the additional phrase, 'and their remnant shall a mighty king exile' (for והאחרון), except on the supposition that the meturgeman has in mind a 'latter' exile analogous to the Assyrian policy.

13. The elevation of events recorded in Joshua to practical equivalence with events recorded in the Pentateuch confirms the anti-Sadducean bias of the meturgeman (see 'Sanctuary' n.10). Cf. 5.13: 'Therefore my people are exiled because they did not know the law . . . .'

14. V. 25 in the Targum reads: 'If the house of Israel set their faces to do the law, would he not respond and gather them from the sons of the Gentiles . . . ?' Note that מביני is here used, cf. n.4.

15. For the thesis of an early 'exilic soteriology', cf. Garnet, *op. cit.* (n.11) and, less convincingly, 'Jesus and the Exilic Soteriology' in: *Studia Biblica 1978* II, JSNTS 2 (Sheffield: JSOT Press, 1980), 111-114.

16. For the history of the development of the Babylonian academies, cf. the five volume work of J. Neusner, *A History of the Jews in Babylonia*, SPB (Leiden: Brill, 1965-1970).

17. One might compare Tg Mic 4.7b, 8. See 'Regnum Dei' ('Sanctuary' n.7), 269.

18. The meturgeman even here permits himself the hope that 'he will remove Gentile dominion from the land of Israel'; cf. 54.1.

19. The importance of this sentence to the meturgeman is shown by the fact that it also occurs at 46.4. 'Exile' also appears at the end of 66.8.

20. Volz, *op. cit.* ('Law' n.16), 26, from which these citations are taken.

21. Volz, 27.

22. Volz, 211.

23. Volz, 43; cf. 48.
24. Volz, 104, citing II Baruch 4.28f.
25. Petuchowski, *art. cit.* ('Law' n.12), 29, 32.
26. Cf. Jerushalmi Taanith 1.1 and Mekhilta de R. Ishmael Pisḥa 14.103 (opinions of R. Eliezer and R. Aqiba precede).
27. Exodus Rabbah 15.16 (following a statement of R. Isaac the Blacksmith); 23.5 (following a statement by R. Levi); Leviticus Rabbah 32.8 (an anonymous Amora's opinion); Numbers Rabbah 7.10 (R. Nathan); Lamentations Rabbah 1.19-20§54 (unascribed); Song of Songs Rabbah 4.8.1 (unascribed).
28. Cf. Tg Jeremiah 30.18 (paraphrased in the 'Jerusalem' section); Tg Hosea 2.2; 14.8 ('*They will be gathered from among their exile*, live in the shadow of their messiah, the dead will live, and goodness abound in the land. The record of their goodness will continue without interruption, as the memory of the trumpet sounds accompanying the ritual libation of wine in the sanctuary house'); Tg Micah 5.3 (where the clause italicized in the last citation appears). In Tg Hosea 3.3, we have a usage which seems at first to be coherent with Tg Is. 43.14 ('Prophet, say to her, Congregation of Israel, your sins caused you to be exiled many days'), but a reference to right worship and a warning from idolatry immediately follow. While formally similar, therefore, it is contextually better related to sanctuary usage than the statement in the Isaiah Targum. These difficulties can only be untangled when the framework of the Hosea Targum is isolated and dated.

NOTES TO SECTION E

1. But not exclusively used. At 8.14 we find the innovative reading: 'because the house of Israel has separated itself from those of the house of Judah.' This, obviously, is very far from a collective reading. Yet the passage (in both the Tg and the MT) already refers to 'two houses' of Israel, so that the usage is more historical than theological. The innovative reading is therefore nothing more than a faithful interpretation of the Hebrew text which employs a frequently used phrase in a somewhat unusual way.
2. Cf. the Exodus typology discussed in the 'Exile' section; for the law as light, cf. Soṭah 5a (R. Eleazar, as cited in the 'Law' section).
3. The meturgeman was giving what he took to be the sense of the statement in Hebrew, 'I have no wrath, who will give me thorns and briars to battle? I will set out against them, I will burn them up together.' The Tagumic interpretation is that Israel is in the position, by doing the law, to activate the now dormant wrath of God against the oppressor.
4. Why not 'house'? Did the meturgeman here speak of an exiled community, rather than the indigenous society? If so, the 'house' usage reading would be earlier, with 'congregation' representing an accommodation to the post-135 reality, in which the dispersion from Jerusalem seemed definitive, and the Babylonian rabbinate (and exilarchate) came to operate with relative

autonomy (cf. 'Exile,' n.16). Cf. 41.14, where MT 'men of Israel' becomes 'families of the house of Israel.'

5.   In the same vein, at 48.19 the interpreter adds 'of Israel' to the statement that the name would not cease, and this follows the lament in v. 18 (both Tg and MT), 'If you had attended to my commandments . . . .'

6.   Comparison with the MT shows that this and those which follow are more circumspect renderings than some which we have seen.

7.   References can easily be multiplied; cf. the index of R.H. Charles, *The Apocrypha and Pseudepigrapha* II (cited in Introduction, n.51). Most Intertestamental passages cited in the present study have been taken from this edition.

8.   Numbers Rabbah 10.2; Song of Songs Rabbah 8.14.1; cf. the exilic soteriology of Numbers Rabbah 16.25.

9.   These rabbis are placed in the third century by Slotki (cf. 'Law,' n.15), and in the fourth by Strack-Billerbeck, *Kommentar zum Neuen Testament aus Talmud und Midrasch* I (München: Beck, 1926), 164. Cf. 'Regnum Dei' ('Sanctuary,' n.7), 269.

10. As it did later in the verse (with Jerusalem), and cf. Tg Jer. 4.31; 6.2, 23. But 'congregation' is not merely a rendering of 'daughter'; cf. Tg Is. 27.2; Tg Jer. 8.20; Tg Hos. 2.15.

NOTES TO SECTION F

1.   The same phrase is introduced in v. 22 for 'a remnant will return,' and similar wording is found at 33.13.

2.   *Op. cit.* (Introduction, n.6), 28, 29. In the LXX, אם תבעיון בעו שבו אתיו becomes ἐὰν ζητῆς, ζήτει, καὶ παρ'ἐμοὶ οἴκει. Presumably אתיו was taken as אתי and (שבו) derived from ישב; these alterations, as well as the singular construction, do not cohere with the Targumic rendering. A variant reading has ἐπιστρέφω in the aorist plural imperative, but the understanding that שוב in this verse refers to repentance is a perennial element in Jewish exegesis.

3.   The meturgeman took the verse as an oracle regarding the result of Israel's disobedience, rather than as 'mockery of the despisers' (so Young, *op. cit.*, volume II ['Sanctuary,' n.2], 275). He was consistent in his interpretation (cf. v. 13).

4.   Uses of תוב for Hebrew שוב in 58.12, 13 are so natural as not to justify speculation as to the theology of the interpreter. On the other hand, it is interesting that, at 59.20, God is pictured as coming to Zion 'to turn (לאתבא) the rebellious ones of the house of Jacob to the law,' rather than as coming 'to those in Jacob who turn (לשבי) from transgression' (MT).

5.   The clause is repeated as a positive statement (not a question) in the second half of the verse in order to represent the last repetitive phrase in the MT. It is apparent that 'blind' has been taken as 'blind to the law' (cf. 42.7, as discussed in the 'House of Israel' section), and therefore 'wicked.'

6.   As in the previous verse, 'to forgive' renders 'to heal.' Cf. 33.13b, 'Know, you penitent, who repented recently to the law, my might.'

7. Cf. on 43.14 in the 'Exile' section; 21.12 and 33.13b are in any case to be classed with the present usage.

8. To this extent, the present discussion may be taken to support the tentative findings offered above. But we would stress that we have not claimed that demands for individual repentance are necessarily late: we are concerned with those demands which are assumed to have been heard and which do not easily accommodate a nationalistic aspect. Cf. E.E. Urbach (tr. I. Abrahams), *The Sages: their concepts and beliefs* (The Perry Foundation: The Hebrew University, 1975), 462-471.

9. Cf. 5.3, cited in the 'House of Israel' section.

10. Cf. RSV and NEB; the present translation accords somewhat with that of Young, *op. cit.*, vol. I ('Sanctuary,' n.2), 469, 472, and is supported by the LXX in respect of the 'inheritance' translation, although the LXX takes the verse *in bonam partem*.

11. The if-clause is in the plural, while the rest of the verse is in the singular, as in the MT. This suggests that the clause is a kind of slogan for the meturgeman.

12. It is worthy of note, though beyond the present purpose, that the refusal theme is even the explanation of God's anger at non-Jews. So, in the oracle of Isaiah to Hezekiah against Sennacherib, we read (37.26): ' . . . the prophets of Israel also prophesied against you, and you did not repent . . . .'

13. Strack-Billerbeck, *op. cit.* I ('House of Israel,' n.9), 164.

14. Moses Aberbach, 'Patriotic Tendencies in Targum Jonathan to the Prophets,' in: *Hebrew Abstracts* 15 (1974), 89-90. Particularly in this context, I regret the delay by Ktav in issuing the book on Targum Jonathan written by Professor Aberbach and Dr L. Smolar.

15. Churgin's position is discussed in the introduction.

16. Cf. S.H. Levey, *The Messiah: An Aramaic Interpretation. The Messianic Exegesis of the Targum*, Monographs of the Hebrew Union College 10 (Cincinnati: Hebrew Union College, 1974), 95. Levey links this rendering to the movement of Judas the Galilean; we take the rendering in Targum Isaiah to be later, and reserve comment on Levey's position.

NOTES TO SECTION G

1. On the strength of this rendering, one can also speak of Abraham as a warning to the nations in the Targum.

2. This is the way in which the זכות אבות idea appears generally to function in Judaism (cf. E.P. Sanders, *Paul and Palestinian Judaism* [London: SCM, 1977], 183-198). It also appears in the Isaiah Targum without specific reference to Abraham. At 43.7a, we read, 'All this for the sake of your fathers that I called my name upon them' (MT: 'everyone who is called by my name'), immediately after a reference to 'Exile,' and in fact this verse itself has, 'I made ready their exiles' (MT: 'I formed them'). The coherence of this motif with the

'Exile' theologoumenon is therefore confirmed. It is also used with 'Jerusalem' at 62.6; the name of the city merely corresponds to the Hebrew text, but the זכות אבות idea is innovatively introduced:

> Tg Behold the works of your righteous fathers, city of Jerusalem, are established and preserved before me . . .
>
> MT Upon your walls, Jerusalem, I have appointed watchmen . . .

In the second half of this verse (and cf. v. 7), the Targum reads, 'the memory of your good deeds is recounted before the LORD unceasingly' (MT: 'Rest not, you who make memory of the LORD'; cf. Acts 10.4). This is well worth noting, because it illustrated that the זכות אבות motif does not represent the divine favour as automatic. Rather, God responds to Israel's obedience in solidarity with the patriarchs. Hence, the meturgeman could even have Hezekiah say, 'because of my memory for good I have been increased in respect of years' (38.10b). Having regard for such passages, we must not imagine that the meturgeman thought that Israel is purely passive when it is said at 64.4d, 'by the deeds of our righteous fathers from of old we were delivered.' To this effect, cf. Urbach, *op. cit.* ('Repentance,' n.8), 497f.; Schäfer, *art. cit.* ('Jerusalem,' n.14), 216f.

3. Volz, *op. cit.* ('Law,' n.16), 103.

4. Volz, 28 (citing Jubilees 12.23f.; 14.5; 15.6f. in respect of Abraham). Cf. p.98, where the 'Frömmigkeit der Stammväter' is seen to be stressed in Philo and II Maccabees. The passage from II Maccabees (15.14f.) is particularly striking, because the prayer of Jeremiah is at least as much an incentive to the young men as a plea to God. The reference to Abraham in the first benediction in the Shemoneh Esreh (both recensions) is incidental, serving to identify Israel's God (cf. Petuchowski, *art. cit.* ['Law,' n.12], 27, 30).

5. The exception, in the literature surveyed, occurs in Leviticus Rabbah 1.9.10, where, after the association with Moses is made, an Amora (R. Abin) is reported to refer Is. 48.15 to Abraham, but in a biographical way.

6. So Mo'ed Ḳaṭan 16b and Shabbath 86b (cf. the notes of D.H.M. Lazarus and H. Freedman, the Soncino translators).

7. P.R. Davies and B.D. Chilton, 'The Aqedah: A Revised Tradition History' in: *CBQ* 40 (1978), 514-546.

8. B.D. Chilton, 'Isaac and the Second Night: A Consideration,' *Biblica* 61 (1980), 78-88.

NOTES TO SECTION H

1. *Op. cit.* (Introduction, n.15), xii. But Stenning's reading of מקדם can no longer be regarded as tenable; cf. M.L. Klein, 'The Preposition קדם (Before): A Pseudo-Anthropomorphism in the Targums,' *JTS* 30 (1979), 502-507.

2. This rendering might also be said to avoid the very slight possibility of anthropomorphism in the MT at this point. 'I will place my spirit upon him'

could imply a congruence of divine and human personalities, while 'I will place my *holy* spirit upon him' merely posits the gift of what 40.13 has told us belongs to all prophets, and 'holy' preserves the distinctiveness of the source of the 'spirit.' The programmatic avoidance of anthropomorphism was especially occasioned by v. 1a, where 'my soul' in the MT was replaced by the meturgeman with 'my memra.'

3.   That he was thinking in this way is also suggested by his rendering of v. 4. Instead of taking the end of v. 3 to supply the subject of this verse, as in the MT, he wrote, 'And the righteous will grow . . . .' צדיקיא will be dealt with in its own section; for the moment, suffice it to say that its introduction establishes that those who are to be blessed in v. 3 are not merely to be seen as passive recipients. For the 'sons' rendering, cf. Max Wilcox, 'The Promise of the "Seed" in the New Testament and the Targumim,' in: *JSNT* 5 (1979), 2-20.

4.   As pointed out above ('Repentance,' n.4), an interesting causative use of תוב (with God as the implied subject) appears in the preceding verse. We might say that the burden of the prophetic preaching of repentance is precisely the holy spirit, in which God himself is active. Cf. H. Parzen, 'The Ruaḥ Haḳodesh in Tannaitic Literature,' in *JQR* 20 (1929-30), 51-76.

5.   See 'My memra,' part i.

6.   P. Schäfer, *Die Vorstellung vom heiligen Geist in der rabbinischen Literatur*, Studien zum Alten und Neuen Testament 28 (München: Kösel, 1972).

7.   *Op. cit.*, 14, 23, 46 (in reference to the possession of the prophetic gift by Israel as a whole).

8.   *Op. cit.*, 62.

9.   *Ibid.* The next sentence continues: 'Sogar die Fälle, in denen der hl. Geist als Subjekt der Handlung auftritt, lassen häufig erkennen, dass die Handlung (das Offenbarungsgeschehen) von Gott selbst gesetzt ist und nicht vom hl. Geist.'

10.   *Op. cit.*, 66.

11.   *Op. cit.*, 139; cf. 15 (citing A.J. Heschel), 75, 135, 136, 140, 143. Cf. J. Blenkinsopp, 'Prophecy and Priesthood in Josephus,' *JJS* 25 (1974), 239-262. As has been pointed out to me by P.R. Davies, the pre-70 provenience of the motif is to some extent supported by the Qumran sources, in which the holy spirit relates to purification (cf. 1QS 3.7; 4.21; 1QH 16.12).

12.   *Op. cit.*, 137, 144.

13.   *Op. cit.*, 145-147 (and the following section).

NOTES TO SECTION I

1.   Cf. the less startling usages at 5.9, 'The prophet said, With my ears I was hearing when this was decreed from before the LORD of hosts . . . '; 6.1, ' . . . the prophet said . . . '; 7.10, 'And the prophet of the LORD continued

speaking with Ahaz, saying'; 8.16, 'Prophet, keep the testimony . . . seal and hide the law'; 21.2, 'The prophet said . . . ' (cf. vv. 7, 8, 10); 22.12, 'And the prophet of the LORD God of hosts . . . '; 28.16, ' . . . the prophet said . . . '; 28.23, 'The prophet said . . . '; 33.15, 'The prophet said . . . ' (cf. the sanctuary usage in v. 16); 35.3, 'The prophet said . . . '; 48.16 (end), 'The prophet said . . . '; 61.1, 'The prophet said . . . '; 63.7, 'The prophet said . . . .'

2.   The claim is all the more startling when read in association with the assertion, 'When the last prophets, Haggai, Zechariah, and Malachi, died, the holy spirit ceased out of Israel, but nevertheless it was granted to them to hear (communications from God) by means of a mysterious voice' (Tosefta Soṭah 13.2, as quoted by Moore, *op. cit.* I [Introduction, n.15], 421). For this suggestion as to the meaning of the ascription, cf. Urbach, *op. cit.* ('Repentance,' n.8), 308-309 (with citations).

3.   'Prophet, explain the prophecy to them, prophet, explain to them what is about to come. The prophet said, There is reward for the righteous and there is retribution for the wicked; if you are penitent, repent while you are able to repent.'

4.   Cf. 7.13, ' . . . Is it a small thing to you to weary the prophets?'; 28.10, ' . . . the prophets prophesied concerning them, that if they repented it would be forgiven them, and they did not receive the words of the prophets . . . '; 28.11, 'For with strange speech and mocking tongue this people were mocking to receive the prophets that prophesied to them'; 28.12, 'To whom the prophets said . . . and they did not wish to receive teaching'; 30.1, ' . . . (they) do not ask my prophets . . . '; 30.2, ' . . . they do not ask after the words of my prophets . . . '; 30.10, 'Who say to the prophets, Do not prophesy . . . '; 37.26 (of Sennacherib), ' . . . the prophets of Israel prophesied concerning you, and you did not repent . . . '; 43.22, 'It was said by means of the prophets, and you did not attend to my service . . . '; 48.8, 'Indeed, you did not hear the words of the prophets . . . '; 50.2, 'Why, when I sent my prophets, did they not repent .?'; 50.10, 'Who among you who fears the LORD, who hears the voice of his servants, the prophets .?'; 63.10, 'And they refused, and provoked the word of his holy prophets . . . ' (n.b., for 'his holy spirit' in the MT); 65.12, ' . . . because I sent my prophets, and you did not repent, they prophesied, and you did not receive . . . ' (so 66.4).

5.   28.24, 'In all time the prophets were prophesying, that somehow the sinners' ears might be opened and they might receive teaching'; 42.19, 'If the wicked repent, will they not be called my servants, and the sinners, to whom I sent my prophets . . . '; 50.4, ' . . . morning on morning he awakes to send his prophets that the ears of the sinners might be opened and they might receive teaching'; 63.11, ' . . . lest they say . . . where is he that caused the word of his holy prophets to dwell among them?' (n.b., for 'his holy spirit' in the MT); 65.2, 'All day I sent my prophets to a refusing people . . . .'

6.   7.9b, 'If you do not believe the words of the prophets, you will not be established'; 11.15b, 'And he will lift up the blow of his might upon the Euphrates by the word of his prophets'; 22.1a, 'The oracle of prophecy concerning the city that dwells in the valley concerning which the prophets

prophesied' (similarly, 22.5); 30.27, 'Behold, the name of the LORD is revealed as the prophets from the beginning prophesied concerning it . . . '; cf. the threat expressed at 28.19 (end), 'Before the curse time comes, you will consider the words of the prophets.'

7.   It should not be imagined that the sentiments cited in n.2 were absolutely normative. Citing Tosefta Soṭah 13.3f, Moore (*op. cit.* I, 422) observes that Hillel was thought worthy to have the holy spirit rest on him, and Ḥanina ben Dosa had to refute the claim that he was a prophet (Berakoth 34a, cited on p. 377). This is not to suggest that the meturgeman claimed he was a prophet; his pretension was quasi-prophetic, perhaps not unlike that of Josephus (cf. J. Blenkinsopp, *art. cit.* ('Holy Spirit,' n.11). At 8.2, the meturgeman referred to 'the prophecy of Uriah the priest.' Cf. J.W. Bowman, 'Prophets and Prophets in Talmud and Midrash' in: *EQ* 22 (1950), 107-114; E. Fascher, ΠΡΟΦΗΤΗΣ (Giessen: Töpelmann, 1927).

8.   Cf. 41.27, 'The words of consolation that the prophets from the beginning prophesied . . . '; 62.10, 'Prophets . . . announce good tidings and consolations to the righteous . . . ' (cf. the section on 'The righteous,' n.14; if those observations are correct, this is another instance of the later usage of a primitive motif).

9.   So many passages have been cited above that it would seem superfluous to further buttress the argument by referring to the uses of 'prophecy' and 'prophesy.' Such a discussion would have to consider 1.1; 2.1; 5.6; 6.7; 8.2, 11; 14.28; 21.1, 11; 22.1, 25; 29.11; 38.4; 51.16; 59.21; 61.1 (for prophecy) and 1.1; 2.1; 6.8; 13.1; 22.1, 5; 28.10, 11, 24; 30.10, 27; 37.26; 40.1, 2, 6; 41.27; 50.2, 5; 65.12; 66.4 (for prophesy).

10.   Cf. Schäfer, *op. cit.* ('Holy spirit,' n.6; the relevant page numbers are given in n.11).

11.   Cf. jSanhedrin 10.2; also in the names of Jacob and Aḥa, where Is. 8.17, 18 are cited, leading up to the observation, 'ce texte prouve combien ceux-ci (sc. ses disciples) étaient chers au prophète qui par affection les appelait ses enfants.' For a general statement of the preeminence of Isaiah among the prophets, cf. Pesiqta Rabbati 33.3.

12.   But cf. the almost wistful statement in Exodus Rabbah 18.12 (discussed more fully in the 'Repentance' section), following a citation of Is. 21.12, 'So Israel has eagerly awaited salvation since the rising of Edom.'

13.   P. 56 n.56 (cf. Introduction, n.53ʲ).

NOTES TO SECTION J

1.   Cf. 5.24b ('for they have despised the law of the LORD of hosts, and rejected the memra of the holy one of Israel') and 37.29 ('because you provoked my memra, and your noising has come before me, and I will set chains on your jaws . . . '). For the relationship between 'memra' and 'law,' cf. Hamp, *op. cit.* (Introduction, n.33), 85, 86. In his exemplary monograph, Hamp pioneered the categorization of usages which we have attempted to

extend here. Cf. Domingo Muñoz León, *Dios-Palabra. Memra en los targumim del Pentateuco*, Institución San Jerónimo 4 (Granada: Santa Rita-Monachil, 1974).

2.   Cf. 57.6c ('will my memra repent because of these things?') and 66.6b ('the voice of the memra of the LORD that completes recompense to his enemies'). Hamp, 182, also explicates the basic meaning of memra in noetic terms. Cf. also Muñoz León's category, '*Sustitución Memrá en lugares que expressan reacciones divinas*' (57f.).

3.   Interestingly, v. 10 includes parallel uses of 'law' and 'prophesy,' and v. 11 parallel uses of 'tradition' and 'memra.'

4.   The motif of the past, consistent refusal to repent (cf. the 'Prophet(s)' section) might be said to cohere with this passage, and with 43.27b ('and your teachers rebelled against my memra'); 59.13a ('we have rebelled, and lied against the memra of the LORD'); 65.3a ('a people that provokes my memra . . . ').

5.   The meturgeman has taken נשא in a very plausible way, but the rendering of לאה niphal with סגי aphel seems rather daring. For an instance of haggadic atonement replacing cultic atonement, cf. 'The Aqedah: A Revised Tradition History' (cited in 'Abraham,' n.7).

6.   Cf. 10.17a, ' . . . his memra will be strong as fire, and his commands as a flame.' The previous clause does justice to the titles 'light of Israel' and 'his holy one' in the MT, so that this rendering is an innovative assertion of the memra's punishing presence. Cf. also 50.11c, 'from my memra this has come upon you . . . ' for 'from my hand . . . ' in the MT.

7.   Cf. 11.4c, 'and he will smite the sinners of the land with the memra of his mouth.' Cf. Muñoz León, *op. cit.* (n.1), 50.

8.   Cf. 26.19, ' . . . and the wicked to whom you gave might, and they transgressed against your memra, you will deliver to Gehinnam'; 31.9b, 'whose splendour is in Zion for those who do his law, and his burning furnace of fire in Jerusalem for those that have transgressed his memra.' In the latter passage, we again see 'memra' used of the divine sense of injury, while 'doing the law' refers more to the fulfilment of an objective standard than to the effect of an action on God. The phrase 'to transgress against his memra' is also used, again in a eschatological context, at 32.5. Cf. 66.24b.

9.   The 'chaff' comes from the first part of the verse in the MT, which the meturgeman there rendered as 'evil deeds.'

10.   Cf. n.4 in the 'House of Israel' section.

11.   צר, taken by the meturgeman as a noun ('oppressor'), as Young, *op. cit.* III ('Sanctuary,' n.2), 440, does. Young also takes נססה to mean 'raising a banner' in the stream, so that his is remarkably similar to the Targumic rendering. Again, we see that what appears at first glance an unusual translation in this Targum turns out to be the result of a sensitive engagement with the Hebrew text as well as of the interpreter's predelictions.

12.   Except for the 'memra' usage, occasioned by 'mouth' at the end of v. 20 in the Hebrew, this rendering parallels the MT quite closely. Cf Muñoz León, *op. cit.* (n.1), 52.

13.   Cf. 32.9b, 'sites that dwell in security, hear my memra'—the following verses make it clear that this security is an illusion; 41.1, 'Hear my memra . . . '—this verse follows a reference to a return of exiles. Cf. also 45.22 ('Turn to my memra . . . '); 46.3, 12; 48.12, 16; 49.1; 51.1, 4, 7. The last group of passages is included because the instances cited appeal for obedience, although various people are addressed by the imperative.

14.   Generally speaking, the 'memra' usages cited in this paragraph can be understood quite easily with reference to the MT, but this passage involves a substantive addition in the usage: 'and to the righteous who do his memra he has made known the words of his good pleasure.'

15.   Similarly (to the remark in the previous note), the Targum reads, 'the reward of those doing his memra' for 'his reward.'

16.   This rendering is particularly interesting, because it involves the reversal of prophecy: ' . . . and the statement of prophecy concerning him will be annulled, for by the memra of the LORD it is so decreed.' Cf. 21.17, ' . . . for by the memra of the LORD God of Israel it is so decreed.' 'God of Israel' is not an innovation, but comes from the MT; the slogan itself is the major innovation, and this passage may also be said to instance its usage in malam partem. Cf. n.12 and Muñoz León, *op. cit.* (n.1), 51.

17.   מימרא is introduced into 28.6 (for רוח) in the context of law courts, and into 4.4 (twice, both times for רוח) in the context of divine judgment.

18.   In v. 35, 'for my sake' becomes 'for my memra's sake.'

19.   For מימר as the word of prophets, see 11.15; 28.23; 63.11. Cf. the expression λόγος θεῖος used by Philo in *De Mutatione Nomine* 31, 169 and *De Somniis* I, 33, 190 (citations in H.A. Wolfson, *Philo: Foundations of Religious Philosophy in Judaism, Christianity and Islam* II [Cambridge: Harvard University Press, 1948], 32). See also Muñoz León, *op. cit.* (n.1), 34, 49.

20.   Cf. 59.16d, 'and by the memra of his good pleasure he helped them,' even though there was no man 'doing good deeds' (v. 16a). A nearly identical rendering (in the first instead of the third person) appears at 63.5. Cf. also 49.15 and 63.14. Cf. Muñoz León, 36.

21.   In each of these cases, memra appears with the term 'help' (סער).

22.   The last clause reads, 'and the memra of God was my help.'

23.   'And his memra was their saviour'; cf. 45.17.

24.   'As cattle that are led in the plain, the memra of the LORD led them.' Coming as it does after reference to the reed sea crossing (v. 12, and explicitly in the Targum), this passage must envisage the period of wilderness wandering.

25.   Cf. 45.25; 62.11, 'the reward of those doing his memra is with him' (cf. n.14 and n.15).

26.   Cf. 59.17, ' . . . he will bring strength and deliverance with his memra to those who fear him'; 62.2b.

27.   Cf. 45.12, 'I have made the earth by my memra . . . '; 48.13, 'Indeed, by my memra I completed the earth . . . '; Muñoz León, *op. cit.* (n.1), 30, n.20. As we have attempted to show, however, the creativity of the memra is not to be

isolated from its certainty as a witness in the thinking of the Isaian meturgeman (compare Muñoz León, 46).

28.   Two memra uses follow in v. 24, and v. 25 speaks of the glorification of Israel by the memra (cf. n.25). Cf. the unusual renderings at 46.4a, 'And forever I am he, and my memra stands forever and ever'; 48.1 (end), 'Does not his memra stand in truth and righteousness?'; 52.6 (end), 'and my memra stands.'

29.   Cf. 54.9a, 'As the days of Noah this is before me, when I swore by my memra . . . '; 63.1, ' . . . to do the just requital of his people as he swore to them by his memra . . . ' (a rather innovative rendering, after 'Bozrah').

30.   In this regard, Barrett's judgment in respect of memra usage ('*Memra* is a blind alley in the study of the biblical background of John's logos doctrine.') may require correction (*The Gospel according to St. John* [London: SCM, 1978], 128). The only example he gives is of the type discussed in part v (citing Gen. 3.8 in Onqelos). Cf. T.W. Manson, *On Paul and John*, SBT 38 (London: SCM, 1963), 149, 'Finally, while it is improbable that the *Memra* of the Targums has anything to do fundamentally with John's Logos doctrine, I cannot help thinking that the linguistic usage of the Targum may have influenced the language of the Prologue.' Cf. J.A. Fitzmyer, *A Wandering Aramean. Collected Aramaic Essays*, SBLMS 25 (Missoula: Scholars Press, 1979), 94, 95, for a warning against basing a pre-Christian theology of the 'word' on the usage of מאמר in the Job Targum from Qumran.

31.   Cf. Moore, *op. cit.* (Introduction, n.8), 419, 'But nowhere in the Targums is *memra* a "being" of any kind or in any sense, much less a personal being . . . It is to be observed, finally, that *memra* is purely a phenomenon of translation, not a figment of speculation; it never gets outside the Targums,' and 'Intermediaries in Jewish Theology' in: *HTR* 15 (1922), 41-61; Strack-Billerbeck, *op. cit.* ('House of Israel,' n.9) II, 302-333. For the position here taken, cf. Hamp, *op. cit.* (Introduction, n.33), 182 (who correctly realizes an intermediary need not be a hypostasis; cf. p. 204); Muñoz León, *op. cit.* (n.1), 31, 46, 54. In an article published after the initial draft of this section was written, C.T.R. Hayward ('The Holy Name of the God of Moses and the Prologue of St. John's Gospel' in: *NTS* 25 [1978-1979], 16-32) argues that '*Memra* is neither an hypostasis, nor a pious periphrasis for the Name of YHWH, but . . . an exegetical term which stands for the Name revealed by God to Moses at the burning bush, the Name 'HYH I AM/WILL BE THERE' (p. 17). In a summary he writes, '*Memra* is God's Name 'HYH, which by midrashic exposition refers to His presence in past and future creation, history, and redemption. *Memra* is God's mercy, by which the world is created and sustained' (p. 24; on p. 31, the term 'covenant' finds its way into the conclusion). While Hayward's thesis is not inconsistent with the present treatment (which is significant, in that his position is worked out in respect of Pentateuchal passages), I do not think it could claim any support from it. Indeed, it may be doubted that the rich variety here detailed can have proceeded from a single, set derivation of memra from אהיה. A similar doubt,

in respect of the Pentateuchal Targums, prevents me from being convinced by Hayward. He writes, 'Only, it seems, when the original meaning of Memra as representing the Name 'HYH had been lost, did it come to be used quite arbitrarily as a replacement of YHWH.' But when a scholarly 'discovery' necessitates the supposition that a derivation was 'forgotten' by the very group which supposedly invented it, the suspicion must be entertained that it is not a discovery at all, but a speculation which does not suit the evidence. Hayward writes, 'First, no one has ever attempted to account for the origin of the term *Memra*' (p. 20). I would have thought that the connection of memra with אמר was evident (cf. Hamp, 88), and that such a simple point of departure would better account for the variety of Targumic usage than the highly precise matrix which Hayward posits. Moreover, while n.30 demonstrates that I am inclined to argue (*pace* Barrett) that memra usage might provide a background to the Johannine prologue, Hayward's attempt to show this is less than compelling. His 'Excursus' on the date of memra usage is quite inconclusive, in that he finds it necessary to assume his own thesis in order to date the usage early (pp. 24, 25; GenAp 22.20-31 reads 'I will be' and אהיה = מימרא, hence, 'we have a direct reference in an Aramaic document to what in Targum is called *Memra*'). Finally, he fails even to suggest a literary connection between John and a Targum, but merely assumes 'as a working hypothesis, that St. John did use the Memra' (p. 28). The phrase 'working hypothesis' scarcely justifies the apotheosis of an assumption into a conclusion.

32. Strack-Billerbeck, *op. cit.* ('House of Israel,' n.9), 317-319, lists occurrences. In Shabbath 119b, R. Eliezer related הדבור to creation, citing Psalm 33.6, but there is no suggestion that the term designates God, and the assertion is not in the nature of a witness (cf. category vii). In Numbers Rabbah 11, Simeon b. Yoḥai refers to הדבור as a voice (category v). Cf. the conclusion offered by Muñoz León (*op. cit.* [n.1], 679) 'que el término Memrá es el primitivo y que Dib-urá es la hebraización de término Memrá en los comentarios palestinenses . . . .'

33. Strack-Billerbeck, 319, lists instances. See also Neophyti Genesis 28.10, cited (but not commented on) in C.T.R. Hayward, *The Use and Religious Significance of the Term Memra in Targum Neofiti I in the Light of the Other Targumim* (Oxford: D.Phil., 1975), 102.

34. Strack-Billerbeck, 318. Cf. Hamp, *op. cit.* (Introduction, n.33), 94.

35. Strack-Billerbeck, 317.

36. As we have repeatedly seen, memra is obeyed by attending to the law; but in the Targum the terms are collateral, while in rabbinic discussion they are genetically related (viz. the word is the law as given on Sinai).

37. Cf. n.33.

38. Cf. n.31, and *Use*, 33, 37, 38, 153, 208. But Hayward puts his position in a far more circumspect manner in the thesis, in that he openly admits the place of the verb אמר, to which I would give primacy, in the development of the usage (VI, 29, 32, 159, 208), and justifies the linkage of memra and covenant in terms of the natural association of memra and oath (VI, VII, 77f., 93, 131; cf. categories iv and vii above). On the other hand, Hayward's contention that אהיה stands behind memra at its point of origin is seen to have an insecure

foundation. He argues that earlier memra usages appeared as the subject of the verb 'to be,' while later usages occurred with various other verbs simply because the former tendency characterizes N and the latter characterizes N^m (18, 21, 26). But as S. Lund and J. Foster (*Variant Versions of Targumic Traditions within Codex Neofiti I*, SBLAS 2 [Missoula: Scholars Press, 1977]) have shown, the relationship between N and N^m cannot be assumed to be as simple as Hayward assumes.

39. *Use*, IX, 50, 167f., 187 (on 1QGenAp; as has already been argued in n.31, this is not—*prima facie*—a memra reading, so that Hayward's claim that it suggests memra usage in the second century B.C.E. [p. 199] is not tenable), 191f., 199. Less important to his position, but tending to confirm memra usage by the first century, are Jubilees 12.4; IV Ezra 6.38; II Baruch 48.8 (173, 179, 184).

40. VI, 62 (indeed, cf. the whole of chapter five, '*Memra* and the Attribute of Mercy,' 53-75). So emphatically are mercy and punishment united in the memra theologoumenon that Hayward suggests that it was used against the 'two powers' heretics (IV, V, 45f. [citing Mekhilta Shirata 4.19-31], 159). In a recent monograph (*Two Powers in Heaven. Early Rabbinic Reports about Christianity and Gnosticism*: Studies in Judaism in Late Antiquity [Leiden: Brill, 1977], 23), Alan F. Segal suggests that memra might have occasioned 'two powers' speculation. Hayward, it must be noted, concludes that we are in no position to settle on any single origin for the usage of the term (200, 201).

41. Hayward, V, 62.

42. Hayward, VIII, IX. He unfortunately does not consider the possibility that דבור represents a degree of continuity with memra usage (cf. IX especially).

43. Hayward, 113; cf. 135f., 142, 143, 152f. On p. 114 (n.4), he makes the point, which we have already made in respect of the Isaiah Targum, that פולחנא may have a cultic signification (cf. 'Law,' n.16). Of course, one might also use the term in its general sense, so that context must be the deciding factor.

44. Hayward, 136.

45. Hayward, 152.

46. Hayward, 157, 158. Hayward himself is not dogmatic about his suggestion. Along with the possibility of an origin in 'two powers' controversy, he lists priestly provenience and the contradictory view of S. Isenberg that memra represents an anti-Sadducean emphasis on God's mercy ('An Anti-Sadducee Polemic in the Palestinian Targum Tradition' in: *HTR* 63 [1970], 433-444). He observes that '*Memra* is such a subtle and versatile piece of exegesis that it may have originated in any of these conditions' (200f.). Cf. also the mention of scribal activity as the matrix of memra usage (p. 209). In an excursus entitled 'Philo's Logos and the *Memra*' (202-206), Hayward sets out to demonstrate that 'the *Memra* of the Targumim has nothing in common with Philo's Logos' (202). Citing Wolfson (whose work is cited in n.19 of the present section) as his guide, Hayward concludes that 'Logos is a philosophical term, and is not really related to *Memra*' (205). But caution needs to be

exercised here. Philo's philosophical tendency is well known, but Alan Segal has pointed out that Philo's task is exegetical; the possibility that rabbinic conventions are reflected in his work is therefore seriously to be considered (*op. cit.* (n.40) 162, and 159-181 generally). Moreover, Wolfson described the Philonic logos as the 'mind of God' (I 231) which informs the 'intelligible world' (I 240; cf. also 229f., 235f., 244f., 253f., 291) and as 'the instrument in the creation of the world' (I 331). These are, of course, only a few aspects among many, and they are developed in a more discursive way than one will find in the Targumim, but the coherence with elements of memra usage in the Isaiah Targum is obvious, and may be more than coincidental. In yet another treatment of memra by Hayward which does not go beyond the argument of his thesis ('Memra and Skekhina: A Short Note' in: *JSS* 31 [1980], 210-213), he takes Domingo Muñoz León to task for having 'failed to grasp that *Memra* is an exegetical shorthand term which represents not only 'HYH itself, but also the *meaning* of 'HYH as God present in past, present and future' (212). Our n.31 would suggest that Muñoz León's putative failure evidences good exegetical sense, and when Hayward makes his case here, he does so without the important qualifications admitted in his thesis (cf. nn.38f.). But he promises a book on memra (p. 210, n.2) which will presumably clarify his thesis and offer sounder arguments for it. In the meantime, we would commend the synthesis propounded by Muñoz León, *op. cit.* (n.1), 639.

NOTES TO SECTION K

1.   Cf. 5.5b, 'I will remove my Shekinah from them . . . '; 8.17, 'The prophet said, concerning this I prayed before the LORD who said he would remove his Shekinah from the house of Jacob . . . '; 49.14, 'because Zion said, the LORD removed his Shekinah from me . . . '; 53.3, 'Then the glory of all the kingdoms will be for contempt and ended. They will be ill and pitiful as a man of pains and destined for sickness, and as when the face of the Shekinah was removed from us . . . '; 57.17, ' . . . I removed my Shekinah from them . . . ' (cf. the 'Exile' section); 64.6b, 'For you removed the face of your Shekinah from us . . . .'

2.   Cf. 12.6b, 'for the great one, the holy one of Israel, has said to cause his Shekinah to dwell in your midst'; 30.20b, 'and he will not again remove his Shekinah from the sanctuary house, and your eyes will see the Shekinah in the sanctuary house' (cf. the 'Sanctuary' section); 33.17a, 'Your eyes will see the glory of the Shekinah of the eternal king in his splendour'; 33.24a, 'And henceforth they will not say to the people who dwell in security around the Shekinah, an evil stroke has come on us from you'; 52.8b, 'for with their eyes they will see the mighty things which the LORD is about to do when he returns his Shekinah to Zion'; 54.6a, 8, 'For as a woman forsaken and grieved of spirit, the Shekinah of the LORD has met,' 'For a little while, a time, I removed the face of my Shekinah from you, and with eternal good things that do not cease I

will have compassion on you . . . '; 60.2b, 'and the Shekinah of the LORD will dwell in you and his glory will be revealed upon you.'

3.   Our question is not answered by the use of the term in v. 5, ' . . . for my eyes have seen the glory of the Shekinah of the eternal king, the LORD of hosts,' since the location of this vision is ambiguous.

4.   Cf. 32.15, ' . . . a spirit from him whose Shekinah is in high heavens . . . '; 33.5, ' . . . who causes his Shekinah to dwell in high heavens . . . '; 37.16, ' . . . whose Shekinah dwells higher than the cherubim . . . '; 38.14, ' . . . whose Shekinah is in high heavens . . . '; 40.22, 'Who caused the Shekinah of his glory to dwell in the mighty height . . . who stretched out the heavens as a small thing and laid them out as a glorious tent for his Shekinah house'; 45.15, ' . . . you have caused your Shekinah to dwell in the mighty height . . . '; 57.15, ' . . . he dwells on high and holy is his Shekinah . . . '; 66.1, ' . . . and where is the house place for my Shekinah's dwelling?' Cf. C.C. Rowland, *The Influence of the First Chapter of Ezekiel on Jewish and Early Christian Literature* (Cambridge: Ph.D., 1974).

5.   Where the point is the return of the Shekinah envisaged in the future, there is obviously nothing curious about the rendering, since it coheres with the meturgeman's expectation of the Shekinah's renewed influence. Cf. 14.2, ' . . . and the house of Israel will possess them in the land of the Shekinah of the LORD . . . '; 18.7 (end), 'whose Shekinah is in mount Zion'; 60.13 (end), 'and I will glorify the dwelling place of my Shekinah.' At 63.17, the restoration of the Shekinah is prayed for: ' . . . return your Shekinah to your people . . . .'

6.   The final phrase ('whose Shekinah is in mount Zion') represents 'who dwells (השכן) in mount Zion' in the MT. This is a straightforward translation, but a mere change in the preposition would have brought the passage fully into accord with the theology expressed in 6.6 (cf. 18.7, cited in n.5).

7.   It has already been observed (in the 'My memra' section, part vi) that the relationship between the rendering of v. 10 and the same verse in the MT is not straightforward from the point of view of mere translation. The MT correspondent of v. 11 reads, 'and in the morning you sow, you make it blossom' (cf. Wildberger, *op. cit.* ['Sanctuary,' n.2], 638). The meturgeman took this difficult clause to be a metaphor of perverted growth, as his treatment of v. 11a as a whole shows. The clause discussed in the 'Repentance' section immediately follows. At 48.15, God is said to have brought Abraham into 'the land of my Shekinah house' (cf. the 'Abraham' section); cf. 64.3, ' . . . eye has not seen what your people have seen, the Shekinah of your glory . . . .'

8.   Cf. 24.16; 38.11 (n.b., 'Shekinah house' appears in parallelism with 'sanctuary house'), discussed in the 'Sanctuary' section, and 33.14b, 'Who will abide for us in Zion, where the brightness of the Shekinah is as a consuming fire?'; 56.5, 'I will give them in my sanctuary house and in the land of my Shekinah house a place and a name . . . .'

9.   This is not to exclude the possibility that a single meturgeman revised his own formulations in the light of recent experience, although if that were the case a more consistent outcome might have been expected.

10.   *Untersuchungen über die Vorstellung von der Schekhinah in der frühen*

rabbinischen Literatur—Talmud und Midrasch, Studia Judaica 5 (Berlin: de Gruyter, 1969).

11. Cf. p. 462, where the later mystical literature is characterized by way of comparison with earlier texts as presenting the Shekinah 'als selbständiges Wesen neben der Gottheit.'

12. See also 467, 468, 480-485. What Goldberg characterizes as late is the replacement of 'holy spirit' with 'Shekinah,' not the basic relationship between the two (cf. 468 and Schäfer's contribution, discussed in the 'Holy Spirit' section). On the relationship between Shekinah and יקרא—כבוד, cf. pp. 469, 470. On p. 470 Goldberg calls for further work on the Shekinah as presented in the Targums in particular. Cf. Domingo Muñoz León, *Gloria de la Shekina en los Targumim del Pentateuco* (Madrid: 1977).

13. For a discussion of how the Shekinah is seen as identified with a finite space, cf. Goldberg, 477.

14. Goldberg, 487. But, as Goldberg shows (pp. 491f.), what was denied in respect of the second Temple was not the presence of the Shekinah, but its efficacy vis-à-vis revelation.

15. Goldberg, 488.

16. Goldberg, 488, 493f. (cf. 164 on Megillah 29a). But cf. Aqiba's dictum in the Mekhilta (Pisḥa 14.97f.), cited in Hayward, *op. cit.* ('Memra,' n.33), 48.

17. In 75b, the same rabbi says that only those who are invited will be able to go up to the Jerusalem that is to come. This illustrates the tendency to individualize eschatology among the Amoraim (cf. 'Jerusalem' in the Targum). In the same place, cf. the comment of R. Eleazar, 'There will come a time when "holy" will be said before the righteous as it was said before the holy one . . . .'

18. We may leave out of consideration the special interest expressed in Babli for the seraphim in Is. 6.3, 6 (cf. Ḥagigah 13b and Berakhoth 4b). See also jRosh Hashanah 1.1-2.

19. Cf. n.18.

20. The view in Exodus Rabbah 50.5 (citing Is. 4.5), that the curtains made of goat hair will protect Israel in the age to come, is probably very early (i.e. near to the time of the destruction of the Temple), but unfortunately it is unascribed.

21. Goldberg, 490. His previous suggestion, to which he refers, is that an older list of defiling sins (bloodshed, fornication, idolatry) has been expanded to include acts which presuppose a period of persecution (defamation and denunciation). For a similar, more generally argued, statement of the case, cf. Urbach, *op. cit.* ('Repentance,' n.8), 40, 43, 54-57.

22. Pp. 13-435.

23. P. 538.

24. Cf., for 'a,' pp. 30f. (citing the unascribed passage in Tanḥuma (Buber) 5 p. 110), 'Sie sollen erkennen, dass ich der Herr, ihr Gott bin, der ich sie aus dem Lande Ägypten geführt habe, um in ihrer Mitte zu wohnen (Ex. 29, 46). Wenn sie meinen Willen tun, dann rührt sich meine Schekhinah nicht von ihnen fort.'), 492 (on the continuing presence of the Shekinah at the site of the

demolished Temple); for 'b,' pp. 125-141; for 'c,' pp. 318-335; for 'd,' pp. 315, 316.

NOTES TO SECTION L

1.   Cf. 4.5, 'And the LORD will create upon all the sanctuary mount of Zion and upon the place of the Shekinah house a cloud of glory; it will be a covering upon it by day and darkness, as flaming fire by night, for with greater glory than he said he will bring upon it the Shekinah . . . '; 6.5 ('Shekinah,' n.3); 33.17a ('Shekinah,' n.2); 60.2b ('Shekinah,' n.2); 60.13 ('Shekinah,' n.5); 64.3 ('Shekinah,' n.7). The term appears alone in a visionary context at 6.1, ' . . . I saw the glory of the LORD . . . ' The usage at 24.23 is similar, but, in that it represents כבוד in the MT, great weight should not be placed on this rendering.
2.   6.3, 6 (cited fully and discussed in the previous section); 40.22 ('Shekinah,' n.4). Cf. 63.11, 'And he spared for the glory of his name . . . '; 66.1, ' . . . the heavens are the throne of my glory . . . .'
3.   Cf. 19.1, where the cloud which afrights the Egyptians is 'the cloud of his glory'; 28.21, 'For as the mountains shook when the glory of the LORD was revealed in the days of Uzziah the king . . . .' At 4.2, it is said that the messiah (for 'branch' in the MT) will be for glory, but יקרא again renders כבוד (cf. n.1).
4.   This is also a passage in which the refusal to repent motif comes to expression. At 66.5, we find the taunt, 'let the glory of the LORD increase' for 'let the LORD be glorified' in the MT.
5.   N.b., not 'their heads,' as in the MT; the meturgeman here addressed his readers as exiles. At 51.11, the same rendering occurs (with 'their heads,' and including the exile reference). Both passages also include the 'House of Israel' theologoumenon, and the latter is cited in full in that section. Cf. 58.8b, ' . . . in glory from the LORD you will be gathered' (largely following the MT).
6.   The first usage is for כבודו in the MT, but the second is for 'her splendour.' Cf. 10.3; 17.4; 22.18, which basically follow the MT. But 51.23 innovatively reads, ' . . . you brought down your glory [for 'your back' in the MT] as the ground . . . .'
7.   'And I sanctified them and glorified them . . . .'
8.   At 16.6, 'their glorious ones' (for MT: 'his pride') appears in respect of Moab. Cf. v. 14, following the MT usage of 'glory,' but then adding, 'and all their glory will end' (at the close of the verse). Cf. 23.9, where the meturgeman had 'the glory of all her [sc. Tyre's] joy' for 'the pride of all ornament'; 'glorious ones of the earth' at the end of the verse simply follows the MT. V. 16, 'Your glory is changed . . . ,' also refers to Tyre (which is mentioned in v. 15). At 25.11, 'his haughtiness' becomes 'his glory' (of Moab). The throne which Babylon is without in 47.1 is a glorious throne in the Targum, and in v. 2 she uncovers, not herself (as in the MT), but 'your kingdom's glory.' At 17.3, the meturgeman simply followed (but expanded on) the MT in his 'glory' usage.
9.   For MT: ' . . . a feast of fat, a feast of dregs . . . .' The meturgeman clearly

took the last word cited *in malam partem*, hence the present translation. This interpretation is carried through in v. 6 and into v. 7, '. . . even plagues from which they will not escape, plagues in which they will perish ('plagues' [מחן] interprets 'garnish with marrow' [ממחים]: again, what at first seems an unusual rendering becomes explicable on comparison with the MT). And the face of the master who lords it over all nations will be destroyed, even the face of the king that rules over all kingdoms.' Patently, this is a reference to the Roman emperor, and it makes best sense if it is understood to address a situation in which the imperial power is preeminent (but not perhaps unthreatened by resistance). The situation is perhaps not unlike that presupposed in Revelation 13 and the fifth Sibylline book, dated by Collins (*op. cit.* ['Jerusalem,' n.16], 94) to the period before the Bar Kokhba revolt. Cf. 53.3, 'Then will the glory of all the kingdoms be for contempt and cease . . . '

10.   23.18b, '. . . for her hire will belong to those who serve before the LORD . . . and for garments of glory'; the usages at 61.6; 66.12 simply follow the MT in this respect.

11.   49.18, 'Jerusalem, lift up your eyes, and see the children of the people of your exiles . . . all of them will be to you as a garment of glory . . . ' (cf. 'Jerusalem,' n.4); 52.2, '. . . sit on the throne of glory, Jerusalem . . . '; 60.15, '. . . I will make you eternal glory . . . ' (for 'pride' in the MT); 60.20, '. . . and your glory will not depart . . . ' (for 'your moon' in the MT).

12.   *Targum and Testament* (Introduction n. 2), 99f. (mistakenly citing v. 2).

13.   G. von Rad, 'δόξα, etc. . . c. כבוד in the OT' in: G. Kittel (ed., tr. G. Bromiley), *Theological Dictionary of the New Testament* ii (Grand Rapids: Eerdmans, 1978), 238-242.

14.   G. Kittel, 'δόξα, etc. . . . e. כבוד and יקרא in Palestinian Judaism' in: *TDNT* ii, 245-247.

15.   Kittel, *art. cit.*, 247. Similarly, cf. II Baruch 54.15, cited by Volz, *op. cit.* ('Law,' n. 16), 362.

16.   Cited by Volz, 372. The other Prophetic Targums present usages which are also cognate with that of the Isaiah Targum (cf. Tg 2 Samuel 23.4; Tg Jeremiah 23.24; Tg Hosea 7.10; Tg Habakkuk 3.4, 8; Tg Zechariah 9.8). On the whole, post-biblical 'glory' usage may be said to stress more the evaluative aspect of the term's meaning (in respect of divine authority) than its visual aspect (as theophany).

NOTES TO SECTION M

1.   Cf. my earlier article, 'Regnum Dei Deus Est' in: *SJT* 31 (1978) 261-270. Some months after the article appeared, Klaus Koch's article, 'Offenbaren wird sich das Reich Gottes' in: *NTS* 25 (1979) 158-165, offered the same basic conclusion regarding the meaning of this theologoumenon in the Prophetic Targumim. But Koch does not distinguish between the levels of usage clearly. Koch also suggests that the Targumic theologoumenon might be of relevance for understanding its New Testament analogue. I had already argued that

Jesus' preaching reflects the Targumic understanding of the kingdom in my 1976 Cambridge Ph.D. thesis, entitled *God in Strength: Jesus' announcement of the kingdom* which was published in 1979 as the first in the monograph series Studien zum Neuen Testament und seiner Umwelt (Freistadt: Plöchl). The use of גלא to speak of the manifest disclosure of what is already a reality—namely God's identity as king—is consistent with rabbinic usage. Cf. G. Dalman (tr. D.M. Kay), *The Words of Jesus* (Edinburgh: Clark, 1902), 97; G.F. Moore, *op. cit.* (Introduction n. 8) II, 374.

2.   Mekhilta Exodus 17.14 (p. 186, lines 4-7 in the Horovitz-Rabin edition [Jerusalem: 1960]).

3.   Cf. J. Neusner, *op. cit.* (Introduction, n. 12).

4.   As I pointed out in the *SJT* article (p. 266), it is of course possible that the 'dwellers' phrase (which is not used by Eliezer, who is after all discussing the desolation of Amalek) is a later embellishment, but the foundational importance of the universalistic aspect of the kingdom (expressed with or without that phrase) seems patent in the two passages here in question. It must be stressed, however, that the universal recognition of the kingdom is not featured in the Targums so as to vitiate the force with which it is expected to come.

5.   We have already had reason to suspect that such diction comes from the Amoraic period (cf. 'Jerusalem,' n. 4, 'Exile,' nn. 4, 14, 28 and 'House of Israel,' nn. 4, 10).

6.   It is also more particularistic than the Exodus-kingdom association in Onqelos (Exodus 15.18), which itself appears to be Amoraic (cf. the fourth century dicta in Exodus Rabbah 29, reported in Strack-Billerbeck, *op. cit.* ['House of Israel,' n. 9] I, 175, 175 as compared to the earlier form in the Mekhilta, given on p. 179; also the prayer אמת ואמונה.

7.   Strack-Billerbeck I, 164, citing jTaanith 1.1.

8.   Esther Midrash 1.2 (85ᵃ), as cited in Strack-Billerbeck I, 175. See also Psalms Midrash 99.1, in the name of the fourth century teacher R. Jehudah, as cited on p. 179.

9.   Strack-Billerbeck I, 172.

10.   Shemoneh Esreh 11 (Palestinian), 'Alenu; Taanith 25b (R. Aqiba), as cited in Strack-Billerbeck I, 175.

11.   Sifra Leviticus 20.26 (Strack-Billerbeck I, 176). Cf. also Dalman, 97, and W. Bacher, *Die Agada der Tannaiten* (Strassburg: Trubner, 1903 [pages indicated are from the 1884 edition, as given in the margins], 228. 'Yoke' is an image for teaching in a saying of Nehunia b. Hakanah (Bacher, 58), and serves to qualify the sense in which 'kingdom' is meant.

12.   M. Berakhoth 2.2 (Strack-Billerbeck i, 177); cf. the Talmuds for later opinions to the same effect.

13.   T.W. Manson recognized that this was a secondary development in *The Teaching of Jesus. Studies of its Form and Content* (Cambridge: University Press, 1955), 137, and yet made it the paradigm for understanding Jesus' preaching (130f.). Cf. N. Perrin, *The Kingdom of God in the Teaching of*

Jesus(London: SCM, 1963), 178-181, and *Rediscovering the Teaching of Jesus* (New York: Harper and Row, 1967), 57-60.

14.   All prayer quotations are taken from Staerk, *op. cit.* ('Law,' n. 12).

15.   Tanḥuma קדשים 1 (Volz, *op. cit.* ['Law,' n. 16], 276) and the thirteenth benediction of the Shemoneh Esreh (Babylonian recension).

16.   But other prayers reflect the yoke motif; cf. תפלת שחרית 3 and אמת ואמונה. Cf. the statement of R. Joḥanan (third century, according to Strack-Billerbeck I, 184) in Berakoth 12a, 'A prayer in which there is no mention of the kingdom is no prayer' (in regard to the interpretation of this dictum, cf. n. 18).

17.   Cf. Perrin, *Rediscovering*, 59. Cf. also Baba Bathra 10b: R. Abbahu (third and fourth centuries); jSanhedrin 11.3: R. Simeon b. Menasia (second and third centuries, although העולם הבא is not applied to this verse directly, but to the list of blessings associated with it). An unascribed comment in Deuteronomy Rabbah explains that Is. 52.7 refers particularly to Jerusalem's peace (6.15).

18.   Cf. 3.33 and Tg Jer. 10.7; Tg Ez. 29.3, 9. 'Kingdom' with the general meaning 'dominion' is to be distinguished by context from 'kingdom' as an abbreviation for 'kingdom of God.'

19.   Cf. *God in Strength* (cited in n. 1).

NOTES TO SECTION N

1.   Cf. the LXX; for an evaluation of proposed emendations, see Wildberger, *op. cit.* ('Sanctuary,' n. 2), 178 and Young, *op. cit.* I ('Sanctuary,' n. 2), 216. By way of background, cf. K. Koch, 'Die drei Gerechtigkeiten. Die Umformung einer hebräischen Idee im aramäischen Denken nach dem Jesajatargum' in: J. Friedrich, W. Pöhlmann, P. Stuhlmacher (eds.), *Rechtfertigung. Festschrift für Ernst Käsemann* (Tübingen: Mohr, 1976), 245-267.

2.   For this conception in the Tannaitic period, see Moore, *op. cit.* II (Introduction, n. 8), 378f. It is to be observed, however, that the reward or punishment here is not rigidly individual (cf. the following paragraph). Indeed, the collective attributes, 'rich' and 'poor,' remind one of the Gospel according to Luke; cf. H. Degenhardt, *Lukas. Evangelist der Armen* (Stuttgart: Verlag katholisches Bibelwerk, 1965). Cf. Targum Isaiah 26.6, 'Feet will tread it, the feet of the righteous, the soles of the poor, the needy of the people.'

Cf. 5.30c, 'but the righteous that are in that hour will be covered from evil'; 7.22b, 'for all the righteous who are left in the midst of the land will be nourished with curds and milk'; 21.12, ' . . . there is reward for the righteous and punishment for the wicked . . . ' (cf. 'Repentance,' in which it is suggested that the last usage may appear in an interpretation from the Amoraic period). One could hardly argue that any whisper of eschatology coheres with the later conception, but it seems reasonable to recognize a distinction between a *diesseitig*, collective eschatology and a *jenseitig*, individualized eschatology. Such works as Matthew and IV Ezra show the latter to be the preferred theodicy after 70 (so Moore II, 323).

3.   Cf. 28.16, 'Therefore thus says the LORD God, I appoint in Zion a king, a strong, powerful and terrible king. I will make him strong and mighty, the prophet says. And the righteous, who believe in these things will not be shaken when distress comes' (the occurrence of the term in a chapter which contains much primitive material is obviously significant); 32.1, 'Behold, a king will reign for truth, and the righteous will be appointed to do just retribution with the nations'; 49.8, ' . . . and I will give you for a covenant of the people, to raise the righteous who lie in the dust . . . '; 53.2, 'The righteous will grow up before him . . . ' ('messiah' appears at 52.13).

4.   A similar interpretation, associated with a similar image in the MT, appears at 24.13. Cf. 51.14, ' . . . the righteous will not die . . . .'

5.   With Young, *op. cit.* II ('Sanctuary,' n. 2), 171-174 and Gray, *op. cit.* ('Sanctuary,' n. 2), 418, the term is probably to be taken collectively, as in the Targum.

6.   So Young and Gray. The difficulty of the MT makes the meturgeman's rather free interpretation more justifiable. It is ignored altogether in the LXX.

7.   The LXX is closer to the Targum in that the woe is pronounced against those who despise the law.

8.   Cf. 25.5b, 'as the shadow of a cool rock in a weary land, so is the spirit of the righteous at rest when the wicked decline'; 55.13a, 'Instead of the wicked the righteous will be established'; 65.13, ' . . . behold, my servants, the righteous, will eat and you wicked will hunger; behold, my servants, the righteous, will drink, and you wicked will thirst; behold, my servants, the righteous, will rejoice, and you will be ashamed,' 14, 'behold, my servants, the righteous, will extol . . . ,' 15c, 'and he will give another name to his servants the righteous'; 66.14b, 'and the might of the LORD will be revealed to do good to his servants the righteous . . . .' Cf. those passages which speak of the destruction of the wicked (2:19, 21; 10:23; 13:5).

9.   Cf. 44.4, 'The righteous will grow tender and delicate as blades of grass . . . .'

10.   Cf. 49.23, ' . . . the righteous who wait for my salvation will not be ashamed.' For further associations with the Shekinah, cf. 33.15, ' . . . the righteous will be installed in it . . . ' (in v. 14, 'it' is Jerusalem, wherein is the Shekinah); 63.17c, 'Restore your Shekinah to your people for the sake of your righteous servants . . . ' (a reference to memra follows); 64.3b, c, 'Eye has not seen what your people have seen, the Shekinah of your glory, LORD, for there is none like you, who is about to act for your people, the righteous, who hope for your salvation.'

11.   For the following portion of this verse, which follows the MT closely, cf. 25.5b, where 'the righteous' also appears. In 32.3, the meturgeman carried on his interpretation, 'And the eyes of the righteous will not be shut, and the ears of those who receive teaching will attend.' Cf. v. 6c, ' . . . the soul of the righteous, who desire teaching, even as the hungry bread, and the words of the law which they as the thirsty water . . . ,' v. 8, 'And the righteous devise truth . . . ,' v. 20, 'Blessed are you, righteous, you have done good works for yourselves . . . '; 40.29a, 'He gives wisdom to the righteous who faint for the

words of his law'; 50.4a, ' . . . the righteous who faint for the words of his law'; 66.5a, 'Receive the word of the LORD, you righteous . . . .'

12.   32.5, 'They will no longer be said righteous to the wicked, and to those who transgress his memra it will not be said, strong.' Cf. 25.4 (end), 'So are the speeches of the wicked to the righteous, as a shower of rain that beats against a wall.'

13.   Particularly, it has already been pointed out (in the 'Repentance' section) that 33.13; 57.19 appear to stem from a later period ('Hear, you righteous, who have kept my law from the beginning, what I have done; and know, you penitent, who repented recently to the law, my might'; ' . . . peace will be made to the righteous who kept my law from the beginning, and peace will be done to the penitent who have repented to my law recently . . . ': the phrase 'law from the beginning' apparently refers to the adherence to tradition, seen as consistent with primeval revelation). The reading at 44.26, 27 is patently Amoraic, 'Who confirms the word of his servants, the righteous . . . who says of Babylon, It will be laid waste . . . .'

14.   This highly individualized view of righteousness, however, would appear to reflect the systematic yetzer teaching of a later period. On the other hand, cf. Damascus Document 2.16, 'that you may walk perfectly in all his ways and not follow after the thoughts of the guilty inclination (yetzer) . . . .' For a brief discussion, with references to fuller treatments, see A.L. Thompson, *Responsibility for Evil in the Theodicy of IV Ezra*, SBLDS 29 (Missoula: Scholars Press, 1977), 49-63 (the citation is on p. 59, but Thompson makes some important cautionary observations).

15.   Noah came to mind as the inventor of wine. Cf. v. 9 (end), 'and my servants, the righteous, will dwell there'; 64.4 (cited in the 'Abraham' section, and following 'righteous' usage in v. 3); 41.2, where Abraham himself is called the 'chosen of righteousness.' The theme of Noah's righteousness was stressed by the second century (see Genesis Rabbah 32.2, cited by Moore, *op. cit.* I (Introduction, n. 8), 400.

16.   Volz, *op. cit.* ('Law,' n. 16), 27.

17.   Volz, 59. Cf. also Enoch 94f. (cited on p. 90) and Wisdom 5.1 (cited on p. 301).

18.   Volz, 31.

19.   Cf. 48.49; IV Ezra 7.95; 8.52 (cited on p. 114) and Enoch 38f. and 40.5 (cited on p. 115), and the examples from the rabbinic period (p. 294).

20.   Volz, 90; cf. 323, 324, 326, 329.

21.   Volz, 326.

22.   Here translated from Staerk's Hebrew, *op. cit.* ('Law,' n. 12), 20.

23.   Presumably, the third century Amora.

24.   W.D. Davies, *Torah in the Messianic Age and/or Age to Come*, JBLMS 7 (Philadelphia: SBL, 1952) 70, 71 (n. 28 citing the article of D. Daube in *JTS* 39 [1938], 45-59. For the antiquity of a legal emphasis in the understanding of Is. 24.16, cf. the LXX reading, Οὐαὶ τοῖς ἀθετοῦσιν, οἱ ἀθετοῦντες τὸν νόμον.

25.   b. Ḥiyya (third century).

26.   Our present interest is in the tendency of Babli as compared to the Targum, but one might also speculate that the secrecy motif in the latter half of the Targumic version influenced R. Judah. In the Song of Songs Rabbah 2.1.2, R. Berekiah applies this verse to the resurrection (cf. the unascribed version of this view in Ecclesiastes Rabbah 1.7.7). The exegesis presented in the Pirqe de R. Eliezer (37: p. 282) is of a different order.

27.   That law was always considered the content of righteousness seems undeniable. But the early meturgeman takes it that the righteous are those who do and teach the law and who will therefore be rewarded. The vindication expected by the later rabbis is put in a more qualified form: if Israel returned to the law, he would be saved (cf. n. 8 of 'Kingdom' and Tg Is. 21.11b, 12, discussed under 'Repentance').

NOTES TO SECTION O

1.   17.23-18.10 in the R.H. Charles edition. It is also convenient here to cite Moore's references (*op. cit.* [Introduction, n.8] II, 367 n.1) to intertestamental writings which express the hope for restoration: Baruch 2.30-35; 4.36-5.9; Ecclesiasticus 13.13-22; Tobit 13.9-18; II Maccabees 1.27; 2.18; Psalms of Solomon 8.33f.; 11; 17.28-31; 'and repeatedly in the Testaments of the Twelve Patriarchs.' On the same page, he also cites the tenth of the Shemoneh Esreh. The 'messiah' usage at 10.27 in the Targum ('. . . and the nations will be destroyed before the messiah') is inspired by etymology (cf. '. . . and a yoke will be destroyed from fatness [שמן]'), although it may be noteworthy that the nations are also pictured as fleeing before the ben David of the Psalms of Solomon (17.25; cf. v. 32).

2.   II, 349. Moore was quite aware of the dictum that the *name* of the messiah was one of the things that preceded the creation of the world (pp. 344, 348, 526), but not, as he points out (p. 344), 'the person of the Messiah.'

3.   In both the passages cited, the idea appears to be a secondary insertion. G.H. Box argued to this effect (in the Charles edition, p. 614); in II Baruch 40 the phrase, 'until the world of corruption is at an end . . . ' follows 'And his principate will stand forever.' It seems quite likely that the early concept of everlasting messianic dominion (as in the Targum) has been qualified. Cf. IV Ezra 7.26-44, where a four hundred year reign is anticipated, and Revelation 20.16, where the time involved is one thousand years.

4.   Cf. 17.32 ('And he will have the heathen nations to serve him under his yoke . . . '). Indeed, statements in the Psalms of Solomon appear to reflect this chapter of Isaiah. For example, the messiah is said to 'destroy the godless nations with the word of his mouth forever' (17.27; cf. v. 29). Isaiah 4.4 (MT) reads, 'and he will smite the earth with the rod of his mouth,' which the Targum renders, 'and he will strike the guilty of the earth with the word of his mouth,' and the LXX has, 'he will strike the earth with the word of his mouth.'

For the description of the messiah in Psalms 17.42, cf. Isaiah 22.1.

5. This may be classed in Stenning's category of 'metaphors for which, in the view of the translator, a literal rendering would be inadequate' (*op. cit.* [Introduction, n.15], xiv).

6. A.S. van der Woude, *Die messianischen Vorstellungen der Gemeinde von Qumran*, Studia semitica neerlandica 3 (Assen: Van Gorcum, 1957); M. de Jonge, 'The Use of the Word "Anointed" in the Time of Jesus' in: *Novum Testamentum* 8 (1966), 132-148.

7. M.D. Hooker, *Jesus and the Servant. The Influence of the Servant Concept of Deutero-Isaiah in the New Testament* (London: SPCK, 1959), 149. For the parallel conclusion in German discussion, cf. L. Ruppert, *Jesus als der leidende Gerechte? Der Weg Jesu im Lichte eines alt- und zwischentestamentlichen Motivs*, Stuttgarter Bibelstudien 59 (Stuttgart: KBW, 1972), 74, 75 n. 7.

8. For the more qualified positions of E. Schweizer and L. Ruppert, see Ruppert, *loc. cit.* As prominent instances of the association, cf. Mt. 8.17; 12.18-21; Lk. 22.37; Acts 8.32, 33; Heb. 9.28; I Pet. 2.24, 25.

9. Cf. K. Elliger, *Biblischer Kommentar Altes Testament. Jesaja II.* XI 4 (Neukirchen: Neukirchen-Vluyn, 1973), 307, 320.

10. Cf. particularly Mt. 3.17 (ἐν ᾧ εὐδόκησα) and 17.5 (the same phrase).

11. Cf. the remark of R.A. Aytoun ('The Servant of the Lord in the Targum' in: *JTS* 23 (1921-1922), 178), 'It should be noted that though it seems to have departed far from the original Hebrew, yet actually the Targum has stuck remarkably close to the letter of the Hebrew.' For the present translation of the MT, cf. D.J.A. Clines, *I, He, We and They. A Literary Approach to Isaiah 53*, JSOTS 1 (Sheffield: JSOT Press, 1976), 13, 20, 21.

12. C.R. North, 'The Servant of the LORD (עבד יהוה)' in: *The Interpreter's Dictionary of the Bible* (New York: Abingdon, 1962), 293. North also acknowledges that the Targumic interpretation is earlier than the 'later' Jewish view 'that the Servant was Israel.'

13. So Jeremias, Hegermann, Seidelin, Strack-Billerbeck, cited by Klaus Koch ('Messias und Sündenvergebung in Jesaja 53—Targum. Ein Beitrag zu der Praxis der aramäischen Bibelübersetzung' in: *JSJ* 3 [1972], 121). More recently: J. Juel, *op. cit.* ('Sanctuary,' n. 1), 182-196. Further material on the Isaiah Targum as a translation is available in Y. Komlosh, 'The Aramaic Translation of the Book of Isaiah as a Commentary' in: *Fourth World Congress of Jewish Studies: Abstracts of Papers—Biblical Studies* (Jerusalem: Hebrew University, 1965), 39-40.

14. Aytoun observed this (p. 177), as does Koch (p. 148), who concludes, 'So hindert nichts, die Notiz vom Sterben des Messias 4 Esr. 7, 29 ebenso von einer Auslegung unseres Targum abzuleiten wie die Bekenntnisformel 1 Kor. 15, 3 . . . .' In this context, it may be appropriate to mention that, at 52.14, the Isaiah Scroll from Qumran reads משחתי for משחת in the MT (M. Burrows, *The Dead Sea Scrolls of St. Mark's Monastery* I [New Haven: American Schools of Oriental Research, 1950]). Cf. W.H. Brownlee, *The Meaning of the*

Qumrân Scrolls for the Bible (New York: Oxford University Press, 1964), chapter 10.
15. Pp. 174, 175.
16. P. 176.
17. This point is made by Koch (p. 148), 'Der Gedanke eines durch Wort und Tat sündenvergebenden Messias ist sonst in spätisraelistischer Zeit und nachher bei den Rabbinen nirgendwo mit Sicherheit zu greifen.' But for the phrase 'forgiving messiah,' which is an exaggeration, since the messiah only prays concerning sin, this is an acute comment. Nevertheless, in view of the rabbinic application of Isaiah 53.12 to Phineas and Moses (cf. Moore, *op. cit.* [Introduction n.8] I, 249, 250), it is perhaps an incautious generalization. Cf. S.R. Driver, A. Neubauer, *The Fifty-Third Chapter of Isaiah according to the Jewish Interpreters*, 'Prolegomenon' by R. Loewe (New York: Ktav, 1969).
18. Cf. v. 4, 'Then concerning our sins he will pray, and our iniquities for his sake will be forgiven . . .'; v. 6, ' . . . it was a pleasure before the LORD to forgive the sins of us all for his sake'; v. 7, 'He was praying . . . .'
19. In particular, cf. 17.27-29, 'He shall destroy the godless nations with the word of his mouth; at his rebuke nations shall flee before him, and he shall reprove sinners for the thoughts of their heart. And he shall gather together a holy people, whom he shall lead in righteousness, and he shall judge the tribes of the people that has been sanctified by the Lord his God. And he shall not suffer unrighteousness to lodge any more in their midst, nor shall there dwell with them any man that knoweth wickedness.'
20. *Revue de théologie et de philosophie* 44 (1911), 5-46.
21. *Art. cit.*, 5, 6.
22. *Art. cit.*, 6-28.
23. *Art. cit.*, 29.
24. *Art. cit.*, 33; cf. Volz, *op. cit.* ('Law,' n. 16), 177 (citing Humbert), 213, 225, 228. But earlier (p. 32), Humbert went so far as to call the meturgeman a chiliast. By this he means that eschatology should not be equated with messianology in the Targum (p. 45), because he concluded firmly 'que le messianisme du Targum dérive logiquement de l'antique piété d'Israël, et que l'apocalyptique judaïque n'a laissé chez lui que peu ou pas de trace.' Humbert's 'hypothèse qui distingue entre la vie éternelle et le royaume messianique' (p. 31) does not seem to apply to the Isaiah Targum, whatever its virtues elsewhere. When he came to mention Tg Is. 53.9, Humbert virtually admitted this (cf. p. 32 n. 2). Cf. Schäfer, *art. cit.* ('Jerusalem,' n. 14), 225f.
25. He saw the essentially human nature of the messiah as another link with Tannaitic thought (p. 38 n. 1).
26. *Art. cit.*, 43. Some of Humbert's statements are remarkably unsympathetic, e.g., 'On le sent, c'est le chauvinisme national et son étroitesse' (p. 13). A better familiarity with the meaning to the meturgeman of such terms as 'Israel' and 'sanctuary' might have prevented him from making such statements.
27. Levey, *op. cit.* ('Repentance,' n. 16), 67. By way of support for his view, Levey cites Pseudo-Jonathan at Gen. 49.10 in order to show 'beyond a doubt

158 *The Glory of Israel*

that in Jewish Messianic thought there is no room whatsoever for a suffering and dying Messiah.' Levey also suspects (pp. 45, 48, 55) that the Isaian meturgeman associates the messiah with Hezekiah. This is inferential, but since Joḥanan b. Zakkai held such views (cf. Berakhoth 28b) one might take it in support of our thesis.

28.   Shemoneh Esreh (Palestinian and Babylonian recensions), fourteenth benediction.

29.   Cf. Habinênu b and תפלת מוסף לראש השנה 1.

30.   *Op. cit.*, 210, citing Schürer.

31.   *Op. cit.*, 176 and 310. For further references to the tangible victory of the messiah, cf. 220.

32.   Berakhoth 48b, translated from Volz, 176.

33.   The point at first under discussion is the Hezekian identity of the messiah. In Sanhedrin 94a, R. Pappias cites the opinion of an unknown Tanna who also held that Is. 24.16 applied in some way to Hezekiah (and cf. R. Joḥanan's view on Is. 9.6 in Shabbath 55a along with R. Judah's in jSanhedrin 10.1). In Genesis Rabbah 97 (N.V.), R. Joḥanan applies Is. 9.6 to the vindication of the righteous, showing that one could start with the messianic theme and move on to the vindication theme, as well as the reverse. For the Hezekian identity of the messiah, see also Ruth Rabbah 7.2 (R. Judah b. Simon); in Numbers Rabbah 11.7 (R. Nathan) he is simply Davidic. The necessary function of the messiah in respect of building the Temple is set out expressly in an unascribed statement in Genesis Rabbah 97 (N.V.).

NOTES TO CHAPTER III

1.   As we have seen, it would have been quite contrary to the programme of the Babylonian Amoraim to encourage the use in synagogue of any such work.

2.   Cf. Hengel, *op. cit.* ('Sanctuary,' n. 19) I, 213 and E.P. Sanders, *Paul and Palestinian Judaism* (London: SCM, 1977).

3.   Goldberg, *op. cit.* ('Shekinah,' n. 10), 455.

4.   Churgin, *op. cit.* (Introduction, n. 6).

5.   The recent concordance to the Isaiah Targum, prepared by Peter van Zijl (*A Concordance to the Targum of Isaiah*, SBLAS 3 [Missoula: Scholars Press, 1979]), was not available to me during the formative period of this project, although I have consulted it in preparing the final draft of the manuscript. Unfortunately, its format (in which words are not listed by their roots) makes it less useful for our purpose than might have been hoped.

6.   That is to say that the present list is not intended to be exhaustive; it derives from our comparison to the Targumic readings of passages culled from indices, as stated in the introduction.

7.   To paraphrase Leopold Cohn, 'An Apocryphal Work Ascribed to Philo of

Alexandria' in: *JQR* 10 (1898) 277-332, 314 and 322. But cf. the 'Abraham' section for a substantive similarity between the L.A.B. and the Targum. Cohn notes a similarity between the L.A.B. and apocalyptic writings (p. 323), and—on internal evidence—dates the document in the period shortly after the destruction of the Temple (pp. 325-327). Cohn identifies the author's purpose as that of strengthening the 'belief in God's providence and in the high figure of Israel by means of a vivid account of the wonderful incidents of the history of the Israelites' (322). The genre of the L.A.B. differs markedly from that of the Targum, but their programmes may be cognate. Although the practice of sacrifice is for the author of the L.A.B. a thing of the past (325), Cenez appears as a figure similar to the Targumic messiah in that he is a military hero who extirpates idolatry and establishes a new altar (295f.). Idolatry and its opposite—faithful martyrdom—are buttresses to this theme of restoration throughout the L.A.B. Cenez is not a ben David, but David himself is assisted by the same angel that helped Cenez (297, 305), and there are other similarities in the haggadic details with which the two are portrayed. Cenez' descent from Joshua (in terms of authority) should not be taken necessarily to imply that he is an extra-rabbinic figure, especially since the L.A.B. seems to have at least some positive relationship with rabbinic discussion (cf. M. Wadsworth, *The Liber Antiquitatum of Pseudo-Philo* [Oxford: D.Phil., 1975]). Someone of the stamp of Bar Kokhba was, after all, no further removed from the ben David than Cenez. Finally, we would note that Cenez, as the messiah of the Targum, is associated with a priest (298). This may be taken to suggest—provisionally, and only as a possibility which needs to be examined—that the L.A.B. and the Isaiah Targum share a programme of messianic vindication which includes the concrete restoration of the cult. Another point of general correspondence between the two documents is that, traditio-historically speaking, they reflect extended periods of development; cf. A. Zeron, 'Erwägungen zu Pseudo-Philos Quellen und Zeit' in: *JSJ* 11 (1980), 38-52.

8.   The Yalkut Shimoni's programme is also midrashic, but its purpose is to serve as an anthology, not a haggadic representation of scripture. A.B. Hyman (cf. Introduction, n. 53h) lists the following among its sources: Babli, Jerushalmi, Tosephta, the Mekhilta, Siphre, Seder Olam, Midrash Rabbah (for various books), Zuṭa (for several books), Pesiqta de R. Kahana, Pesiqta Rabbati, Pirqe de R. Eliezer. The collection, although late, does serve to bring together some of the major rabbinic exegetical motives. For example (referring to Lorje's edition, where the Yalkut is conveniently set out by Isaian chapter), Yalkut Is. 24.16 explicates כנף as distinct from 'mouth' (cf. Sanhedrin 37b, cited in 'The righteous'), showing that R. Judah's was an influential interpretation. Likewise, this verse is cited in reference to Isaiah 9 in the Yalkut, with special emphasis on רזי־לי רזי־לי (cf. Sanhedrin 94a and 'Messiah,' n. 33). The programmatic coherence of the Yalkut with opinions expressed in intramural rabbinic literature is to be contrasted with the

problematic relationship of the Targum to the same corpus. To some extent, the differences between the Yalkut and the Targum can be explained with reference to their dates of formation, but it is also evident that each represents its own genre. This implies that each speaks from, and to, its own context: research into 'developing techniques and tendencies in rabbinic discussion,' to which I allude below (in the text), must seek to clarify the setting in life of the documents whose material it wishes to compare.

9. Cf. also Y. Komlosh, *art. cit.* ('Messiah,' n. 13).

10. Staerk, *op. cit.* ('Law,' n. 12).

11. Volz, *op. cit.* ('Law,' n. 16).

12. Moore, *op. cit.* (Introduction, n. 8). Cf. Urbach, *op. cit.*('Repentance,' n. 8).

13. Schäfer, *op. cit.* ('Holy spirit,' n. 6).

14. Cf. n. 3.

15. Hayward, *op. cit.* ('Law,' n. 16; 'Memra,' n. 33); cf. Hamp, *op. cit.* (Introduction, n. 33) and Muñoz León, *op. cit.* ('Memra,' n. 1).

16. McNamara, *op. cit.* (Introduction, nn. 1, 2). But cf. the important challenge recently presented by Lester L. Grabbe in 'The Jannes/Jambres Tradition in Targum Pseudo-Jonathan and its Date' in: *JBL* 98 (1979), 393-401.

17. Volz, 255.

18. The work of Aberbach and Grossfeld (*op. cit.* [Introduction, n.17]) might be cited as undertaking a similar programme, although their treatment of Genesis 49 in Onqelos is less focussed from the point of view of determining provenience (cf. 'Repentance,' n.14, and my review in *JSOT* 8 [1978], 61-70). Methodologically, the present work stands closer to that of J.J. Collins (cited in 'Jerusalem,' n. 6).

19. Cf. the Introduction, and particularly Stephen A. Kaufman's contribution (n. 47), which is a reasoned summation of the impact of the contributions of Fitzmyer and Kutscher.

20. Humbert, *art. cit.* ('Messiah,' n. 20).

21. Aytoun, *art. cit.* ('Messiah,' n. 11).

22. Levey, *op. cit.* ('Repentance,' n. 16).

23. Koch, *art. cit.* (Introduction, n. 45).

24. Hayward, *op. cit.*('Law,' n. 16; 'Memra,' n. 33); *art. cit.* ('Memra,' n. 31). Similarly, while we greatly appreciate the descriptive achievement of Muñoz León, *op. cit.* ('Memra,' n. 1), his assumption of Neophyti's antiquity vitiates his conclusions.

25. It should be mentioned, of course, that his decision to deal with all of the Prophetic Targumim made it impossible for him to deal with a single Targum with the specificity we have attempted to achieve.

26. *The History of the Jews in Babylonia* I: SPB (Leiden: Brill, 1965), 67 (cf. 77-79).

27. *Op. cit.* II (1966), 52, 53.

28. *Op. cit.* V (1970).

29. So Hugo Mantel, 'The Causes of the Bar Kokba Revolt' in: *JQR* 58 (1967-1968), 224-242. Mantel favours the notice of Eusebius over those of Dio Cassius and Spartianus: 'It was not the decrees of Hadrian that caused the Bar Kokba revolt, but the reverse is true: Hadrian's decrees constituted a reaction of the Romans to the Jewish revolt' (p. 225). Accordingly—and taking into account clear evidence for heavy troop movements—he argues that the war began 'probably in 126 or 125' (p. 239). Commenting on a title deed discovered at Murabba'at, Joseph Fitzmyer concludes that 'the revolt began on, or at least was officially reckoned from I Tishri A.D. 132' ('The Bar Cochba Period' in: *Essays on the Semitic Background of the New Testament* [London: Chapman, 1971], 305-354, 330). But Fitzmyer recognizes that this text refers to the effective administration (cf. p. 341), not necessarily (or even probably) to the actual beginning, of the movement which resulted in a temporarily successful formal revolt. Moreover, Fitzmyer praises Eusebius' chronological accuracy in placing the climax (not the end) of the revolt in Hadrian's eighteenth year, a reckoning he argues is substantiated by the recent finds. Fitzmyer also notes (p. 345, n. 100) the troop movements which, on his understanding, 'took place before the war began.' To some extent, the difference between Mantel and Fitzmyer involves the definition of 'war.' But even in Fitzmyer's chronology (pp. 317-318), Hadrian's order to build a shrine to Jupiter Capitolinus came in 130, so that, if (*pace* Mantel) this occasioned the revolt, the germ of the movement antedated 132. In any case, as P. Schäfer observes in a recent article ('R. Aqiva und Bar Kokhba' in: *op. cit.* ['Law,' n.18], 65-121, 120), 'Die wenigen messianische Aussprüche, die Aqiva neben der sog. Messiasproklamation zugeschrieben werden, lassen eine national-irdische und damit politisch gefärbte Messiaserwartung erkennen, die zudem auf einen nahe bevorstehenden Zeitpunkt gerichtet ist (Naherwartung).' Such a general situation, not the description of it particularly offered by Mantel, is all that our thesis requires. In her recent treatment of the question, E. Mary Smallwood, while undecided in regard to the immediate causes of the revolt, is quite clear that it developed to some extent in response to the Diaspora Jewish wars of liberation earlier in the century (cf. *The Jews under Roman Rule from Pompey to Diocletian* [Leiden: Brill, 1976], 421-466). Cf. van der Kooij, *op. cit.* ('Sanctuary,' n.21), 186f., 192f. The author attempts, however, on the basis of a narrow range of evidence to prove that the priest Eleazar from Modi'im composed both Onqelos and Jonathan (cf. 203f.). But the only concrete connection between Eleazar and the Isaiah Targum he can adduce is the זכות אבות motif (cf. 'Abraham,' n. 2) which was obviously not peculiar to Eleazar's usage. Although van der Kooij and I agree on the date of the Targum in its initial form, his omission to consider its relation to Rabbinica as a whole leads him into a defective understanding of its literary development and provenience. Most recently, cf. P. Schäfer, 'The Causes of the Bar Kokhba Revolt' in: *Studies in Aggadah, Targum and Jewish Liturgy in Memory of Joseph*

Heinemann (Jerusalem: Magnes, 1981), 74-94 and *Der Bar Kokhba-Aufstand:* Texte und Studien zum Antiken Judentum (Tübingen: Mohr, 1981).

NOTES TO APPENDIX

1.	Cf. Levey's own translation of a similar phrase in Tg Is. 9.6 on p. 45.
2.	Cf. 'Law,' n. 16 and 'Abraham'; 'Memra,' n. 43.
3.	He applies the same argument to the Amos Targum, citing 9.11 (p. 157, n. 116). On the same page, Levey cites the later Hillel's opinion, according to which Israel is not to enjoy a messiah (Sanhedrin 99a). The opinion is justified by the implication that Hezekiah was the messiah, a view already shared by Johanan b. Zakkai (Berakhot 28b). But Johanan also looked forward to the coming of 'Hezekiah, king of Judah' and, as Levey suggests (pp. 45-46, 48, 55), such a teaching may be reflected in the Isaiah Targum. Cf. 'Messiah.'
4.	Cf. 'Jerusalem,' n. 4; 'Exile,' nn. 4, 28, and Tg Joel 2.14 (treated in 'Repentance').
5.	Levey, 92, citing Moore, *op. cit.* (Introduction, n. 8) II (1946), 343f. (on p. 157).
6.	He also ingenuously admits, 'All this, of course, is speculation, but speculation with some measure of plausibility.' For similar conclusions in respect of the date of the Targum, cf. Wieder, *art. cit.* (Introduction, n. 17); Brownlee, *art. cit.* (Introduction, n. 30); Marcus, *op. cit.* (Introduction, n. 30).

INDEXES

INDEX OF REFERENCES

170 *The Glory of Israel*

Isaiah

	106, 139, 141
63.11	139, 142, 149
63.12	142
63.14a	62, 142
63.17	127, 147
63.17c	63, 106, 153
63.19	128
64.3b, c	153
64.4	154
64.4d	137
64.66	146
65.1	63, 64, 106, 127
65.2	139
65.3a	141
65.4	5, 121
65.8	84
65.9(end)	154
65.11	35
65.12	42, 105, 139
65.13	153
65.14	153
65.15c	153
66.1	147, 149
66.4	42
66.5	149
66.5a	154
66.6	25, 61
66.6b	141
66.7	88
66.8	133
66.9	31
66.12	105, 150
66.14b	153
66.24c	83

Jeremiah

| 3.1 | 40 |
| 3.7 | 40 |

Jeremiah

3.12	40
3.22	40
4.1	40
4.31	135
6.2, 23	135
8.20	36, 135
8.21	28
10.7	152
14.19	65
23.5	17, 86, 96, 115
23.24	150
24.7	40
26.18	23
27.5	65
27.6	65
30.9	113, 116
30.10	113
30.11	65
30.18	22, 28, 134
30.21	96, 113, 114
31.6	86
31.11	36
31.12	22
33.5	74
33.15	17, 96, 115
33.21, 22	96
51.39	56
51.51	23
51.57	56

Ezekiel

3.14	56
7.7	79
7.10	79
14.7	65
14.13	65
17.22-24	113
17.23	86, 113
17.24	65
20.3	65
29.3	152

Ezekiel

29.9	152
34.24	65, 113
34.26	22, 113
34.30	65
37.27	74
38.35	74
39.16	45

Hosea

2.2	114, 134
2.15	36, 135
3.3	36, 134
3.4	114
3.5	96, 116
6.1	40
7.10	40, 150
7.13	64
10.12	17, 40, 56
11.2	56
13.14	36, 37, 74
13.15	65
14.1	64
14.7	114
14.7, 8	116
14.8	22, 114, 116, 134

Joel

| 2.14 | 22, 43, 162 |
| 3.1, 2 | 50 |

Amos

4.6	40
4.8	40
4.9	40
4.10	40
4.11	40, 64

Obadiah

21	79, 80, 81, 151
21a	78
21b	78, 79

INDEX OF AUTHORS